M46
C16

The Story of Canterbury

The Mediæval Town Series

ASSISI. By LINA DUFF GORDON. [5th Edn.

AVIGNON. By THOMAS OKEY.

BRUGES. By ERNEST GILLIAT-SMITH. [4th Edn.

BRUSSELS. By ERNEST GILLIAT-SMITH.

CAIRO. By STANLEY LANE-POOLE. [2nd Edn.

CAMBRIDGE. By the Rt. Rev. C. W. STUBBS, D.D. [2nd Edn.

CANTERBURY. By G. R. STIRLING TAYLOR.

CHARTRES. By CECIL HEADLAM, M.A. [2nd Edn.

CONSTANTINOPLE. By WM. H. HUTTON. [3rd Edn.

COVENTRY. By MARY DORMER HARRIS.

DUBLIN. By D. A. CHART, M.A.

EDINBURGH. By OLIPHANT SMEATON, M.A.

FERRARA. By ELLA NOYES.

FLORENCE. By EDMUND G. GARDNER. [9th & Revised Edn.

JERUSALEM. By Col. Sir C. M. WATSON.

LONDON. By HENRY B. WHEATLEY. [3rd Edn.

LUCCA. By JANET ROSS and NELLY ERICHSEN.

MILAN. By ELLA NOYES.

MOSCOW. By WIRT GERRARE. [3rd Edn.

NUREMBERG. By CECIL HEADLAM, M.A. [6th Edn.

OXFORD. By CECIL HEADLAM, M.A. [2nd Edn.

PADUA. By CESARE FOLIGNO.

PARIS. By THOMAS OKEY [2nd Edn.

PERUGIA. By M. SYMONDS and LINA DUFF GORDON. [6th Edn.

PISA. By JANET ROSS.

PRAGUE. By COUNT LÜTZOW. [2nd Edn.

ROME. By NORWOOD YOUNG. [6th Edn.

ROUEN. By THEODORE A. COOK. [3rd Edn.

SANTIAGO. By C. G. GALLICHAN.

SEVILLE. By WALTER M. GALLICHAN. [2nd Edn.

SIENA. By EDMUND G. GARDNER. [3rd Edn.

TOLEDO. By HANNAH LYNCH. [2nd Edn.

VENICE. By THOMAS OKEY. [3rd & Revised Edn.

VERONA. By ALETHEA WIEL. [3rd Edn.

Thomas Cranmer.
Archbishop of Canterbury.
From the painting by G. Fliccius in the National Portrait Gallery

DA690
C3
T3

The Story of Canterbury

by G. R. Stirling Taylor

Illustrated by Katherine Kimball

London: *J. M. Dent & Sons, Ltd.*
Bedford Street, Covent Garden, W.C.
New York: E. P. Dutton & Co. 1912

43511
OCT 1?

All rights reserved

CONTENTS

ILLUSTRATIONS

Illustrations

To the Isle of Thanet
21
...he Old Church of St. Andrew.

The Story of Canterbury

CHAPTER I

The City of Canterbury

IT will be convenient if we consider first what exactly is the scope of the subject of this book: we want to decide the point of view from which we shall contemplate a town which has lived through a history of something approaching nineteen hundred years. Unless we find some central idea for our study, we shall be lost in the multitude of divergent facts which have happened during that long time. The affairs of wayward human beings do not always sort themselves in order round a central point, but in the case of Canterbury they have been more considerate for the historical reader. This city has a predominant note which governs all the rest of its voices.

The mediæval town of Canterbury was one of the most famous centres of the Roman Church. It was, of course, the seat of the Primate of England; but it was, still more, the place where lay the sainted remains of Thomas Becket, whose reputation brought to his tomb pilgrims from all Christendom. In the history of Canterbury, we find a summary of many of the chief characteristics of mediæval times. For, be it remembered, a fact which the modern reader will perhaps forget, the Church of Rome in the Middle Ages was an overwhelming power which wound itself about every part of the social structure. In mere bulk of material wealth, the Church in England had got into its possession a vast amount of land—then the main form of property. When Henry VIII. dissolved the monasteries, it was discovered that they had held one-third of the total landed estates of the country: and the "regulars" of the monasteries were only one part of the ecclesiastical class.

It was not only in material wealth that the Church was so supreme in mediæval society. It was also predominant in learning. There was no science then to dispute with it the control over men's minds. Thus the Church held the keys of many of the gates to success in this life: it also held the keys of the world to come. The layman still believed with his whole heart in the rewards and terrors of religion: at least the sceptics were only an insignificant few in the great mass. The Pope was a mighty king of the earth; even the parish priest was the agent of a heavenly host which distributed the pleasures and pains of humanity at its good will.

In their material and in their mental life the men and women of the Middle Ages were conscious of the Church at every turn. The central interest of this mediæval town of Canterbury is that it represents, in a very particular way, this great Church which was such an urgent feature of mediæval life.

A study of the present topographical features of Canterbury, even after this long lapse of modern life, will go far towards reconstructing for us a typical town of the Plantagenet and Lancastrian and Tudor periods; and a survey of its historical records may do much to give reality to that old-world manner of thinking, and that old-world way of living, which constituted the life of the pilgrims who went to Canterbury—and these were gathered together from all the lands of mediæval Europe.

Just because Canterbury was the seat of the premier Archbishop of England it must not be suspected that its history will therefore give an erroneous and exaggerated idea of the influence of the Church. Every important mediæval town had its great church, and many smaller parish churches and religious foundations. Take the case of London—a city of merchants before verything else, for in early days it was not even the place of the royal Court. London, by the end of the 1100-century, had a bishop's cathedral, twelve great conventual churches, and one hundred and twenty-six parish churches, and all these when the population could not have exceeded thirty or forty thousand people at the most. It is true to take London life as typical of the traders of the Middle Ages, just as it is fair to take Canterbury as a picture of the ecclesiastical life in any normal town.

There is one hint which may be given to the student or traveller in Canterbury. It is not wise or discriminating to think of the town merely as something grouped round a central great cathedral. That would be an unbalanced view of the whole. Of course the Cathedral of Christ Church is by far the greatest event and fact in the town; yet it is probable that the real atmosphere of the old days will be breathed more naturally by the traveller if he is careful to visit that delightful series of little flint-walled parish churches which are still scattered all over the city. There are still a dozen or so of these, many of them with more apparent signs of age about them than the mighty Cathedral. Besides, the great church is so stupendous that even the most imaginative of minds will find it hard to regard it as anything more than a "show" place: it seems so far away from the reality of life, much farther away from most of our modern minds than it was from the thought of even the humblest pilgrims who believed that it held, in very truth, the wonder-working shrine of St Thomas. The reality of a mediæval church was more than the wonders of piers and vaulting, and the jewellery of glittering glass—it was its possession of the holy relics of the saints, whose worship brought peace and health to those who cast themselves before their shrines.

This note of religious conviction in the Middle Ages was not quite what we understand by that term to-day. If we seek to understand the pilgrim mind, we may turn to Geoffrey Chaucer's tales of the Canterbury pilgrims; and, certainly, the men and women who set out from the Tabard Inn of Southwark were not of the turn of mind which would feel itself at restful ease in the Bible-classes and mothers' meetings of this twentieth-century religious life. If the Church was a more pervading fact in life than it is now, it had also a broader influence, not so limited in its appeal to ordinary human beings. One makes the observation without expressing an opinion as to the merits of its broadness. The mediæval Church held close within its bounds the sinners as well as the saints of its day: there was scarcely the same distinction between the two sets. This same Church held almost all the learning and culture; and a greater part of the governing class was drawn from its priests. There was rebellion from the laws of the Catholic Church during the Middle Ages; but it was little more serious than a schoolboy playing truant. Until the great chaotic upheaval of the Reformation, which came with sudden dramatic violence, the Church was an all-pervading thing in the everyday life of the ordinary man and woman. And Canterbury is the chief seat in England of this all-powerful Church.

There was a second reason for the importance of this town: the most important of facts can easily be exaggerated; few statements of historical generalisation can stand alone without many qualifications; and so with this subject. After all, Canterbury began its serious career as the capital of the Kings of Kent, when Christianity was no more than a mythical rumour, if as much as that. Some will claim that the Canterbury of the Romans was important enough to be called its origin, in which case this city began as a posting-station and fort on the great Roman road leading from the landing-places on the coast of the Channel towards London and the North. This function of a posting place for inns and entertainment long remained, indeed, a definite part of its right to historical prominence. We shall have to record frequent hospitality to travellers of fame, mainly on their way between London and the Continent.

There is one other hint which may be useful in getting a right perspective when one is looking over Canterbury. If we first consider the tiny church of St Martin outside the walls, we shall be nearer the beginnings of Canterbury than if we go straight to the great Cathedral; and we shall be more in the mood for understanding that a town, like a human being, is a thing which grows—it does not spring into life full made. The study of a town is increasingly interesting and understandable if we realise this fact of gradual growth.

With these general words on the atmosphere of Canterbury—the scope of its possibilities as a piece of history—we shall proceed to consider its records in the chronological order, attempting to weave its continuous story as a whole: considering the archbishop's church of Christ Church and the abbot's house of St Augustine; the smaller houses of religious bodies; the City Corporation; and the interference of the kings from Westminster—all these elements making together the tale of the town. In the latter part of the book, the separate buildings will be viewed from the topographical standpoint of the visitor who desires to perambulate the town in detail. The history is placed first; for without its written record Canterbury is, with all the beauty of its churches and the picturesqueness of its streets, only the skeleton of its more glorious past.

The seriously minded reader, who really desires to make the story of Canterbury a living thing, with all its atmosphere of the days that have now given place to new men and new manners, will, of course, have to travel and think beyond the walls of this city. Canterbury is, after all, only one link of a chain of ancient places in this neighbourhood, to which it was very intimately bound. For example, this chief town and its origin and purpose will never be understood, in all its vitality, until one has journeyed to it along one of those ancient roads of which it was the centre. Even to this day, within a few minutes' walk of the West Gate, we can still tread the same path along which came the tin merchants from the Cornish mines, which was England's first venture in international trade—unless, perhaps, we began our commercial career as slave-dealers. In later days, this road devoted itself to the more spiritual duty of bearing the pilgrims who came to worship at Becket's shrine; it became known as the Pilgrims' Way, a name which it retains to this moment in many parts of its course. This Celtic road can be found on the east side of the city, between Patricksbourne and Bekesbourne, as it continued its way towards the shipping place at Dover, or its near neighbourhood. Compared with these prehistoric ways, the Roman roads—which still are easily traced from the landing-places at Richborough, Dover, and Lymne—are almost modern innovations. At the end of these three roads can still be found the ruins of the Roman castles which guarded their ports; and on the north-east coast of Kent is the ruin of Reculver, another Roman fortress, which Ethelbert made his

DISTANT VIEW OF CANTERBURY CATHEDRAL

palace when he gave up his Canterbury house to St Augustine, to serve as the foundation of the church which is now the Cathedral in its later form. Then, again, all Kent is dotted with the manors and buildings which were the possessions of the great priory of Christ Church or its rival abbey of St Augustine. Thus, there are still remains of the archbishop's palaces at Addington and Otford. The latter had been in the possession of the see since Offa of Mercia gave it as a gift in 791.

But it is impossible to do more than just hint at all the places within the county which are really part of the history of Canterbury in the broader sense, for they are beyond the practicable scope of this book. Still they should be always in the background of the reader's mind: a good history or guide to Kent will supply the details. If a map of Kent is marked with a red line under every name intimately connected with Canterbury as a manor of the monastery or in the domain of the archbishop, then it will be seen how, after all, the city is but the centre of the greater district of Kent, which was once the whole kingdom of the Saxon king who had Canterbury for his chief seat of government. If we try to think of Canterbury as once the capital of a material kingdom, we shall then go on to understand how in later days it became the capital of the immaterial kingdom of the Church.

CHAPTER II

The Beginnings of Canterbury

The Britons

IT is only a mind overflowing with conceit for the supremacy of man that will expect to find the human race present at the birth of Canterbury. Viewed in a properly logical perspective, Canterbury is the creation of vast geological and physical forces to which little men have bowed, forces which they have turned to what use their strength permitted. The beginning of Canterbury was the marshy valley of the Stour River, as it is now called, at the psychological moment in its course, as it were, where its water was spread wide enough to make it shallow and fordable, and yet not too wide to make it unduly inconvenient. In these prehuman days, the tide of the sea swept over the marsh which is now the dry land of many of the city streets. This spot was just on the border line between the open country of the plains of Kent and the thickly wooded and hillier land which lay away beyond to the south, where the woods were a barrier to easy habitation and use. But the top ridges of these hills were more barren; and along the North Downs of Kent came that oldest of all British roads, which carried the tin, dug from the Cornish mines, to the ships which were to take it over the Channel or perhaps even round the Bay of Biscay to the Mediterranean peoples. It was this road which, in the far-distant centuries, was to become the Pilgrims' Way.

Thus, the first use that man found for this spot, which became Canterbury, was as a ford over the Stour River, by which most easily to reach the sea, or, on the contrary, to journey inland. It is even possible that from this place to the coast the journey may have been accomplished in boats. It must be remembered, also, that the east coast of Kent was not then as far distant from Canterbury as it is now; for Thanet was then an island, with a narrow arm of the sea reaching between Reculver and Richborough. The land road, as we have seen, continued beyond the Stour in the direction of the coast near Dover. Thus, like many other famous cities, Canterbury was born as the place of a ford.

Of its pre-Roman days we have, of course, no contemporary, written records, and very little else in unwritten signs. Besides the roads just mentioned, and extensive fortified places and mounds in the near neighbourhood (such, for example, as those at Tunford, near Chartham, which was probably a more important Celtic centre than the less defensible Canterbury, in the early days), we are probably rash in deciding that the Dane John Mound, still standing in the city, is a relic of the British inhabitants. It stands within a few moments' walk of the south railway station, which has itself taken the place of another similar mound which stood on that spot until the railway came; and there were the remains of a third smaller mound, not many yards from the Dane John, to the south-east.

However, many authorities deny that these earthworks are of British construction, and ascribe them to Danish or even Norman days. But it is more or less certain that British Canterbury had established itself as a place of some importance when Cæsar landed on the Kentish coast in B.C. 55. It is highly probable that it was at this place that he met the first resistance on the day after the landing of his second and more ambitious expedition. If this is so, it is a pertinent illustration of what we have decided to be the central fact of Canterbury's origin—namely, an all-important spot on the main road into the interior, the first place which Cæsar reached in his advance. He probably found a comparatively humble village, although Nennius, a Welsh priest who wrote about A.D. 800, tells us that the Britons called it "Cær Ceint," the fortified city.[1] Geoffrey of Monmouth, writing in the days when it was fashionable to imitate the history of Rome as nearly as possible, says that Canterbury was founded, in the year B.C. 900, by a British king named Lud-Hudibras, but this was merely a rather snobbish attempt to go one better than Rome's Remus and Romulus.

The Romans

With the Romans we arrive at the period of written records, and, also, we now begin to possess fairly abundant remains of contemporary buildings. The first writer to mention Canterbury by name is Ptolemy, who lived about the year A.D. 150. He says: "In the most eastern part of Britain are the people of the Cantri, and among them three towns, Londinium, Darvenum, and Rutupiæ," which, in modern names, are London, Canterbury, and Richborough. Richborough was the favourite landing-place in Roman days, and they called it "statio tranquilla": it was their making of a great military road from this port to London, passing the Canterbury ford on the way, which made the latter town of such importance. But this was not all they did; for they had two lesser ports on the Kentish coast, one at

[1] Mr Godfrey Faussett thought that this was merely the Welsh form of the Saxon name, Cantwarabyrig, as it was adopted long after the latter had become fixed.

Dover, another at Lymne; and they constructed roads from these places to join the London Road at the point of the Canterbury ford. In the "Antonini Itinerarium," the Roman military survey of road, compiled probably during the first century of the Roman Empire, Canterbury appears under the name of Durovernum, and is described as being twelve miles from Rutupiæ, fourteen from Dubræ (Dover), and sixteen miles from Portus Lemanæ (Lymne), while Canterbury is termed a fort. The "Tabula Pentingerii," which dates from about the reign of the Emperor Theodosius the Great (A.D. 378-395), marks Canterbury as being a fortified city of a considerable size, and calls it Buroavernus. These varying Roman forms of the name of Canterbury are all probably based on a Celtic Durwhern, of which the root is *dur*, meaning water, referring to the river on which the town stands; and the fact that the Romans adopted a British name is almost proof that there was an established town already there when they arrived.

What was the extent of this Roman city of Duravernum is a disputed question. That there were quite extensive buildings of stone is certain; and Roman bricks are repeatedly found built into later walls all over the city. Some antiquarians hold that the earliest Roman walls only enclosed a comparatively small part of this area, which is now merely the centre of the town, extending probably from Sun Street, just outside the present Archbishop's Palace, to the corner where Watling Street crosses St Margaret's Street, and reaching westwards as far as the first arm of the Stour, which runs under the High Street, where St Thomas's Hospital still stands. Others again think that the present walls on the south and east side are in the same position as the Roman walls. The Roman wall in Sun Street and again at the St Margaret's Street corner of Watling Street seems to be accepted by most authorities, so we have that distance as a minimum. Perhaps the two theories can be easily reconciled by the reasonable assumption that the town grew during the Roman occupation, just as there was an earlier and a later Roman wall round London. But even if we accept the larger estimate, Roman Canterbury still would remain only half as large as the space included within its mediæval walls, for the Cathedral and all the present city westwards beyond the King's Bridge in the High Street were then outside the walls at their fullest theory. Indeed, the ground which now lies between the King's Bridge and the west railway station was in Roman days probably in a marshy state.

It seems highly probable that the position of the North Gate of the Roman city was very near the west towers of the present cathedral; and Mr Faussett has made the illuminating suggestion that the Roman Christian church, which Bede said was the foundation of the later church of Augustine (which became the Cathedral) may well have been placed on that spot, just outside the walls, to be near the Roman cemetery which lay there.[1]

There is evidence of five burial-grounds used by the Romans of Canterbury, of which the one outside this North Gate, and the one beyond the present West Gate, near the church of St Dunstan, were the chief. A very massive piece of Roman masonry was discovered across the High Street, in front of the Fleur-de-Lys

[1] Mr T. G. Godfrey Faussett's brilliant paper is printed in the *Archæological Journal*, vol. xxxii. (1875), under the title "Canterbury till Domesday." It should be compared with "Ancient Canterbury," an article by Mr John Brett, published in the *Journal of the Archæological Association*, vol. xxxiii. (1877), and "Roman Canterbury," by Canon Scott Robertson, printed in *Archæological Cantiana*, vol. 15 (1883). In this last is given a complete list of all the Roman remains discovered in Canterbury, with a map marking the place of their discovery.

Hotel and the neighbouring houses. Mr Pilbrow, who was in charge of the excavations, described them, somewhat hastily perhaps, as the foundations of the Roman citadel of the town; but whether this be so or not, we may be certain that we have here the place of an important building, out of which, more than a century before, had been recovered a fine piece of tessellated pavement. The position of this building, right across the High Street, is a useful reminder that this present main thoroughfare of Canterbury was not the original chief street, which in Roman days was probably, as we might well expect, the older Watling Street, which still runs through the city, bearing the name of the most famous Roman road in the British Isles.

But Roman Canterbury now lies buried eight or ten feet under the surface; and it is impossible to get a very living picture of it to-day. Still, it served as the foundation of what was to come, and it is necessary to remember that the earlier city is still lying beneath our feet throughout, at least, the central parts of the town.

The Arrival of the Saxons and Angles

With the departure of the last Roman legions from Britain, about the year A.D. 407 (hurrying back to defend their Italy from the invading Goths), a long silence falls on the history of Canterbury. The Romans went, and the Saxons and Angles and Jutes and their kinsmen took their place, without leaving us much evidence of their manner and times of conquest. But it seems clear that it was all around Canterbury that the first invaders landed and fought. It was at Ebbsfleet, a few miles away on the Isle of Thanet, that Hengest and Horsa landed in A.D. 449. Then followed battles all over Kent; and in A.D. 473 Hengest is still recorded as fighting the British. From this year the history of Kent disappears in the sand until 565, when Ethelbert became King of the Kentishmen, with Canterbury as his capital city, under the name of Cantwarabyrig, the town of the men of Kent (or Cantwaraburh, as it is sometimes written).

Bede in his "Chronicles" calls this city "the chief place of King Ethelbert." He denotes it by its old Roman name, or a derivation therefrom, Doruvernis; but then he was merely adopting the form which had been reintroduced by the priests from Italy, who were returning to the terminology of their predecessors, the Romans. Until they revived this word, the Roman name of Canterbury had been lost in the long silence which followed the Saxon conquests; whereas, on the contrary, the Saxon names of Richborough, Dover, Reculver, and Lymne were modifications of the older Roman names which were never lost. The loss of its very name is one of the proofs that the city itself was deserted for many years after the Britons, and those whom the Romans had left behind, fled before the advance of the Teutonic invaders led by Hengest and Horsa. Canterbury was on the great road along which the invaders must necessarily travel on their way inland: if the city could not be held against the foe, then it had to be abandoned entirely, for there could be no neutrality in such an exposed position. Another fact which makes it likely that Canterbury was deserted for a long time, is the well-preserved condition of the Roman pavements and other foundations, which suggests that these must have been covered by earth and vegetation before the ground was again occupied by human beings.

So there is reason to believe that when Ethelbert made Cantwaraburh his capital, he was taking possession of what had become a deserted place. The Teutons had not been town-dwellers in their early career in England; they had been a country folk. Such centres as they had in Kent were probably near Richborough, with its great Saxon cemetery near by at Ash; or Faversham, with another similar great Saxon burial-place in its neighbourhood: but these were, after all, near towns, not in them. But around Canterbury no indications have been found of any pagan Saxon burials within two or three miles, one more proof that the city was deserted until almost the days when Christian burial customs supplanted the older pagan forms. So with Ethelbert, we repeat, Canterbury began a very fresh chapter in its life history.

Ethelbert, its new ruler, was a man of outstanding importance in the England of his day. "Aedilberct, King of the Cantwara," as Bede calls him, reigned for fifty-six years, and established himself as the chief or over-king of all the smaller kings who ruled south of the Humber—for England was yet far from acknowledging a permanent kingly house as supreme over all the land. He was what they termed a Bretwalda (or Brytenwealda), the Britain-wielder who at that time had seized the chief place among the tribes of the Heptarchy. And, as we have seen, his capital city was Canterbury, which fact denotes a more intimate acquaintanceship between the city and its monarch than we understand in these days when kings spend their autumns in Scotland and their springs in Norfolk, and their summers hidden away mysteriously behind the walls of a palace in a great city where even kings get overwhelmed by its vastness.

Canterbury was still a little market town, as we should call it to-day: even five hundred years later, it is said to have had only 8000 inhabitants; and it had far fewer at the period of which we are writing, although at the later date it had been long harried by Danish attacks. When it did show distinct signs of energetic growth, it was mainly owing to the large addition to its walls when the Christians of Augustine's following built themselves a church and monastery outside the North Gate of the old Roman city: this was the beginning of the Cathedral, and the first great event in the history of this city. We must now consider at length the story of Augustine's arrival and work in Canterbury.

CHAPTER III

The Story of Augustine

THERE is a well-known tradition, which is probably authentic as well as persistent, that Gregory, a Benedictine monk, stood one day in the great forum of Rome, watching the ways of some handsome lads who had been brought captives for sale in the slave market. Their golden hair and comely faces caught the fancy of the monk, and he inquired whence they came. From Britain, he was told, and that they were pagans. "Alas," sighed the Benedictine, "that the Devil should have for his subjects such shining faces; alas, that such perfect bodies should hide hearts so empty of heavenly beauty." Then he asked the name of their race: and the merchants answered, "They are called Angles." "Fitly named, indeed," said Gregory, "for they have angelic faces. "And what is the name of their province?" The answer was "Deira." "Good again; saved *de ira*—from wrath—into the mercy of Christ. And the name of their king?" "Aelle." "Then, alleluia, let the praises of God be sung in that land."

In the year 590 this merry ecclesiastical punster was made Pope of the Roman Church, and as Gregory I. he realised his desire of a mission to the heathen in England. It was in 595 that he instructed his steward in Gaul to buy young English slave boys in order that they might be trained in the monasteries to be missionaries to their fellow-countrymen. It was professional conversion with a vengeance! Whether the purchased boys turned out an unsatisfactory lot, we do not know; but in the next year, 596, Gregory chose Augustine, the prior of the monastery of St Andrew's in Rome, and sent him on a mission, with many monkish followers, to turn the English to the worship of a new God. However, on their way through Gaul, towards their destination, they heard such alarming travellers' tales of the pagan barbarity and inhospitality of their future hosts, that the monks thought better of their valour, and despatched Augustine back to Rome to get the Holy Father's permission to return. But the Pope would not hear of such a thing; and off they set once more toward England, where, after many precautions, they arrived, in the spring of 597, on the shores of the Isle of Thanet.

As is naturally to be expected, they first endeavoured to come to terms with the great King Ethelbert at Canterbury. It was not a difficult matter, for his wife, Bertha, the granddaughter of Clovis, the famous King of the Franks, was already a Christian, and her husband was of such easy-going paganism that he allowed her to keep a private chaplain who conducted Christian services in a church of St Martin on the east side of the city. According to Bede's account, Augustine's interpreters informed Ethelbert that the monks "were come from Rome with a joyous message that would assure a certainty of joys in heaven everlastingly with the living and true God." Ethelbert thought such a prospect sufficiently alluring to offer the messengers all necessary hospitality on Thanet until he had considered the situation. A few days later the king set out from Canterbury, and, crossing to Thanet, he demanded an open-air conference with the monks, for he thought there would be more chance of witchcraft in a closed building. So it was that Augustine preached his gospel before the pagan Ethelbert at this first meeting. The king was not to be led away by a sudden impulse, and he replied with caution: "Your words and promises are fair, but they are also new to me and my companions, and of vague meaning; therefore I cannot agree to them as to forsake that which I have believed so long with the whole race of my fellow-English. But since you are strangers from afar in my kingdom, and are wishful to preach to us those things which you believe true, we desire not to do you hurt, but rather to give you good cheer and all those things which are necessary to your maintenance: neither do we forbid you to gain over as many as you can to your faith."

Then Bede continues to tell how Ethelbert gave the monks a home in Canterbury, and how they set out to take possession of it in solemn order: "As they drew near to the city, after their manner, with the holy cross and the image of our Lord and King, Jesus Christ, they sang together this litany—'We beseech thee, O Lord, for Thy great mercy, that Thy wrath and anger be turned away from this city, and from Thy holy house, for we have sinned. Hallelujah.'" That is the first piece of detailed story in the history of Canterbury, and it marks the beginning of its career as the first town in the records of the Church of England, and that is the central fact in the life of this city.

We now begin to get definite information as to the position and uses of some of the oldest buildings in Canterbury. For this information Bede is our chief authority.[1] He tells us that Augustine and his monks

[1] The revised translation, with an introduction, life, and notes, by A. M. Sellar (G. Bell & Sons), is a very useful edition of Bede's "Ecclesiastical History of England," without the reading of which it will be hard to get into the atmosphere of our early history.

took up their abode in Canterbury, where they performed constant fasting and prayers, despising all wealth except what was necessary for their daily sustenance. "There was," says Bede, "on the east side of the city, a church dedicated of old to St Martin, which was built whilst the Romans were still in the island; wherein the Queen, who was a Christian, was accustomed to pray." It was in this church of St Martin, which we can enter to-day with the strong conviction that many of its stones stand as they did when Augustine and Bertha knelt therein, that the monks performed their first devotions. But soon the king himself became a convert, and henceforth they had a wider range for their efforts: "nor was it long before he gave his teachers a settled residence, fit for their rank, in his chief city of Canterbury, with such possessions of varied kinds as were necessary for them." We know, from the "Vita Augustini," that it was his own palace in Canterbury that Ethelbert presented to the monks. This palace almost certainly stood on some part of the ground which now is enclosed within the area of the Cathedral close and its monastic buildings and Archbishop's Palace. It may well be that the royal palace itself gave way for the episcopal one. One very good reason for assigning the palace to this corner of the city is the name of the gate which once existed in the city wall at the east side of the Cathedral. This postern was called Queningate, that is the Queen's Gate, a name which still attaches to the spot, though the gate is no longer there. Now, since we have already seen reason to believe that there were no royal personages dwelling in Canterbury until Ethelbert came there, and since we also know that after giving his palace to Augustine he retired to Reculver, where he made his palace instead, and further since Canterbury henceforth had no permanent royal residence, therefore, the queen of this gate must presumably have been Bertha, Ethelbert's wife. And there is the most plausible explanation why she would have good reason for using a gate in such a position, for it was on the way to her devotions at St Martin's Church, outside the walls towards the east. So that there are very good reasons for holding that the present Archbishop's Palace is on or very near the site of Ethelbert's palace, which he gave to Augustine and his monkish followers.

Being thus well established in Canterbury, Augustine journeyed back to Arles, where the archbshop, Vergilius, received the orders of the Pope to consecrate him Archbishop of all the English. The name of Canterbury was not allotted to him; indeed, Gregory had always intended that London should be the residence of the new high priest of England. But, unfortunately, London was not yet established in the faith; and before it was so settled Canterbury had won for itself the right to be the archbishop's seat. So the fame of Canterbury was rather a mere chance, after all—as much of fame is, perhaps. Then Augustine, after his consecration, returned to his followers in England, and they set about the building of a more permanent abode. Bede tells us that within the city of Canterbury he "recovered therein, with the support of the king, a church, which people told him had been built of old by the believers in the days of the Romans; and he consecrated this in the name of the Holy Saviour, our divine Lord Jesus Christ, and then established a residence for himself and all his successors."

Such is the first record of the foundation of the monastery of Christ Church and its chapel, which became Canterbury Cathedral. The church which had been built by the Roman Christian, was almost certainly the same one which we have seen in our glance at the Roman city, just outside the North Gate of Canterbury, which stood somewhere between

ST MARTIN'S CHURCH

the present western towers and the Christ Church Gate of the close. So that the Cathedral of to-day is the direct descendant of the Roman church which Augustine restored.

But this church was as yet scarcely the most

TOWERS OF ST AUGUSTINE, CANTERBURY

important sacred building of the neighbourhood. For about the same time Augustine "also built a monastery not far from the city to the eastward, in which, by his advice, Ethelbert erected from the foundation the church of the blessed apostles Peter and Paul, and enriched it with divers gifts; wherein the bodies of the same Augustine, and of all the bishops of Canterbury, and the kings of Kent, might be buried. Nevertheless, it was not Augustine who consecrated that church, but Laurentius, his succcessor." This monastery became in later days known as St Augustine's Abbey, after its reconsecration by Dunstan.

The probability is that Ethelbert begun this monastery of SS. Peter and Paul before he had decided to surrender his palace to the monks. There is evidence that it was on this spot that he worshipped his earlier gods before his conversion. Thorn, the historian of St Augustine, writing towards the end of the 1300 century, records that in the year A.D. 598 "there was not far from Canterbury, towards the east, about midway between the church of St Martin and the city walls, a temple or idol-place, where King Ethelbert, according to the custom of his people, was wont to pray, and with his nobles to sacrifice to demons and not to God; which temple Augustine purged from the defilements and impurities of the heathen, and having broken in pieces the idol that was in it, he changed it into a church, and dedicated it in the name of St Pancras the martyr; and this was the first church hallowed by Augustine." Thorn goes on to say that there was still, in his day, an altar in the south porch where Augustine had celebrated mass on the same spot whereon had formerly stood the idol which Ethelbert had once worshipped; and he tells the tale of how the dispossessed spirit of this pagan altar had tried to overthrow the church in revenge for his defeat.

The masonry, which to this day remains of the ruins of this church of St Pancras, is apparently of the very early Saxon period; and there is, therefore, good reason to believe that in these ruins we have the actual remains of St Augustine's church. It was probably a smaller and temporary chapel which was useful while the greater SS. Peter and Paul church was being built. There is also a good deal of Roman material in these ruins of St Pancras; so Augustine may well have built it of the remains of an earlier Roman Christian chapel, which Ethelbert had adopted in his heathen days.

We have now arrived at a point when we can visualise Canterbury as the centre of a flourishing Christian community, with St Martin's and St Pancras's built, and Christ Church and SS. Peter and Paul's monastery in the process of building; and all this in the few years before Augustine's death in A.D. 605. And of all these, Saint Martin's Church undoubtedly claims presidence, for it was the first Christian temple in Canterbury; whether we hold (which is quite possible) that it was founded in the days of Roman Christianity, or whether we take the less ambitious view that it was put up by Queen Bertha and her chaplain Lindhard, whom she brought with her from her Frankish home when she came here to marry the pagan Ethelbert, in the year 575. Bede himself says it was of Roman building, and he wrote from notes supplied by a dweller of Canterbury. Nevertheless, the dedication to St Martin is a difficulty, for he did not die until A.D. 402, and the Romans had left England within a few years of that date: which does not leave much time or chance for its building during the troubled days of their departure, and before the chaos of the Saxon arrivals. But there is little doubt that the present church of St Martin has much of its structure just as it was when Queen Bertha and Bishop Lindhard showed religious hospitality to Augustine and his followers when they first arrived.

But it will be impossible to realise the position of

Canterbury in these first days of its ecclesiastical history until we remember that although Augustine had come as a missionary to the pagans of Kent and the eastern parts of the island, yet there was an already established Christian Church in the west of England and Ireland. British bishops had attended the Council of Arles in A.D., 314; and their Church had not been destroyed by the Saxon invasions, but had rather been swept back into Wales. So flourishing indeed was this Celtic Church that it produced a first-class heretic named Pelagius, who taught free-will and made very light of the fall of Adam and predestination: but the Council of Carthage, 412, said this was unsound doctrine. St Patrick and Gildas had taught the faith in Ireland, and Columba had retaliated by being the missionary from Ireland to Scotland. So, mainly shut up in Wales and Ireland, was Celtic Christianity with its back to the wall against Saxon pagans.

With this pre-Augustine Church of Britain the missionary of Canterbury had to deal; for had he not been appointed archbishop over the whole island? So after he was fairly settled in Canterbury, he set out to come to terms with Welsh bishops, who had stubborn views as to the exact way to shave the head, and the proper time to hold Easter celebrations. These do not seem altogether vital questions to most people; yet the old chronicles record a tale of Augustine only gaining the Celtic bishops' consent to discuss the matter, by performing a miracle on a blind man. So a great debate of bishops and doctors of ecclesiastical law was arranged to take place before Augustine. But he bore himself with a superior air that got on their nerves, not even rising from his chair when they approached him. So they rejected his terms and refused to acknowledge him as their archbishop. Soon after this conference Augustine died, 605, and when

Ethelbert died in 616 the first generation of Canterbury's ecclesiastical history ended.

The new king-lord of Canterbury, the son of Ethelbert, went back to the earlier faith of his race; and the new archbishop, Laurentius, got so disheartened or alarmed that he made all arrangements to leave England for good: but on the last night, as he lay in St Augustine's monastery—so runs the tale—he saw, or dreamed of, a vision of St Peter, who scourged him for his cowardice. In the morning they say his shoulders were marked deep by the lash; and when he showed them to the relapsed King Edbald, that unworthy man shook with fear of the divine signs, and promised to put away his idols and be baptised. By this time, Mellitus, that companion of Augustine who had been made bishop of London, had been driven out of his see by relapsed converts, and he lived in Gaul until he was appointed to succeed Laurentius as archbishop in Canterbury.

All these men, namely, the three archbishops, also King Ethelbert and his wife Bertha and Edbald their son, also Lindhard the chaplain of St Martin's, were buried in Augustine's monastery of SS. Peter and Paul: the three archbishops in the chapel on the north side of the aisle, and the rest on the corresponding chapel on the south side. There was a reason for thus choosing SS. Peter and Paul's rather than Christ Church, within the walls; for the early Saxons followed the Roman custom of forbidding burials within the city, which were not allowed until the time of Archbishop Cuthbert (consecrated 740). It was the presence of these revered bodies, above all, of the body of Augustine, which gave the Abbey of SS. Peter and Paul so great a superiority over the priory of Christ Church at this period: a superiority which it increased when King Canute presented the body of St Mildred, as we shall see, in 1027; this supremacy, indeed, held until the martyrdom of Becket and the possession of his relics by the Cathedral, swamped every other ecclesiastical vested interest in the town, and well nigh in all Europe. But that is to anticipate. As early as 610 we find a papal order from Rome granting to SS. Peter and Paul's Abbey that no bishops should intrude therein except they were freely admitted to perform services in the abbey church. Here we find the beginning of that great rivalry between Christ Church with its archbishops and priory on one side, and on the other the abbots and monks of the Augustine order without the walls.

The conversion of the rest of Great Britain to Christianity was not much due to Augustine and his successors; but we shall see how they were able, after a considerable struggle, to assert the right of Canterbury to remain the overruling archbishop's seat in England.

CHAPTER IV

Saxon Canterbury

SPITE of all the assertion of the ecclesiastical lords of Canterbury to be chief bishops of all England, when Archbishop Honorius died in 653, Rochester, a few miles away, was the only bishopric which would acknowledge their claims. Indeed, Canterbury for a long time was beaten in vigour by the ecclesiastics who came southwards from Iona, the Isle of Columba, and at first would not acknowledge obedience to the rules of the Roman Church. Northumbria and its kings were now beginning to take the place of the kings of Kent, as the most powerful rulers in England. Edwin, who married the daughter of Ethelbert of Kent, had listened to the arguments of his wife and her chaplain, Paulinus; he was baptised, and made the chaplain bishop of York. But Penda, the pagan king of Mercia, slew Edwin, and his wife fled back to Canterbury with Paulinus: and only the faithful deacon James was left in all Northumbria to represent the new faith.

Then the Scottish monks came south and seized the empty place—one of the earliest instances of Scotchmen coming south with success. The temporary strength of the Celtic Church must necessarily be mentioned in a history of Canterbury, for it was not without a struggle that the latter city asserted itself in triumph. The monks of Iona had the juster claim, if hard work was the test, for they converted the greater part of England. But the history of Canterbury has

HARBLEDOWN CHURCH—THE APPROACH TO CANTERBURY LONDON ROAD

some right to the story; for the man who had a chief part in the victory of the Roman Church of Canterbury over the Celtic Church of Iona was Saint Wilfrid, whose body lies buried in the Cathedral; for Archbishop Oda claimed that he conveyed to Canterbury the holy relics of the saint from Ripon, where they had first been buried. However, it must be admitted hat the evidence is conflicting; and Ripon has always claimed that the body removed was that of the second Wilfrid. So we must stand before the spot pointed out in the corona of Christ Church, with a truce of doubt.

It was at the Council of Whitby, 664, that the great debate was fought out by the rival parties. The Northumbrian king, Oswy, presided: Wilfrid spoke for Rome, and the Bishop Colman for the Celts. Wilfrid was hot and contemptuous in his speech; he was one of those men who are convinced they are certainly right. The apparent points in dispute seemed somewhat technical—whether Easter should be at one date or another. The king had found that he was in the midst of his Easter festival while his Roman-minded queen was fasting during her Lent. It is clear that households could not be run conveniently on that principle. But what determined the Whitby debate in favour of the Roman practices was when the king heard from the disputants that St Peter was on the side of Rome. "I will not go against Him who holds the keys of Heaven, lest, perchance, when I come to the gate, I find none to open to me." This careful consideration of his future eternal welfare perhaps turned the course of English ecclesiastical history. Had the king decided otherwise, Canterbury might well have been permanently swamped by York —and England might have been a "Non-conformist" country from its start: in other words, the Reformation would have come eight hundred years before Henry

VIII. desired to get a divorce from Catherine of Aragon. Such are the thoughts one should revolve in the mind before the St Wilfrid spot in Canterbury Cathedral.

We now take up once more the direct story in Canterbury, in the person of the great Archbishop Theodore: one of the outstanding holders of the see. His appointment was somewhat by chance; for Wighard, a priest of Kent, had died of the plague in Rome, almost at the moment of his consecration, by the Pope, as archbishop. A Greek monk of Tarsus, Theodore, was rather unexpectedly chosen to take the vacant place. There were complications, however; for being of an Eastern and unorthodox order, Theodore's head was shaven after the wrong pattern; and four months waiting was necessary until his hair had grown sufficiently to permit of its rearrangement after the manner of the Roman tonsure. But in 668 he was consecrated, and started off for Canterbury, accompanied by his friend Hadrian, who was, in part, sent by the Pope to guard against any unorthodox lapses on the side of the newly-shaven Greek.

This is not the place to tell how Theodore first put the Church of England in an organised state, and on a national basis. Rather strangely, the man who had won over England for Rome, against the claims of the Celtic Church of Ireland and Scotland, namely Wilfrid, was the man who hampered the unity of England by asserting the claims of York against the Archbishop of Canterbury, when the latter ordered the see of York to be sub-divided. Theodore eventually had his way, but not until Wilfrid had appealed to Rome—the first time in English history that the Pope had been asked to overrule the orders of an English archbishop, confirmed in this case by the approval of the king and Witan. The decision of the Pope in Wilfrid's favour was disregarded in England; indeed, when he returned from Rome with the papal bull, he was promptly thrown into prison and dispossessed of his goods: and after his release he wandered for long as an exile; amongst other places he went to Sussex and converted the pagans of that district which had not yet been touched by any evangelists from the neighbouring see of Canterbury: an instance of the slackness of the southern ecclesiastics.

In the words of Bede, Theodore "visited all the island, wherever the tribes of the English dwelt, for he was gladly received and heard by all persons; and everywhere attended and assisted by Hadrian, he taught the right rule of life and the canonical custom of celebrating Easter. This was the first archbishop whom all the English Church consented to obey." In Canterbury itself, Theodore and Hadrian, both men of learning above the standard of their time, gathered together a school whose scope reached far beyond mere ecclesiastical study. Bede says: "they gathered a crowd of disciples, and rivers of wholesome knowledge daily flowed from them to water the heart of their hearers; and together, with the books of Holy Scripture they taught them also the metrical art, astronomy, and ecclesiastical arithmetic [whatever that may be!]. A testimony whereof is that there are still living at this day some of their scholars, who are as well versed in the Greek and Latin tongues as in their own." It was indeed time to strive after the raising of the standard of culture in the south; for the monks of Lindisfarne, Jarrow, Wearmouth, and York were taking a first place for scholarly accomplishment; and Caedmon, the herdsman of Whitby, had died in 680 with an immortal name for his poems; and Bede and Alcuin were soon to come. Theodore died in Canterbury in 690, eighty-eight years old, and he was buried in the Abbey of SS. Peter and Paul, beside Augustine and his fellows. When his body was translated, in the year 1091, Gocelin says that it was in a very perfect state, with its cowl and pall.

With the death of Theodore, there was a long lapse in the glory of Canterbury: and the best events and men in the English Church were in the province of the North. In 734 the Pope sent the pall to Egbert, the Bishop of York; that is, he conferred on him the rank of an archbishop. It had been Gregory's original plan that England should have two archbishops—neither of them to be of Canterbury, by the way—one at London and the other at York. Thus, this arrangement of 734 was the later accomplishment of the first scheme. The Bishops of Canterbury were not yet strong enough to assert their superiority; and it was not until the strong Lanfranc appeared that the premiership of the southern archbishops was formally acknowledged. For a short time, from the year 786 until 802, there was even a third archbishopric at Lichfield, because Offa, the king of Mercia, did not care to acknowledge the Archbishop of Canterbury, who was to him, probably, little more than the creature of the inferior kingdom of Kent, now become a part of the greater kingdom of Wessex: and he was sufficiently powerful to get the papal legate to sanction the scheme of a new archiepiscopal see. In short, all during the 700 century it was a slack time in the history of Canterbury. The archbishops of this period are insignificant: Brihtwald (693-731) who succeeded Theodore, was formerly the Abbot of Reculver a few miles away; Tatwyn (731-34) was also a monk, from Mercia in this case; Nothelm (735-39) was a priest from London, not a monk apparently, a friend of the Abbot of St Augustine's in Canterbury; Cuthbert (740-58) had been Abbot of Lyminge. This last archbishop had been the first to break through the regular custom of burial in the church of SS. Peter and Paul,[1] and the feud between the

[1] "For when Cuthbert went to Rome to receive his pall and full powers from the Pope Gregory, he obtained permission that all archbishops might be buried in the church of

monks of St Augustine's and the priory of Christ Church burst into its first flame when Cuthbert was buried in the Cathedral. For the relics of holy men were a valuable asset to a religious corporation; they meant the offering of riches and honours with which to buy the intercession of the saints. Cuthbert was well aware what would be the result of his innovation; and he told the clergy of the Cathedral to conceal his illness and death until he was safely buried. The clergy were careful to follow the same plan when Brecgwin, the next archbishop, died in 765; and the funeral bell did not ring until the ceremony was over. Whereupon Jaenberht, the abbot of St Augustine's, marched to the Cathedral at the head of a band of armed men and demanded the body, not knowing it was already buried. Perhaps it was as a slight consolation that the same Jaenberht became the next archbishop (766-91). Indeed, he pressed his claim for the body so determinedly that the members of Christ Church thought his election would be the best way of stopping his appeal to Rome. It was during Jaenberht's term of office in the see of Canterbury that Offa, King of Mercia, invaded and conquered the kingdom of Kent; and when the conquering king suggested the transfer of the archbishopric to Mercia, Jaenberht is even recorded to have appealed to Charles the Great to invade England; but the authority for this statement is doubtful. However, as we have

Canterbury, and that a cemetery might be made within the city. For it had been customary, from the earliest time until the death of this Cuthbert, that all the kings of Kent, the archbishops and the monks of Christ Church and also the citizens, should be buried in the churchyard of SS. Peter and Paul. For the first men who were sent from Rome into England were accustomed to say that a city was not for the dead, but for the living. But now, by the will of God and at the request of the blessed Cuthbert, by the authority of Pope Gregory, and by the consent of King Eadbrith, it was ordained that all archbishops might be buried in their own church" (Gervase: "Actus Pontificum").

already noted, Offa had his way to the extent that he got his new Mercian see, but Canterbury remained an archbishopric, although a great part of its province was cut away to be placed under the control of Lichfield: leaving to Canterbury the sees of London, Rochester, Winchester, Selsey and Sherborne. Remembering the exciting events which followed his predecessor's burial, Jaenberht was careful to die within the precincts of St Augustine's Abbey, where he was buried as became a loyal member of his order.

Ethelhard, his successor (793-805), was put there by the influence of the powerful Offa of Mercia, and when an insurrection broke out against the Mercian rule in Kent, and Offa died, the archbishop had to fly from Canterbury, and take refuge in Mercia. When the revolt was settled, the Kentishmen allowed him to return; and he received a kindly letter of congratulations from Alcuin, with the slightly satirical suggestion added, however, that he ought to do penance for having run away from his Cathedral. Now that the great Offa was dead, the way was clear for the suppression of the new archbishopric of Lichfield; and Ethelhard journeyed to Rome and brought back the Pope's bill confirming the supremacy of Canterbury once more over all the province of Lichfield. This archbishop was buried in the Chapel of St John the Baptist, in his Cathedral.

CHAPTER V

The Period of the Danes

There is a sufficient excuse for marking the end of the 700-century and the beginning of the next century a dividing line for a new chapter in our history: though there are nor many real dividing lines in history—most of those inserted are chiefly for purposes of rather trifling convenience. However, the appearance of the Danish invading pirates on the English coasts, about the year 790, did indeed substantially affect the course of the history of Canterbury, which, in fact, was always so bound up with the national affairs. The first brunt of the attack fell on Northumbria and the north and eastern kingdoms: this unexpectedly brought to a sudden close that period of brilliant learning and religious enthusiasm amongst the northern churchmen, which had threatened the position of the see of Canterbury. In the "Anglo-Saxon Chronicle," under the year 794, it is recorded that, "the heathens ravaged among the Northumbrians and plundered Ecgferth's monastery at Wearmouth"; and after Halfdene's invasion of Northumbria in 875 there was scarcely a church saved between the rivers Tyne and Tweed; and the monks had fled from Lindisfarne with the body of St Cuthbert, the head of St Oswald, and their other sacred relics; and after long wanderings found refuge in 883, in the territory of Chester-le-street (near Newcastle).

But Canterbury was not in a position to take full advantage of the troubles of the see of York, for it had sore troubles of its own. Two years after the record of the "Anglo-Saxon Chronicle" just quoted, it goes on: "796. In this year Ceolwulf, king of the Mercians, ravaged Kent as far as the marsh, and took Praen their king, and led him bound to Mercia." This was in the time of Archbishop Ethelhard, with whom we closed the last chapter. His successor, Wulfred (805-832), showed that the see of Canterbury was not much more than of local power, in spite of its apparent regaining of the Lichfield province. Wulfred was a large land-owner of Kent, and perhaps as powerful as the local kings, who were still under the control of Mercia. Indeed, the archbishop was strong enough to take off the coinage of Canterbury the name of the king of Mercia; whereas the coins of Ethelhard had borne that mark of subjection. Cenwulf, the Mercian king, seized the monasteries of Reculver and Minster, which were both possessions of the church of Canterbury. The archbishop appealed to the Pope, and a long struggle followed; during which something approaching a suspension of the ecclesiastical authority resulted. Wilfred was compelled to give way, until the death of Cenwulf put the more friendly Ceolwulf in his place. But the end of the difficulty about Mercia was solved by the rise of the kings of Wessex to a supreme power which was acknowledged by the Mercians, as well as by the men of Kent; and Egbert, King of Wessex, became Bretwalda of England. Under the year 823 the "Anglo-Saxon Chronicle" says: "King Ecgbryht of the west Saxons, and King Beornwulf of the Mercians, fought at Ellendum, and Ecgbryht gained the victory, and a great slaughter was there made. He then sent Æthelwulf, his son, from the army, and Ealhstan, his bishop, and Wulfheard, his aldorman, to Kent with a large force, and they drove Baldred the King north over the Thames; and the Kentish people and those of Surrey and the south Saxons and the east

Saxons turned to him": and Ethelwulf became the King of Kent under the supremacy of Wessex. It is impossible to avoid mentioning all these general historical facts in a history of Canterbury, for we must continually remember that this city is still, during this early part of its life, the chief town of the kingdom of Kent, as well as the seat of the archbishops of the south of England. So complete was the triumph of the Wessex king in Kent that there was no need for him to have resource to all the manœuvring by which the kings of Mercia tried to place the chief metropolitan of the church at Lichfield.

But worse than the enemies from Wessex were at the door of Canterbury, and the "Anglo-Saxon Chronicle" for the year 832 has the brief and solitary statement: "In this year heathen men ravaged Sheppey." The Danes, whom we have seen already harrying the Northumbrian coast nearly half a century earlier, thus suddenly reappeared after a long pause which they had filled by ravaging Scotland and Ireland. Now they are going to affect Canterbury directly as well as indirectly; for Sheppey is on the Thames a little above the cathedral city.

Canterbury was now under the ecclesiastical lordship of the Archbishop Ceolnoth, who held the see for the long period between 833 and 870. His predecessor, Feologeld, who had held the see for a few weeks in 832 (the "Chronicle" says: "he was hallowed on the fifth day of the Ides of June and he was dead on the third of the Kal. of September"), had been the abbot of a Kentish monastery—he may perhaps be regarded as the last of the archbishops who had merely a restricted local significance, or a choice which in any real sense depended on the strength of local power. Whereas Ceolnoth seems to have been a West Saxon, the nominee of Egbert; and we find him signing a treaty of perpetual alliance between the Church of Canterbury and the Kingdom of Wessex.

Canterbury had need of a powerful ally, for the Danes were extending their raids along the south coast of England. In the year 838 it is recorded that "among the Kentish people many men were slain by the Danes." Under 851 the "Chronicle" records: "In

TOWER OF ST MARY MAGDALENE, BURGATE

this year the aldorman Ceorl with the men of Devonshire fought against the heathen men at Wicganbeorh, and there made great slaughter and gained the victory. And in the same year King Æthenstal and the aldorman Ealchere fought in ships and slew a great force at Sandwich in Kent, and took nine ships, and put the others to flight." Thus we see the peril getting nearer and nearer: then the chronicler goes on to give the most momentous statement of all: "And the heathen men, for the first time, took up their quarters over winter in Thanet. And in the same year came three hundred and fifty ships to the mouth of the Thames, and landed, and took Canterbury and London by storm." Five years later, 856, the Chronicle says: "In this year heathen men first took up their quarters over winter in Sheppey." In other words, Canterbury was gradually being surrounded by the Danes. In 865 the Danes again took winter quarters on Thanet and, says the "Anglo-Saxon Chronicle," "made peace with the people of Kent; and the people of Kent promised them money for the peace; and during the peace and the promise of money the army stole itself away by night, and ravaged all Kent eastwards." There is a suggestive fact confirming this statement in that an exceptional number of coins of Ceolnoth's minting have been discovered; which makes it probable that he was driven to melt down some of the treasure of the see in order to get money for payment of the ransom to the Danes.

There are various inserted passages in the "Anglo-Saxon Chronicle" which, if a true record, go to show us the state of the Canterbury monks at this time. The statement runs that in the first year of Ceolnoth's bishopric there was a severe epidemic among the monks of Christ Church, and only five of them were alive at the end of it; and Ceolnoth replaced the regular monks by substituting secular canons or clerks, who were free from the strict vows of the monks. It illustrates the beginning of the struggles between the "regulars," bound by the rigid vows or regulæ (rules) of their orders; and on the other hand, the secular priests who had committed themselves to no vows, but who were nevertheless subject to the laws and canons of Rome and its ecclesiastical officers. In the former case, disobedience was the breaking of a personal sacred vow; in the latter case, it was the defiance of a rule laid down by some one to whom the priest certainly owed obedience, but no solemn vow had passed beyond recall. Whether there is much distinction to the ordinary lay mind between the two positions does not matter; the old ecclesiastical mind saw a difference and it was the root of much discussion in the history of Canterbury, as we shall see later. Another inserted passage in the "Chronicle" relates that when Ceolnoth's successor, Ethelred, was moved to the see of Canterbury from his former see of Wiltshire (which, if true, is another proof of the new influence of the Wessex kings over the Church) he immediately, on establishing himself in his cathedral, took thought how he might drive out the secular clerks and replace them by regular monks. But no definite steps appear to have been taken in the matter, and the sequel will follow later in this story. This archbishop Ethelred may be remembered as one of the witnesses to the will of Alfred the Great.

His successors, Archbishops Plegmum (890-914), and Athelm (917-923), and Wulfhelm (923-942), were without personal significance: but with Oda (942-959) we reach a man of importance. For the moment there was a lull in the attack of the Danes, for terms had been made with them. Oda himself is significant of these terms, if it be really true that he was a Dane, who had been adopted by one of Alfred's nobles. His clever brain marked him out for a learned profession—which meant the priesthood in those days. So a priest he became, and for this his piety well fitted him; though in earlier life he had been a soldier, as was likely in the case of the son of a Danish pirate. Athelstan made him Bishop of Ramsbury; but this holy office did not prevent his following the king to the battle of Brunanburg, in 937, and apparently he actually fought there, or at least attended the king in battle. Then, in 942, he was offered the archbishopric of Canterbury, but replied that he had no right to it, since he was not a monk. King Edmund quickly remedied that default by despatching Oda to a monastery with instructions to the abbot to make the bearer a monk forthwith. So archbishop he became immediately he possessed a cowl. He found the cathedral of Christ Church at Canterbury in sad need of repair, and he set men to work which lasted three years. The main structure was still the building which Augustine had begun. But his spiritual repairs were more extensive than his material rebuildings: for he made a determined effort to enforce the stern discipline within the walls of the monasteries; and be also taught the ethical duties of laymen outside when he preached to the king and his nobles on their obligations towards the weak. But his most original propagandist work was in the matter of the relations of the mother, for here he announced doctrines which have of late been revived as part of the Suffragist creed. Oda, for example, ruled that a man before marriage should allot a fixed sum as her dowry, and give security that he would continue to maintain her while she was his wife; further, on his death, the wife was to be entitled to half the husband's estate, and to the whole if there was a child of the marriage. This early expounding of the endowment of motherhood is of interest coming from a Dane of the 900-century; a large part of his life and theories was closely linked with the history of his more famous successor, Dunstan, and will be told therewith. Oda was buried in the Cathedral of Canterbury; finally resting, after the rebuilding by Lanfranc, under the feretory of St Dunstan.

We now turn to the greater Dunstan (archbishop 960-988) who was one of the most vital of the beings who have been closely connected with the history of Canterbury. He was born near Glastonbury somewhere about the year 925, of a royal or noble Anglo-Saxon family, though his aristocratic descent is not absolutely certain. Apparently his father, Heorstan, was a Saxon landowner near Glastonbury; and his mother, Kynedritha, was a lady at the court of Athelstan. Dunstan was educated at the abbey of Glastonbury, one of the most ancient religious houses in the country; for there had been almost a continuous existence there, from the rule of the Celtic churchmen until the Roman system arrived from the East. Irish influences were still strong even in Dunstan's day, and it was perhaps from the Celtic ecclesiastics who lived and taught then, that Dunstan may have gained his mystical and poetic strain which coloured all the deeds of his life. He was surrounded by the altars of Irish saints who were buried there; he breathed an atmosphere of miracles. When a boy he took part in serving in the church, and became learned in the Scriptures.

But his relations at the Royal Court took him away from the abbey to the palace: a transition which was not to his taste. As he professed to see visions, and evidently knew more of the spirit than the body, the young bloods of the Court treated him in much the same way that a poet would be treated in the officer's mess of a guard's regiment. At least, they did what corresponded to a "rag" in Saxon times, they accused him of communicating with evil spirits, and got him expelled from the Court: their parting shot being to deposit him in a muddy pond.

Dunstan now tried a more clerical atmosphere and lived with his kinsman the Bishop of Winchester, who persuaded him to take the vows of a monk. Dunstan's decision was only made after a struggle, for a pledge of celibacy was against his desire; and he was only brought to it by a serious illness which almost ended in his death. He now seems to have lived mainly at the abbey of Glastonbury, where he made himself a skilled worker in many of the crafts—such as painting, music, furniture-making, and metal work. This love for the handicrafts and arts remained with him throughout his life: he was a man not unlike the William Morris of these later days.

ST DUNSTAN'S CHURCH

Then he built for himself an anchorite's cell, which was half a place of worship, half a workshop.

When Edmund came to the throne in 940, he called the youth Dunstan to his Court, where his book learning was valuable. But once more he aroused jealousy and once more he was ordered to leave, on the old charge of communications with devils. However, the order was withdrawn, as the tradition goes, because the king was in deadly peril from a runaway horse and the precipice of the Cheddar Cliffs; and on the brink he remembered that he had been harsh to Dunstan. "Oh, God, if Thou wilt save my life, I will be reconciled to Thy servant." The prayer was answered, the horse pulled up in time, and the vow was kept: and the king rode with Dunstan to Glastonbury Abbey and made him abbot.

The reform of monasteries and their monks was in the air at this time. In 910 William, Duke of Aquitaine, had founded the monastery at Cluny, the first religious house where an attempt was made to recall the older strictness of the rules of St Benedict, which had lapsed into neglect all over Europe. This widespread desire for reform suited Dunstan's temperament: not altogether, or even mainly, because it was bound up with acetism, but rather, one fancies, because it also meant an increase in learning and the arts and sciences which appealed to this broad-minded ecclesiastic. Anyhow, whatever was his motive, we find Dunstan, the youthful abbot who was scarcely twenty years of age, if so much, reforming the abbey of Glastonbury. The monastery was partly composed of monks, partly of secular priests: but even the monks were under the slackest discipline; as for the strict Benedictine rule, it was yet unknown in England. It was rather a home of learning and scholarly study that Dunstan tried to make his abbey; and the attempt was successful. And all this time Dunstan's mystical nature was laying the foundation of the innumerable tales which afterwards were credited as miracles.

Under the next king, Edred, the abbot still stood in high favour; and in his monastery was deposited the royal treasure. But with the accession of Edwy, a mere boy, in 955, there was a change. The "Anglo-Saxon Chronicle" in this year says of Edwy: "He drove St Dunstan out of the land." Apparently the abbot did not go far; for in the year 957 the "Chronicle" repeats: "In the same year Abbot Dunstan was driven away over the sea." The quarrel seems to have shown itself even as soon as the coronation festival. When the young king left his nobles at table to enjoy himself in the more congenial society of the damsel Ælfgifu, with whom he was in love, and her mother, Æthelgifu, the archbishop Oda proposed that some of them should follow the king and reprove him and bring him back to the banqueting-hall. Dunstan and the Bishop of Lichfield were commissioned to carry out the delicate business: and back the boy came with his crown replaced on his head by Dunstan. Of course the picturesque historian likes to make this scene the reason of the abbot's fall from favour. But it was probably based on something wider: partly the rise of a reaction against the severe discipline of Dunstan and his reforming friends. In any case, Dunstan fled from England to Flanders, leaving Oda the archbishop to deal with the king who had married his lady. But in the "Chronicle" of 958 it is recorded: "In this year Archbishop Oda separated King Eadwig and Ælfgyfu because they were too near akin"; and the same year the king died, and Edgar, his brother, succeeded to the throne. In the next year, 959, it is written: Edgar sent after St Dunstan and gave him the bishopric of Worcester and afterwards the bishopric of London.

Dunstan, during his exile, had lived in the great monastery of St Peter's at Ghent, where the strict Benedictine rule was observed; and it was when he returned and took high ecclesiastical office, as recorded above, that Dunstan systematically set to work in an attempt to reform the religious houses of England. His power was great, for in 961, the "Chronicle" relates: "In this year died Oda, the good archbishop; and

St Dunstan succeeded to the archbishopric" ; and he was also easily first in the secular councils of the kingdom. We can imagine his case if we think of the Prime Minister and the Archbishop of Canterbury being one and the same person to-day There was another fact which increased his greatness ; for at this time the kingdom of Kent, which had already lost its local king, now even lost the right to an ealdorman, and the archbishop had no lay rival within his diocese.

Dunstan's direct connection with Canterbury had now begun ; and the chroniclers tell us that on the first day on which he offered Mass as archbishop, a dove came down before him from the sky ; and in his sermon Dunstan called his predecessor, "Oda the Good," a name which has clung to his memory through the ages. When Dunstan came to Canterbury the ecclesiastical officers of the Cathedral were, in part at least, secular clerks, free from all the strict vows of the Benedictines, with which Dunstan had become familiar in Ghent. This archbishop has, somehow or the other, got the reputation of one who fiercely forced the monastic rules on every ecclesiastical body within his reach. There is no evidence for this historical verdict ; indeed, there is evidence the other way ; or, at least, the negative fact that there is no record that Dunstan removed any of the secular canons from the lax monastery of Christ Church, Canterbury, which served his own cathedral. It is certain that there was a determined effort at this time to introduce the true Benedictine rules into English monasteries—with its strict celibacy, its almost total silence, its prohibition of private property, the use of rough clothing, and the disuse of any flesh food which came from a four-footed beast—all these regulations were after the mind of Dunstan. But whereas his brother bishop, Ethelwold of Winchester, was harsh to the last degree in enforcing these reforms, Dunstan was always on the side of moderate patience and gentle argument. He was a man of real and wide culture, and it was not the letter of the law he desired so much as the practical result of a more efficient and better behaved and more learned Church in England. We are probably right in saying that the following canon of Edgar's reign—when Dunstan was all in all as chief minister of the kingdom—sums up Dunstan's ideal ecclesiastical system: "Every priest shall teach manual arts with diligence; no learned priest shall reproach him that is less learned, but shall mend him if he know how; no noble priest shall despise one of less noble birth, for all men are of one origin, if it be rightly considered."

At this time the history of Dunstan would be, in great part, the history of England, and there is no space for it here. But in the last few years of his life the rule of a new king, Ethelred (978), who heeded him not, took away much of his power; and Dunstan lived in retirement in Canterbury, where his doings were recorded by a priest who was his intimate friend. He was constantly taking his part in the Cathedral services, and teaching in the school attached to the monastery. Then he returned to his earlier love for the handicrafts, and spent much time in the library in annotating the manuscripts. His gentleness became proverbial in Canterbury; and more than a hundred years later we find schoolboys craftily begging to be let off a whipping for the sake of their "sweetest father, Dunstan." The details of his death were carefully recorded, within twenty years of its occurrence, by Adelard, with many mystical embellishments. It appears that on Ascension Day, 988, he preached three times and administered the sacrament, although he was very near his end and his strength was going fast. On the following Saturday he called the monks around him and received the last rites, then began to recite the psalm: "Memoriam fecit mirabilium

Suorum misericors et miserator Dominus; escam dedit timentibus Se," and passed away as he uttered it. And, as fitly became a master of the handicrafts, he was buried in the Cathedral, near the high altar, in a tomb made in his lifetime and most probably after his own planning. However, there is another account which says that he chose the place of his burial only two days before his death—just before the steps of the altar—and there a tomb was afterwards built. The story of St Dunstan is one of the most illuminating and alluring of all those whose bodies lie in the city of Canterbury. The place of his later shrine—to which the body was translated when the Saxon church was rebuilt—is now in the choir of the Cathedral, at the south end of the steps leading up to the high altar. It rouses important memories in the history of Canterbury.

His last interference in national affairs is worth recalling here, for it concerned events which happened in the very near neighbourhood of this city; and it illustrates this man and his times and the kind of excitements which must have thrilled the citizens of Canterbury when Dunstan was living so quietly within the Cathedral walls. Almost without warning the young King Ethelred appeared before the walls of Rochester, the neighbouring bishopric city, and laid siege to it, the reason given being "certain dissentions"—apparently a quarrel with the bishop. Ethelred excused himself, a few years later, on the ground that he had been misled by a wicked person named Ethelsin, "an enemy of God and man." However, at the time the king was very fierce in the attack; and it was only the energetic appeal of Dunstan that saved his fellow-bishop's property and city; and even then it needed a bribe of one hundred pounds of silver by the archbishop before the king would stop the siege. There is a touch of humour in the record that when the king had accepted the money and raised the siege, Dunstan promptly wrote to him, saying that a man who would take a bribe under such circumstances would come to a bad end very quickly. Which scarcely seems the game: to offer a bribe and then curse the fellow for accepting it and carrying out his obligations thereby undertaken. When an archbishop condescends to worldly ways and means, it is scarcely fair to turn round on his opponent with heavenly principles. Having used the devil's silver, the archbishop had a certain moral responsibility in the matter.

The next few succeeding archbishops were not of importance. Of both Sigeric (990-994) and Ælfric (995-1005) it is said that they expelled the secular canons from Christ Church, the Cathedral monastery. But it is probable that the so-called expulsion was only a token that these two men, the former of whom was a friend of Dunstan, continued the same lines of monastic reform that the latter had desired. It is also probable that the tale of their driving seculars out of Canterbury Cathedral was merely a later-day forgery for the end of glorifying the monks. Of this trick they have been repeatedly found guilty.

This is an entry in the "Anglo-Saxon Chronicle": "995. In this year appeared comets, and Archbishop Sigeric died; and Ælfric, bishop of Wiltshire, was chosen on Easter day by King Æthelred and by all his witan. This Ælfric was a very wise man so there was no more sagacious man in England. Then went Ælfric to his archiepiscopal see, and when he came thither he was received by those men in orders, who of all were most distasteful to him, that was, by clerks." Ælfric died away from his see, and it was, not until the reign of Cnut that his body was brought for burial in the Cathedral. His will is of interest, for it is a vivid reminder of the exciting times we have now reached in the history of Canterbury. He left to the king his

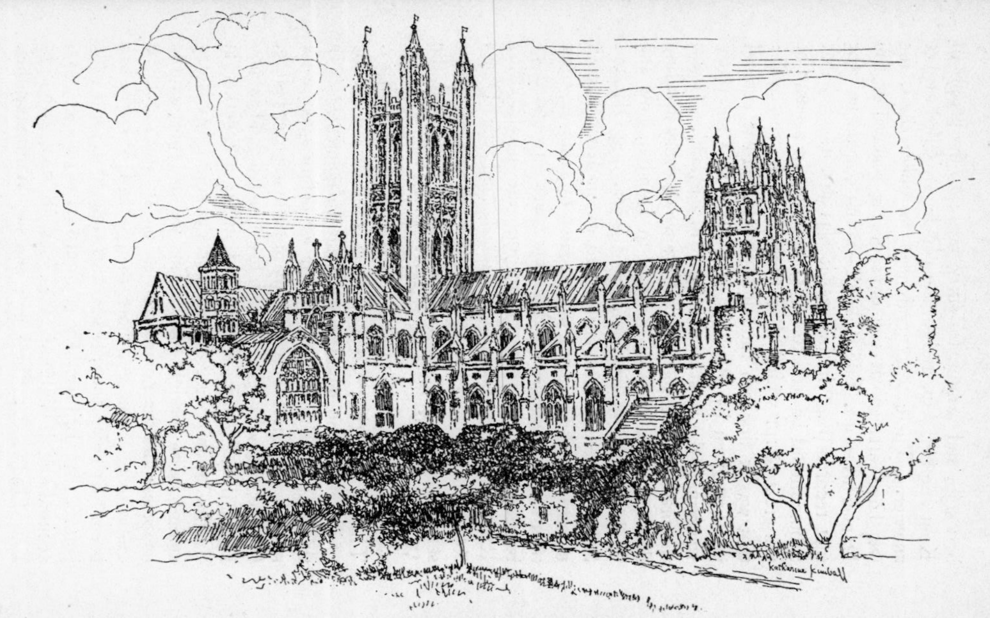

GENERAL VIEW OF CATHEDRAL

best ship, and armour for sixty men; to the people of Kent another ship, and to the people of Wiltshire yet another. There was good need for these ships, for we have arrived at the days of the renewal of the Danish invasions. The "Anglo-Saxon Chronicle" for 991 records that "in this year it was first decreed that tribute should be paid to the Danish men on account of the great terror which they caused by the sea-coast: that was at first ten thousand pounds. That counsel was first given by Archbishop Sigeric." Canterbury was almost the most exposed spot in England. It was the first tempting place for pillage which every invading fleet must pass near on its way to London, now the wealthiest city in England. In the year 994 Olaf and Sweyn were repulsed in their attack on London with ninety-four ships; and, when beaten off, they let their men loose in Kent, and Canterbury was surrounded by burning and harrying. In 999 the neighbouring Rochester was taken and sacked, and the Danes "then took horses and rode whithersoever they themselves would, and ruined and plundered almost all the West Kentish."

Then in 1009 came the fatal day of Canterbury. The record of the "Chronicle" is as follows: it is a tale of treachery and muddling and mismanagement. "In this year the ships about which we before spoke were ready; and there were so many of them as never before, from what books tell us, had been in England in any king's day. And they were all brought together at Sandwich, and were there to lie and hold this country against every foreign foe. But we had not yet the happiness and the honour that the naval force should be useful to this country, more than it had often before been. It befel, then, that at this same time, or a little before, that Brihtric, the aldorman, Eadric's brother, accused Child Wulfnoth, the South Saxon, father of Earl Godwine, to the king; and he, Wulfnoth, then went out and enticed ships to him; until he had twenty; and he then ravaged everywhere by the south coast, and wrought every kind of evil. Then it was made known to the naval force that they might easily be surrounded if they would go about it. Then Brihtric

CASTLE, CANTERBURY

took to him eighty ships, and thought that he should get himself much talked off, that he should get Wulfnoth alive or dead. But as they went thitherward, such a wind came against them as no man before remembered, and beat and thrashed all the ships to pieces, and cast them upon the land: and immediately came Wulfnoth and burned the ships. When this was all known to the other ships where the king was, how the others had fared, it was as if all counsel was at an end, and the king and the aldermen, and the high witan went home and thus lightly left the ships; and the people then that were in the ships brought them again to London, and they let the toil of all the nation thus lightly perish. When this naval force had thus ended, then soon after Lammas [August 1st] came the great hostile army, which we have called Thorkell's army, to Sandwich, and soon went their way to Canterbury, and would soon have subdued the town, if they then more speedily had not craved peace of them. And all the East Kentishmen made peace with the foe, and gave them three thousand pounds."

It was a hopeless policy to think that these Danes were to be bought off with money: sooner or later they would carry their attack to the point of the sword, and it came to that very quickly. In the year 1011 the "Chronicle" is writing: "Nevertheless, for all this peace and tribute, they went everywhere in flocks, and harried our miserable people, and robbed and slew them. And then, in this year between the Nativity of St Mary [September 8th] and St Michael's mass [September 29th] they besieged Canterbury and entered it through treacherous wiles, for Ælfmær betrayed it, whose life the Archbishop Ælfheah had before saved. And they then took the Archbishop Ælfheah and Ælfweard the king's reeve, and the abbess Leofrun and bishop Godwine. And the abbot Ælfmær they let go away; and they took there within all the men in orders, and men and women. It was not to be told to any man how many people there were. And they remained in the town as long as it pleased them, and when they had searched all the town they went to their ships, and led the archbishop with them. And they had the archbishop with them as long as to the time when they martyred him."

This Ælfheah, or St Alphege, as he is more generally known, had succeeded to the see of Canterbury in 1006. He had owed his early preferment, to the see of Winchester, to his friend Dunstan. There was a special reason why he should be known and disliked by the Northmen soldiers; for in 994, when they were wintering in England, under Olaf Tryggwesson of Norway, Ælfheah had gone to them as ambassador for the English king. While there, he had apparently baptised Olaf in the Christian faith; the latter had already been made a convert in his own country, and with the baptism he gave a promise that he would not allow his Norse army to invade England during his lifetime. He kept his promise; and that seems a very good reason why all good warriors should bear a grudge against Ælfheah.

Be this as it may, Canterbury was sacked, and we have other details to add to those of the "Chronicle" given above. The city stood the siege for twenty days before the walls were passed. Then, while the citizens were being massacred, the monks remained barricaded in their church; and it was only when the archbishop went forth to appeal for mercy for his townsmen that he was seized and thrown back again within the church door; and "these children of Satan piled barrels one upon another, and set them on fire, meaning thus to burn the roof. Already the heat of the flames began to melt the lead which ran down outside." Whereupon, the monks came forth and were immediately slaughtered by the invaders, all except four of them.

Ælfheah was dragged off in order that a ransom might be demanded for him, and this the archbishop at first promised to find. But he soon remembered that it was his people, not himself, who would have to find the money, and go without instead; so he determined that he would take no steps to raise the ransom. But the captors had hopes from other sources, for the archbishop could scarcely be deserted by the Christians of England: so the negotiations dragged on for seven months. During this time the pious ecclesiastic was preaching the words of his faith to these Danes; and not without effect—indeed, the martyrdom was not a premeditated act on the part of the captors; it was during a drunken feast which happened to fall on the day on which Ælfheah had originally promised to bring his ransom. The murder began with the pelting of the archbishop with the skulls of the oxen which they had devoured at the feast, and the pelting grew until it became a riot of stoning by tipsy men. Thorkell, one of the chief of the Danish leaders, who probably had been converted by Ælfheah's teaching, offered his maddened comrades all the gold and silver in his possession if they would cease from their work of death. But they would not heed him; and the archbishop became a martyr: the actual death-blow was dealt, strangely enough, in pity for his tortures by a Dane, whom the victim had baptised but the previous day. Probably they never really meant to kill him; and now that he was dead they gave every help in carrying the body to London, where it was buried with all reverence in St Paul's Cathedral—for Canterbury was as yet too completely in the hands of the Danish freebooters. To finish the story now, it was the greatest of the Danish kings, Canute, who, eleven years after the murder, gave orders that the body of the man his own fellow-countrymen had killed should be carried with full pomp to Canterbury Cathedral, which was its fittest resting-place, and Canute himself attended the ceremony. The tomb as it is now placed, after its translation from the earlier Saxon church, is at the north end of the steps in the choir leading up to the high altar, opposite the burial-place of Dunstan, which we have already found at the south end of the same steps. Years afterwards Lanfranc and Anselm, the Normans, had a long debate as to whether Ælfheah had the right to a place amongst the saints. Lanfranc said he had no such right: but, then, he wished to pull down as many of the English saints from their pedestals as possible. Anselm on the contrary saw that the archbishop had died in the cause of justice, and that was a cause worthy of a martyr's crown. And Lanfranc gave way; so the name of St Alphege (as it was canonised) remains on the list of the saints.

"And in the year after that in which archbishop Ælfheah was martyred, the king appointed bishop Lyfing to the archiepiscopal chair of Canterbury. And in this same year, before the month of August, came King Sweyn with his fleet to Sandwich." Thus records the "Anglo-Saxon Chronicle" under the date 1013. This Archbishop Lyfing, or Living (1013-1020), saw the beginning of a new order, for he, crowned Canute, the leader of the Danes, as King of England, and one very disturbing element in the history of Canterbury was thus soothed down in peace and unity. Until this event we must try to picture Canterbury for all the years round about A.D. 1000 as living in perpetual terror from the attack of Danish warriors. Archbishop Ethelnoth (1020-1038) marks the change still more firmly, for in earlier days he had been a chaplain of Canute's court. He was also the dean of the Cathedral monastery at Canterbury, that is of Christ Church. Since the days of the fatal siege and massacre of 1011, when only four monks had been spared in all Christ Church, the monastery had become laxer than ever in its attention to the monkish rules, for the new men who had come in were less instructed in those rules, and less inclined to obey them, in any case. In short, the so-called monastery of Christ Church was now, practically, a house of secular canons, not a house of monks under vows of celibacy and communal property, in spite of all that Oda and Dunstan had striven for the stricter discipline.

Canute was now an earnest Christian to all appearances, and doing everything he could to make his peace with the Church. The "Anglo-Saxon Chronicle" records, under the date 1033, the translation of the body of the martyr, Archbishop Ælfheah, to Canterbury: "In this year King Cnut, within London, in St Paul's monastery, gave full leave to Archbishop Ethelnoth and Bishop Brightwine, and to all God's servants who were with them, that they might take up from the burial-place the archbishop St Ælfheah. And they did so on the sixth of the Ides of June. And the renowned king and the archbishop and suffragen bishops and earls, and very many men in orders and also laymen, conveyed in a ship his holy body over the Thames to Southwark, and there delivered the holy martyr to the archbishop and his companions; and they then with an honourable band and winsome joy, conveyed him to Rochester. Then on the third day came Emma, the lady with her royal child Harthacnut; and they then all, with great magnificence and bliss and song of praise, conveyed the holy archbishop into Canterbury, and so honourably brought him to Christ Church on the third of the Ides of June. Again, after that on the eighth day, on the seventeenth of the Kal. of July, Archbishop Ethelnoth and Bishop Æfsige and Bishop Brightwine and all those who were with them, deposited St Ælfheah's holy body on the north side of Christ's altar, to the glory of God and the honour of the holy archbishop, and to the eternal health of all who will then with devout heart and with all humility seek daily his holy body. May

God Almighty have mercy on all Christian men through St Ælfheah's holy merits."

We have in this record a good example of the spirit of saintly intercession, which was the real basis of the splendour of such a church as Canterbury. The people were taught to believe that their "eternal health" could be gained if they "daily sought" the shrines of the saints. It was the offerings of worshippers and pilgrims that made Canterbury and other religious places rich. A church was great in proportion to the number of the holy relics and bodies it contained. Another of Canute's gifts to Canterbury was more material, the "Anglo-Saxon Chronicle" telling us that in the year 1029 he gave "to Christ Church at Canterbury, the haven of Sandwich and all the dues that arise therefrom"; and another chronicle adds: "His crown of gold which is kept at the head of the great cross in the nave of Christ Church."

Archbishop Eadsige (1038-1050) was another of Canute's chaplains, and his appointment, following that of Ethelnoth, is a reminder of how much Canute interfered in the affairs of the Church. Whereas, before, the appointment of an archbishop had received the sanction of the Witan, as representing the people, now Canute made bishops of his own will—which does not necessarily mean that the appointments were any the worse.

With Robert the next archbishop, who received the see of Canterbury in 1051, we reach another turn in the wheel of history, for he was a Norman abbot of Jumièges who had won the heart of Edward the Confessor, by services rendered to the latter when he was an exile in Normandy. This Robert was the first and foremost of the foreign favourites who were opposed by the so-called English nationalists, led by Godwine and his sons. This is not the place to discuss the contest, for it has no particular connection with Canterbury: suffice it to say that when Godwine appeared in England, back from exile in 1052, Robert of Canterbury buckled on his armour, fought his way out of London accompanied by the Bishop of Dorchester, and escaped to the coast, where he took ship and eventually saw the Pope in Rome, and got a document reinstating him in his lost see. But he never returned to England again; for the "Anglo-Saxon Chronicle" says: "The Archbishop Robert was without hesitation declared wholly an outlaw with all the Frenchmen, because they had made discord between Earl Godwine and the king." Archbishop Stigand succeeded to the archbishopric of Canterbury.

Stigand was, strictly speaking, never archbishop at all, for Robert was still alive. But a bird in the hand was worth two in the bush, and he clung to his unstable position until William got a great council to depose him in 1070. On the whole he seems to have been a bad lot, and since he was living on false credit, as it were, he imitated the manners of some other adventurers and plunged heavily: thus, he kept possession also of the bishopric of Winchester, when it was illegal to hold two sees at the same time; he also bought and sold ecclesiastical preferments, and even is said to have seized the lands of several abbeys for himself. He died a well-treated political prisoner, at Winchester, and was buried there. So he is rather an outlaw in the history of Canterbury.

With his successor, Lanfranc, we begin a very new period which we will consider, after we have first examined the state of the city of Canterbury at the end of the Saxon times.

CHAPTER VI

The City of Canterbury at the time of the Norman Conquest

THERE will be such an important period of re-building to record immediately after the coming of the Normans that it will be helpful to see how far the Saxons and Danes had got with the architectural development of Canterbury. We have seen the Celtic beginnings submerged under the Roman city, which in its turn decayed and was almost covered in its own ruin before the Saxons took up the tale.

The Saxon walls apparently included a wider area than those built by the Romans. The matter is not without doubt, but probably the next extension of the wall brought within the city what is now, roughly speaking, the Cathedral and its close, and the monastery with all its buildings and grounds; also the domain of the Bishop's Palace, up to, or a little beyond Princes Street. In other words, the Saxon walls on the south and east, from St Mildred's Church to Northgate, were in the position they occupy to-day. But at St Mildred's Church the wall turned in a north-eastern direction, running along the east bank of the Stour river, not far from the line of Stour Street; then crossing the High Street, and continuing almost parallel with Palace Street (and not far west of its present course), until it reached the north wall near the North Gate. We will glance at the main features and buildings within these walls and in the country just beyond them. The principal gate of the early Saxon city was, in all probability, Burgate (which stood where the present Burgate reaches Broad Street). Its name suggests its pre-eminence as the chief gate of the burh, or borough. Both the gate in the High Street (which West Gate supplanted further along the same street when the walls were extended by the Normans) and Newingate originated in Saxon times; and the street connecting these became, for the first time, the main thoroughfare of the town.

The Cathedral had by no means, in these Saxon days, the easy supremacy it has to-day. St Augustine's Abbey (or the Abbey of SS. Peter and Paul, as it was called until Dunstan re-christened it with the addition of its founder's name, which has supplanted the others in popular use) was at first as great or even greater than the archbishop's church. But we will consider the Cathedral first, as it was before the great fire of 1067, which practically destroyed the whole church and monastery.

It is not clear how much new work Augustine had added to the building he found on this spot modelled after the old basilica of St Peter's in Rome, neither do we know when it became a purely Saxon edifice; for it is impossible to believe that the church of Augustine's day, even if he rebuilt it, could have remained sufficient for long. We know definitely that it was rebuilt in part in the days of Archbishop Oda, when, according to the records of Eadmer (who was a scholar in the Canterbury school in the time of Lanfranc), "the roof of Christ Church had become rotten from extreme age, and rested throughout upon half-shattered pieces: wherefore he set about to rebuild it, and being also desirous of giving to the walls a loftier reach, he ordered his assembled workmen to remove altogether the disjointed structure above, and commanded them to supply the lacking height of the walls by raising them." Eadmer goes on to relate the traditional story, how that Oda prayed that no rain might fall into the church so long as the roof was off; and that, in answer to this prayer, for the space of three years "did no rain fall either within the walls of

OLD TOWER AND WALL OF CANTERBURY

the church or even within the walls of the city": whereby the services of the Cathedral were never interrupted in the least degree. "And truly," adds the chronicler, "it was a sight worth seeing to behold the land beyond the walls of the city drenched with water, while the walls themselves did keep quite dry." It is of course possible that a prolonged drought may have given some basis for this exaggerated tale.

Then in the year 1011, as we have seen, the Danes set fire to the Cathedral, but according to one chronicler it was "neither consumed by the fire, nor were its walls or its roof destroyed. We know indeed that it was profaned and despoiled of many of its ornaments . . . but when the enemy had laid hands upon the archbishop, they abandoned their fire." So apparently very little harm was done at this time, to the building at least. Gervase says that this was the first time that the Cathedral was damaged by fire.

The second time was when it was almost totally destroyed by the fire of 1067, a disaster which is recorded by Eadmer, who was probably an eye-witness. What is more to our purpose in this chapter, he has described in some detail the church which was thus burned in 1067; and as this is the building in which were enacted the deeds which we have been recalling, and in which lived and prayed the personages of whom we have been writing, we will conveniently give this description by Eadmer at length. He says—

"This was that very church which had been built by the Romans, and which was duly arranged, in some part, in imitation of the church of the blessed Prince of the Apostles, Peter. The venerable Oda had translated the body of the blessed Wilfrid, Archbishop of York, from Ripon to Canterbury, and had worthily placed it in a loftier tomb, to use his own words, that is to say, in the great Altar which was built of rough stones and mortar, close to the wall at the east end of the presbytery. Afterwards another altar was placed at a convenient distance before the aforesaid altar, and dedicated in honour of our Lord Jesus Christ, at which the Divine mysteries were daily celebrated. In this altar the blessed Ælfheah [St Alphege] had solemnly placed the head of St Swithin, which he had brought with him when he came from Winchester to Canterbury, and also the relics of other saints. To reach these altars, one ascended several steps, from the choir of the singers, by a crypt which the Romans called Confessionary. This crypt was fashioned underneath in the likeness of the Confessionary of St Peter, the vault of which was raised so high that the part above could only be reached by many steps. Within, this crypt had at its east end an altar, in which was the head of the blessed Furseus, as it was said of old. Further, the single passage which ran westwards from the curved part of the crypt, reached from thence up to the resting-place of the blessed Dunstan, which was separated from the crypt by a strong wall; for that most holy father was buried at a great depth in the ground before these steps; and at the head of the saint stood the matutinal altar. From this spot the choir of the singers stretched westwards into the main part of the church, but shut off from the multitude by a proper inclosure. Then, beyond the middle of the main body [the nave] of the church there were two towers which jutted out from the aisles of the church. The south tower had an altar in the middle of it which was dedicated to the honour of the blessed Pope Gregory. At the side was the principal door of the church, which is still called the *Suthdure*, as it was called of old by the English; by which name it is often mentioned in the law books of the early kings. For all disputes from the whole kingdom which cannot be referred to the King's Court or to the hundreds or to the counties, are judged in this place. Opposite to this tower, on the north side, was the other tower, built in honour of the blessed Martin, and about it were the cloisters for the monks. And as the first tower was devoted to the worldly business of the law, so in this second tower the younger brethren were instructed in the knowledge of the offices of the Church, for the different hours and seasons of the day and night. The west end of the church was adorned by the oratory of Mary, the blessed Mother of God; which was so built that it could only be reached by steps; and above these there was an altar consecrated to the worship of that Lady, which had within it the head of the blessed virgin Austroberta. When the priest performed the Divine Mysteries at this altar he had his face turned to the east, towards the people who stood below. Behind him to the west was the pontifical chair, moulded with rich workmanship, of large stones and cement; it was far removed from the Communion table, seeing that the chair touched the exterior wall of the church. And this was the plan of the church of Canterbury. These things we have shortly described, in order that the men of this and coming generations, when they find them mentioned in the old writings and perceive that the existing things do not agree with their narrative, may know that all these things have passed away, and that new ones have taken their place. For after the innumerable vicissitudes which this church underwent, the whole was finally consumed in our own days by fire."

This description by Eadmer is still of the greatest interest to the sightseers as well as the students of to-day, for it gives that sense of continuity which is so necessary if one wishes to realise the great age of this building. At the very beginning of their visit they enter the church by the "Suthdure," or south door, which Eadmer knew as its main entrance; and we still find this main porch beneath the south-west tower. The cloisters are still abutting on or very near the foot of the north-west tower. There are still the steps leading up to the high altar: indeed the main structural distinction of the present church, namely the rising of the eastern end high above the body of the nave, seems to have been already the essential structure of the Roman Saxon building. A reference to the reconstructed plan drawn by Professor Willis in 1845 for his masterly "Architectural History of Canterbury Cathedral" shows this Saxon edition of Christ Church as in the main a rectangular building with a circular apse at each end, of which, the west apse perhaps originally held the chief altar, as was customary in the earliest churches. Beyond the construction of the building itself, perhaps the principal fact to grasp is that the most honoured body in this church of the Saxons was St Wilfrid, with Oda and Dunstan for minor worship. It will not be until St Thomas takes their place with overwhelming significance that this church will become the immense creation it is to-day, though we shall see vast additions in the time of the Normans.

At the east end of this Saxon Cathedral there was a separate (but almost touching) church dedicated to St John the Baptist. This had been built by Archbishop Cuthbert about the year A.D. 750. His main purpose was to have it for a place of baptism and also for judicial trials, which had formerly been held in the Cathedral. But there was another important use which he had in his mind : he had obtained from the Pope a dispensation allowing the future burials of archbishops to take place in their own Cathedral instead of, as formerly, in the Abbey of SS. Peter and Paul, outside the walls of the city. It was in his new church of St John that Cuthbert himself was buried, and his immediate successor, Bregwin, was buried near him. It is probable that there was soon, if not at first, a structural connection between Christ Church and this church of St John; and when we are told that the archbishops were buried in the former, it is possible that they were in fact placed beside the two mentioned. Eadmer tells us that St John's was destroyed at the same time as the main Cathedral by the fire of 1067: and with them went the monastery buildings, all except the refectory and the dormitory, with the cloisters attached to them.

So much for the great church within the walls of the Saxon city. Small though was the area contained by these walls, it already held a large number of parish churches within it before the Norman Conquest. The churches of St Mildred, St Mary Bredin, St Margaret, St George, St Andrew, St Mary Andrewsgate, St Michael Burgate, St Mary Magdalene, the church of the Four Martyrs, St Mary Queningate, St Alphege, St Mary de Castro, St John the Poor, and St Edmund—fourteen in all, were of Saxon foundation. In a subsequent itinerary of the city of Canterbury, the tourist will be guided to these as existing churches or their sites, and it will then be realised at what an early date in its history Canterbury had shown its ecclesiastical bias, or it would be more correct to say, its mediæval bias, for the Church had gripped the mind of all mediæval society.

All these, be it remembered, were churches within the walls. Outside the Saxon city lay others of equal importance. The great Abbey of SS. Peter and Paul was in the first rank of English monasteries, and its church was probably as large as Christ Church itself, at this time, and of almost higher veneration for its holy relics of kings and saints. In its near neighbourhood were the independent churches of St Pancras, St Martin (most venerable of them all), and St Paul. To the west of the city were St Peter's, All Saints', and St Dunstan's.

Thus within its walls, or just outside them, were already twenty-two churches in the Saxon period. Canterbury had already taken a form which is not unfamiliar to its present citizens and visitors. There will be vast developments in the future history, but the main outline can be traced in the topography of the Canterbury of Dunstan. The extension of the western walls will be the only great structural change to record; the rest of the history will concern its gorgeous elaboration of details.

Although the Kings of Kent had given up their palace to Augustine and his monks, and his palace had become the place of their monastery, yet Canterbury remained as a city in the immediate domain of the Crown; and the Saxon governor was the portreeve, who was the representative of the king, although the citizens may have had some say in his election; but the matter is uncertain. He may have been entirely the choice of the king; or he may have been chosen by the citizens from men whom the king approved. The Domesday Book records that there were in Canterbury, in the days of Edward the Confessor, 51 burgesses who paid rent direct to the king; and 212 others over whom he had sac and soc, that is, the rights of jurisdiction that a lord of a manor had over his tenants; and, further, there were three mills owned by the Crown. But there were several other minor lords, such as the archbishop; and to keep a balance between the world and the Church, a "certain concubine of Harold's" held four houses in Canterbury. But the city as a whole was the property of the Crown from its earliest occupation by Ethelbert, the King of Kent.

CHAPTER VII

The Norman Conquest and Lanfranc

WE have sketched the outlines of Canterbury as they existed at the moment when William, Duke of Normandy, invaded England in 1066. A sudden change in the national history coincided with a somewhat drastic series of new events in this chief city of Kent. The arrival of the Normans and the rule of Lanfranc, their choice as archbishop of Canterbury, mark the beginning of a new order, so far as there can be any new starts in the evolution of social affairs. This beginning was marked by a fresh set of ideas, and by a new material cathedral which took the place of the one we have just examined in the records of Eadmer. These innovations we must now consider.

The Norman Conquest had a very intimate connection with the affairs of Canterbury; for the cute mind of William of Normandy saw the advantages of making his piratical invasion look as much like a holy war as was possible. So he got the Pope to bless the expedition against England, and one of the best reasons the Pope had for granting that blessing was the fact that the sitting Archbishop of Canterbury, Stigand, was not, according to the technicalities of ecclesiastical law, the archbishop at all, but merely an unlawful usurper who had seized the place of Robert of Jumièges, when the latter, as we have seen, was driven out of England by the Nationalists under Godwine. Anyhow, this was a good enough excuse for William and his fellow politician, the Pope, or rather, it was one of several plausible reasons for heading the Norman army with the holy banner of Rome. Stigand had accepted his office (illegal at the best, because Robert was still alive) at the hands of an illegal pope; it was a crime within a crime against ecelesiastical orthodoxy.

So when England was beaten at the Battle of Hastings, the lord-bishop of Canterbury must have known very well that his position was critical; and he took an early opportunity of meeting William at Wallingford, and handed in his submission. But the energetic Conqueror had already been to Canterbury, though Stigand had taken care not to be at home when William came. For immediately after the Battle of Hastings William had marched on Dover, and after seizing that stronghold, he next went straight to Canterbury. As the Norman army approached the city, the inhabitants sent a deputation to meet William, and offered to surrender to him without resistance. So the Normans entered Canterbury without striking a blow. Almost directly he left Dover, William had been seized with a sudden illness; and this appears to have kept him a few days in Canterbury, which can thus claim to be the first town inhabited by the Conqueror in his new kingdom. But it was not long before the Norman army and its duke set out from Canterbury, and marched towards London to strike the decisive blows, which they began by the burning of Southwark, which then was an independent town at the south end of London Bridge. When William returned to Normandy, in a few month's time, he took with him, theoretically as friendly followers, but in reality as hostages, Stigand and Ægelnoth, Abbot of Glastonbury, and many nobles in his train. But so far no formal change was made in the archbishop's position.

Under the year 1067 the "Anglo-Saxon Chronicle" records: "The king came again to England on St Nicholas's mass-day, the sixth of December; and on that day Christ Church at Canterbury was burnt." This was the fire which destroyed the Saxon church In the words of Eadmer: "While misfortunes fell thick upon all parts of England, it happened that the city of Canterbury was set on fire by the carelessness of some individuals, and that the rising flames caught the mother church thereof. How can I tell it?—the whole was consumed, and nearly all the monastic offices that appertained to it as well as the church of the blessed John the Baptist, wherein aforesaid the remains of the archbishops were buried. The exact nature and amount of the damage done by that fire no man can tell. But its ravages may be known, insomuch as the devouring flames burned up nearly all that was then preserved most precious, whether in ornament of gold, silver, or of other sorts, and sacred and secular books. Those things that could be replaced were the less to be regretted, but an overwhelming grief weighed down this church because there were also reduced to ashes all those charters granted to it by the popes of Rome and by the kings and princes of this kingdom, by which they and their successors were bound to defend and uphold the church for ever. Copies of these documents were sought for and collected from every place where such things were preserved; but their bulls and seals were irrecoverably lost with the church in which they were deposited." So far concerning the destruction of the stones of the Cathedral.

The change in men and manners was soon to follow. The "Chronicle" for 1070 says: "In this year Lanfranc, who was Abbot of Caen, came to England, and a few days later became Archbishop of Canterbury. He was ordained on the fourth of the Kal. of September [*i.e.* August 29th] in his own episcopal see, by eight bishops, his suffragans. The others who were not present showed by messengers and letters why they could not be there." Stigand had been allowed to

NORMAN STAIRCASE—NOW PART OF KING'S SCHOOL

retain possession of his see until this time, though his illegal position had all along made everyone reluctant to have any business dealings with him; for example, in the way of receiving the consecration to a bishopric at his hands. Now, when the papal legates came to England in 1070, they deposed Stigand from the see of Canterbury, and Lanfranc took his place.

The history of the life of Lanfranc is indispensable if one wishes to understand the atmosphere of Canterbury in these days of which we are now writing. He was born, about 1005, a native of the Italian town of Pavia, the son of Hanbald, a senator and leading magistrate. Lanfranc was trained as a lawyer also; and quickly attained renown for his legal knowledge and eloquence. He determined to go forth to the world as a teacher; and he was still young when he emigrated to France, and he settled at last, in the year 1039, in the town of Avranches, in the north of that country; whither he soon gathered a famous school around him. Then came a period of mental unrest; secular learning no longer satisfied him, and he decided on the whole-hearted action of becoming a monk in the most humble monastery he could discover. The tale goes that he set out from Avranches with one of his scholars, Paul, who is generally believed to have been his own son. They were seized on the way by robbers; and his inability to remember the words of the divine service as he stood propped and bound to a tree trunk, where the robbers had left him, made him more than ever alarmed about his soul's salvation. The next morning he was released by some travellers and directed to the monastery of Bee, where a religious house had been founded by the soldier Herlwin, who was at that time acting as the abbot. He took a fancy for the newcomer, and in 1045 Lanfranc was made prior of Bee, just when he was meditating taking another step of renunciation by becoming a hermit. As at Avranches, scholars from all over Europe had gathered to listen to his teaching, men who afterwards became renowned in the Church.

His fame was known to the Duke of Normandy, and William soon made him his confidant and adviser in affairs of State. But Lanfranc had a will of his own; and when he stubbornly refused to allow the marriage of William with Matilda of Flanders, the Duke promptly ordered him out of the country. Lanfranc set off for exile on a lame horse, and it chanced that on his way from Bee he met his angry master, to whom he audaciously tossed the passing remark that he would obey his commands more quickly if the Duke would give him a better horse. Whereupon came a very sudden change in the situation, for William enjoyed the spirit of the jest, and pardoned the jester; and Lanfranc in return promised to plead for the papal sanction of the offending marriage, when he arrived at Rome, whither he was journeying. The tale suggests that there was much more than a pious divinity in the heart of this monk; he was a delicate blend of the man of the world and the saint—which his subsequent career amply confirms. His arguments were sufficient to get the dispensation for the Duke of Normandy's marriage (which, by the way, was already a matter of six years old). But he did another good stroke of business in Rome; for he met the notorious Berengar of Tours in a great debate concerning the exact significance of the Sacrament of the Lord's Supper. Berengar was the new leader of the mystical school which denied that there was any material change in the consecrated bread and wine by which they became the real blood and body of Christ. This mysticism was an unorthodox interpretation, and someone had to be found to confute the heresy. As it happened Berengar had written to Lanfranc on the subject, and there were malicious gossips who said that Lanfranc was tainted with Berengar's views. The unfortunate letter was read to the council in Rome, and Lanfranc was ordered by the Pope to prove his innocency by arguing against Berengar in public. This he did with acknowledged success; and Lanfranc became known in papal circles as the champion of orthodoxy and sound thinking—as such things are judged in ecclesiastical circles.

We now see how it happened that Lanfranc, the favourite of both Pope and Norman Duke, was chosen, in 1070, as Archbishop of Canterbury on the deposition of Stigand. He soon had set himself to the work of radically changing the state of the Church in England. His patrons were of the highest rank, one the Pope, the other the king: with such backing he need not submit to dictation. His first struggle was to compel the Archbishop of York to acknowledge the supremacy of Canterbury—a matter which had never been properly settled, since Gregory had originally intended that there should be two English archbishops of equal and independent power. Though in practice, Canterbury had always been acknowledged superior. The "Anglo-Saxon Chronicle" records that in this year, 1070, "Thomas, who has been chosen Bishop of York, came to Canterbury that he might be ordained according to the old custom. When Lanfranc craved confirmation of his obedience by oath-swearing, he refused and said he ought not to do it; the archbishop became wroth, and ordered the bishops who were come thither to end the service, and all the monks to unrobe themselves; and by his command so they did. So Thomas for that time went back without the blessing. Then soon after this it befel that the archbishop Lanfranc went to Rome, and Thomas along with him. When they came thither, and had spoken about other things, Thomas began his speech, how he came to Canterbury, and how the archbishop asked obedience, with oath-swearing, from him, and he refused it. Then the archbishop Lanfranc began to show openly and distinctly that he with right craved that which he craved, and with strong discourses confirmed the same before the Pope Alexander and before all the council that were then gathered; and so they went home. After this, Thomas came to Canterbury, and all that the archbishop craved of him, humbly fulfilled, and then received the blessing." What really happened was that the Pope referred the dispute to an English synod representing the nation, both clerics and laymen; and it was the ruling of this council which settled that Canterbury was the premier see of England. It is now fairly certain that this decision was obtained mainly by the production of documents forged by Lanfranc as false evidence of the privileges of Canterbury; after all, it is usually a man of the world—as well as a saint—who arrives at such a seat of power as an archbishop's see.

Then, as became a monk and a strictly orthodox theologian, Lanfranc was on the side of the Pope Gregory VII. in his determination to make the Church a sternly isolated caste, cut off from the rest of the people by the vow of celibacy. Likewise, Lanfranc preferred the monastic cathedral foundation to the unvowed secular chapter of canons. Here, at last, he seems to have been able to do what so many archbishops, as we have seen, had attempted before, namely, to make the Cathedral of Christ Church, Canterbury, a stricter monkish house; whereas before it had been, at the least, a mixed body of unorthodox regulars and seculars. Now, it appears that Lanfranc gradually ordered that all the canons should take the monastic vows; though he does not seem to have been at all harsh or sudden in this ruling. It was not until a long course of gentle guidance away from the easy luxurious life which had become usual at Christ

Church that Lanfranc drafted a new set of rules for the governance of the monastery. This new Christ Church, in fact, was so much a half-way house that by some historians it is said that Lanfranc introduced a sterner rule and by others that he allowed a laxer one. The truth of the matter seems to be that his new monks (whom he raised in number to 150, instead of the 50 or so who had been there before) were less strict if one approaches them from the side of the orthodox Benedictine monastery, while they were more strict than the secular chapter of clergy. Lanfranc found the monks of Christ Church having a very easy time of it; a generous diet, sports in summer, and gambling for the cold indoor season; he endeavoured to make them useful members of society; he told them to teach, to do handiwork, to read, to write, to attend to the needs of the poor.

But perhaps the most marked change in the governance of Christ Church was that by which Lanfranc divided the property of the Cathedral into two parts; one to be devoted to the upkeep of the monastery, the other to the support of the archbishopric. Theodore, the first great administrative archbishop, as we have seen, had begun in some way to distinguish between the property of the monastery and the archbishopric, but the details are somewhat vague. The archbishop, by Lanfranc's changes, now ceased to be the prior of the house; Lanfranc built a palace, outside the monastery, for himself and his successors; and now began that custom by which the archbishop stayed much at his country residences scattered about his diocese, such as Otford and Aldington, Lyminge and Charing. In fact, the archbishop was henceforth to be in practice a secular priest and not a monk, though he was long to remain the latter in theory. When he, further, dealt a severe blow against one of the central principles of monasticism, the holding of all property as communal, by instituting the prebendal system, then the house of Christ Church stood out in clear contrast against the Benedictine monks of St Augustine's Abbey outside the walls. For by the prebendal system the various estates of the monastery were allotted to the maintenance of certain specific offices: no longer were all goods to be shared in common.

THE CASTLE, CANTERBURY

The enforcement of celibacy was rather a hopeless task in England, where married clergy during Saxon times had been the general rule, not the exception. So Lanfranc, who was certainly a man of the world, as well as an ecclesiastic, was content with a ruling of a synod of Winchester which forbade any future consecration of married men as priests, but allowed those who were already married to keep their wives. In the case of the regular canons of a religious house—even though not strictly monks—the rule was, however, absolute at once; they must not have wives.

It is with no sudden break in the discussion of these affairs of ecclesiastical discipline that we reach Lanfranc's quarrel with the Benedictine Abbey of St Augustine, which had for so long been the rival of Christ Church and its bishops. Lanfranc was the servant of the King of England, and a supporter of a national church of which the archbishop was the supreme head and the papal representative. Now, the great abbots, such as those of St Augustine's, were determined to ignore the jurisdiction of the bishops, claiming that they had the right of direct dealing with the popes of Rome. Also, it happened that the English monasteries took the side of the English race as against the Normans. So, for many reasons, Lanfranc was the opponent of the Benedictine Abbey outside his Cathedral gates. It was in 1087 that his most determined attack was made, or some may prefer to say that then he was most violently resisted.

According to the "Anglo-Saxon Chronicle" Lanfranc had consecrated Wido as Abbot of St Augustine's; but when he himself, accompanied by Odo, the Earl of Kent, arrived at the door of the abbey with Wido, the monks flatly refused to admit the new abbot. Lanfranc at once ordered them to be drawn out, which was promptly done and Wido was placed in the abbot's chair, while the rebel prior and the other leaders of the rebellion were ordered off to the castle in chains, and the other monks retired to St Mildred's Church just outside the castle walls. Then Lanfranc sent these latter a message that if they cared to return to their monastery before nine o'clock, they would be received and forgiven. At first they hesitated, but the approach of the hour of dinner convinced several of them that it would be more comfortable to dine at home than starve for their principles outside: so these gave way, and swore before the tomb of St Augustine that they would be obedient to Wido. The rest, Lanfranc scattered over England in other monasteries until they repented of their obstinacy, whereupon they were allowed to return to St Augustine's. But one or two of them, who attempted flight, were punished with all the vigours of the monastic discipline. For Lanfranc was no gentle saint when it came to serious opposition to his rule, as was again evident when, a little later, another conspiracy was hatched against Wido, in which Columban, a monk of the abbey, was the chief character. When charged with the offence before the archbishop, he confessed that it had been his intention to murder Wido, his abbot. So Lanfranc ordered Columban to be tied to a stake, naked, before the gate of Saint Augustine's, and flogged, and his cowl cut off; and that then he should be driven from the city of Canterbury.

We have now glanced at the chief events in Lanfranc's ecclesiastical and political policy—it must be continually remembered that he was second only to William, his master, in political power—it is time to turn to the vast changes he made in the physical condition of his Cathedral. He was appointed archbishop, we have seen, in 1070. He therefore found on his arrival in Canterbury that there were only the ruins of the famous Saxon Cathedral, and the services were being conducted in the "house of small size," which Eadmer tells us had been built over the remains of the treasured body of St Dunstan: "and in this there were daily performed over his holy relics the masses and other services." Eadmer was convinced that it was mainly by the intercession of St Dunstan that even the refectory and dormitory of the monastery had been saved from the fire. It was natural that the monks should be respectful to such a valuable asset.

After this great burning of 1067, the bodies of the

archbishops, Cuthbert and his successors, who had been buried in the chapel of St John the Baptist, as we have seen, remained undisturbed in the ruins for three years, until Lanfranc arrived. According to the chroniclers: "When he came to Canterbury and found that the church of the Saviour, which he had undertaken to rule, was reduced to a fragment by fire and ruin, he was filled with consternation." However, he soon set to work, and, "neglecting his own accommodation, he finished with all haste the houses which were necessary for the monks. For those which had been used for many years were found too small for the larger numbers of the monastery." It will be remembered that Lanfranc had added a hundred monks to the fifty who were there before. "He therefore pulled to the ground all that he found of the destroyed monastery, and having dug out their foundations from under the ground, he built up others which greatly excelled them in beauty and magnitude. He built cloisters, celerer's offices, refectories, dormitories, with all other necessary offices; and all the buildings within the enclosure of the curia, as well as the walls thereof. As for the church, which the aforesaid fire, and its age, had made completely unserviceable, he set about to utterly sweep it away, and build a greater one. And in the space of seven years he raised this new church from its very foundation, and made it nearly perfect. But before the work began, he ordered that the bodies of the saints which were buried in the eastern part of the church, should be removed to the western part, where the oratory of the blessed Virgin Mary stood. Wherefore, after a three days' fast, the bodies of the most precious priests of Christ were taken up, and, in the presence of a vast multitude of people, were borne to their chosen place of burial. To which I, Eadmer, can bear witness, for I was then a boy at the school."

But this removal of the bodies of the saints to a

less ruined part of the destroyed church could, of course, be only a temporary arrangement; and, as the work of rebuilding proceeded, the masons eventually arrived at this temporary resting place, which, in its turn, had to be removed. Eadmer continues: "It became necessary to take down the remainder of the old work where the bodies of these saints were lying. Having prepared, therefore, the refectory of the brethren for the celebration of Divine Service, we all proceeded thither from the old church in festal procession, bearing, with honour and reverence, our most glorious and sweetest fathers, Dunstan and Elphege."

Professor Willis has pointed out how these records of the continual moving of the bodies from one spot to another prove that the Norman church of Lanfranc was built on the same site as the older Saxon predecessor; and further, how the Norman church was new from the ground, otherwise it would not have been necessary to move the buried bodies at all.

This careful account of the moving of the saintly bodies should be noted; for it is a vivid illustration of the central fact about a great mediæval church; namely, that it was the collecting place of a number of relics which were held to be invested with holy power. In a very real sense, the mediævel man and woman believed that before the tombs of the great ecclesiastics they were in the presence of those who could intercede for the worshippers before the heavenly powers. So once again, Eadmer continues these all-important events, as they seemed to his mind: "When the High Altar [of the old church] was pulled down, the relics of the blessed Wilfrid were discovered and placed in a coffin. But after some years it was the united wish of the brethren that the relics should be placed in a more permanent resting place; so a tomb was prepared on the north side of the altar, where the relics were placed. And when the other altars, which we have named, were pulled down, all the holy places were discovered. That all this happened as I have said, without any doubt, I can certify, for I witnessed it with my own eyes."

Then, when the new church was finished, the most important work was the reburial of the old saintly relics within its walls; and Eadmer tells us that: "After a few years the bodies of the archbishops were carried into the newly built church and placed on the northern side, upon a vault, where each day the mystery of the Sacrifice of Salvation was celebrated." Then he tells a simple but miraculous tale, which fitly illuminates the mind of the age in which the chronicler lived: "In our own time, it happened to one of the elder brethren of the church, Alfwin, by name, who filled the office of Sacrist, that he, on the night of the festival of St Wilfrid, was resting in a certain lofty place in the church beyond the choir, and before the altar, where at that time the relics of the blessed Wilfrid were placed in a shrine. Then, as he lay between sleeping and waking, he beheld the church filled with light, and angels performing the service; and he beheld those of them whose duty it was to read and sing ascending the winding stair, to ask a blessing before the altar and body of the blessed man; which done, they straightway descended and resumed the usual offices of the church with all solemnity." Unless one can understand the caste of mind which could relate that story as a rational and credible event, it will be impossible to get in any real contact with the spirit and life of a great mediæval church. The secret of the history of Canterbury Cathedral, and the reason of its vastness, was that the worshippers and pilgrims who visited it believed that there was more chance of a miracle happening with its walls than in most places. So, if one cannot, at least, sceptically sympathise with

RUINED ARCHES—GARDEN, CANTERBURY CATHEDRAL

a belief in the supernatural, then it will be well to give up the contemplation of Canterbury. Without that sympathy it will still be a great architectural monument, perhaps; but, the life and blood will have gone from its structure: it will be a mere skeleton—something cold and dry.

What remains of this church of Lanfranc's we shall see when we consider the Cathedral in detail in a later chapter; but for all practical purposes it has disappeared, although the tower at the north-west corner stood until as late as 1834, and there are parts, such, for example, at the north-west corner of the central tower and part of the dormitory, which still give reality to the history of this first Norman building.

It so happened that the nave of this Cathedral of Lanfranc's building was described in detail by a monk of the church, Gervase, who wrote during the years 1188-1199, when the nave was still standing, though the choir had long gone. It is well worth reading his words in full: "I will first describe the work of Lanfranc; beginning from the great Tower, for not the whole of that church has been destroyed, although a part of it had been altered. The tower is raised on great pillars, and placed in the centre of the church, like the centre in the middle of a circle. It had on its summit a gilded cherub [which perhaps gave it its early name of the Angel Steeple]. On the west of this tower is the nave or aula of the church supported on each side by eight piers. Two lofty towers with gilded pinnacles end this nave. In the middle of the church hangs a gilded crown. This tower was separated, as it were, from the nave by a screen with a loft, and in the middle of this, on the side towards the nave, was the altar of the Holy Cross. Above this loft-screen, and placed across the church, was a beam bearing the great cross, with two cherubim and the images of St Mary and St John the Apostle. In the north aisle was the oratory and altar of St Mary. In this nave we lived for five years after the fire [of 1174]. The aforesaid great tower had from each side a transept, one on the south and another on the north, in the middle of each of which transepts was a strong pillar, which sustained a vault which reached out from the walls on three of its sides. The two transepts are almost exactly the same in design. The south transept was used to carry the organ above its vault, and an apse extended from the east side of the transept, above and below the vault. In the lower part was the altar of St Michael, in the upper part was the altar of All Saints. Before the altar of St Michael, to its south side, was buried Archbishop Ceologild; to the north side lay the body of the holy virgin, Siburgis, whom Saint Dunstan caused to be buried in this church because of her sanctity. Between this apse and the choir the space is divided into two sets of steps: one leading down to the crypt, and the other leading up to the higher parts of the church. The northern transept has likewise two apses; in the upper one is the altar of St Blasius, in the lower is the altar of St Benedict. In this lower one, on the right hand side of the entrance, was buried Archbishop William, who dedicated this Christ Church with such magnificence; and on the left lies his predecessor, Archbishop Ralph, who had prudent wisdom and famous eloquence—yet did Pope Calixtus prefer Thurstan of York and Abbot Hugo of St Augustine's to him. In the same apse, before the altar, on the right, lies Archbishop Egelnoth, and on the left Wulthelm. Behind the altar, on the right, is Athelm, and on the left Ceolnoth. And with such is the aforesaid apse graced. Between this apse and the choir there are two flights of steps, one leading to the crypt, and the other which goes up to the eastern part of the church. Between the space of these steps and the aforesaid apse is a solid wall, before which that glorious companion of martyrs and guest of the Apostles, Saint Thomas, died in the body by the swords of raging men, but whose unconquerable soul he gave to heaven to be crowned with the glory and honour of the everlasting kingdom. This place of the martyrdom has a door opening out of the opposite cloisters, by which entry came those four notaries of the devil, that they might place the acknowledged seal of martyrs by the anvil and the hammer, that is, that they, the head of St Thomas, lying between the pavement and the swords, might receive the stamp of the Most High, the palm of martyrdom. The pillar, which stood in the middle of this transept, likewise the vaults which rested on it, were in after years taken down in respect for the martyr, in order that the altar, which was raised on the spot of the martyrdom, might be seen from a greater distance. Round the transept, at the height of the aforesaid vault, a passage was constructed from which pallia and curtain might be hung. From the transept to the tower were many steps, and many also from under the tower up to the choir. Also there was a way from the tower down to the nave through two doors. Thus much for the church of Lanfranc."

This was all of Lanfranc's Cathedral which Gervase had ever seen; for the old choir had been replaced before his time by the new choir of Anselm and his successors. So he can only add: "You must know, good reader, that I never saw the choir of Lanfranc, neither have I been able to meet with any description of it."

There are many notes in Gervase's chronicle, as given above, which will show the modern visitors how the earlier planning remains to-day as the basis of the present Cathedral. They will see these more clearly when they go through the church in detail; but an

THE TREASURY, CANTERBURY CATHEDRAL

example of what one means may be pointed out in the steps leading down to the crypt and up to the choir, all which are still almost where they were in Lanfranc's time.

But in the matter of buildings Lanfranc's chief innovation was the archbishop's palace, which he set up for the first time: a natural sequence from the dividing up of the Cathedral property—which we have already noted—between the monks on one side and the archbishop on the other. Since they all, archbishop and monks, were no longer to live a united, communal life, it was therefore necessary that the archbishop should have a residence of his own. Hence this first foundation of the palace. It stood on the same site where stands the palace to-day, but nothing of Lanfranc's building is left: though there were perhaps still remains standing in 1800, according to Hasted's history written at that date. This palace of Lanfranc's was replaced within a hundred years of his time by another Norman rebuilding, and this second one lasted in practical use, with alterations, until the time of the Stuart Civil War of the sixteen hundreds.

Take him all round, this Italian archbishop, who left such a mark of his time in Canterbury, was evidently a man of genius and charm; there was a polished, worldly culture about his religion which raised him far above the sphere of a bigot, as perhaps it also took him far away from the sphere of the saint. The estimate of a man who was born within a year or two of Lanfranc's death, William of Malmesbury, expresses the judgment of his own time, and it is only a little too flowery for the judgment of history: "A man worthy to be compared to the ancients in knowledge and in religion; of whom it can be truly said, 'Cato the third is descended from heaven'—so much was the whole western world exerted to the knowledge of the liberal acts by his learning, and so earnestly did the monkish class labour in the work of religion, either from his example or authority." It will be observed in this estimate that his knowledge and culture are placed before his religious virtues: and that may be

HARBLEDOWN CHURCH, CANTERBURY

Lanfranc's true position. His value to England was that he was a man of education as balanced against the crude Saxon Stigands and their fellows, whom the Norman conquerors displaced. He died 1089, two years after William Rufus began his reign; his last hours were passed in his palace at Canterbury, and his body was buried in the Cathedral. It was placed in the Trinity Chapel of Anselm's church; and when this choir was burned in 1174 the body was carried to the spot in the north-east transept, where the name of the archbishop can still be seen cut on the wall, in the recess of the altar of St Martin, near the words "Edina Regina," for the body of that Saxon queen (died 960) was also carried to the same spot. Gervase says: "The larger bones with the remaining dust were collected in a leaden coffin, and deposited at the altar of St Martin. But all trace of any tomb has now disappeared. We must remember that this archbishop was never canonised, as for example Dunstan and Anselm and Becket were; which fact may account for the somewhat modest place in the church which he did so much to make famous. Too much wordly wisdom is not helpful towards a saint's halo, which needs temperament more than brains.

We shall come across the works of Lanfranc in the city beyond the Cathedral close; for he was far-reaching in his scope. His biographer, Milo Crispinus, who was his contemporary, says: "He built two hospitals for strangers and the poor without the city walls; one on the north, the other on the west, with all necessary buildings; and to those he allotted such yearly payments out of his own estate as seemed good to him. He also founded prebends in his manors to be given to the poor yearly." These two hospitals were St Gregory's and St Nicholas of Harbledown, to be noticed in our journeys in the neighbourhood.

So we may take leave of Lanfranc with the knowledge that he was one of the most important citizens of Canterbury, though he was not so picturesque to the popular fancy as many of his predecessors and successors.

CHAPTER VIII

Anselm and his Period

WE pass rapidly from one great archbishop to another; for the period of Anselm ranks with Lanfranc's both in the ecclesiastical and in the architectural history of Canterbury, while in the realm of piety Anselm far surpasses his predecessor.

Anselm was the son of very blue-blooded parents, and he was born at Aosta about the year 1033. His early career was very different from the eminently level-headed Lanfranc's. Although he had the latter's brilliancy of brain, yet there was a neurotic strain in him. His tutor made him work too hard, and Anselm became sickly. Then, before he was fifteen, he had an intense craving to become a monk, and prayed he might get seriously ill, so that his father should yield, out of compassion, to this desire. Then he got well, and the whole tone of his mind seemed to change; and outdoor sports and indoor lighthearted-ness (of a questionable kind, if we are to believe his own literal words) took the place of his turn for piety. When he was twenty-three he got rather disgusted with himself and set out to seek a more satisfactory life. Eventually he arrived at Lanfranc's famous school of Avranches, now the talk of Europe for its learning. Then he passed on to Bec, which, also, Lanfranc had made a centre of knowledge. Here Anselm worked himself ill with study, and the desire for a monk's life again seized him. So a monk he became in 1060, and succeeded Lanfranc as prior of Bec when the latter went to Caen; Anselm became abbot when Herlwin, the founder, died; and thus he remained until 1093. So he was thirty-three years a monk of the monastery of Bec.

His gentle spirit found the world a difficult place to live in without pain. He did not care to order his fellows to do this or not do that. He did not want to become abbot, and when the office was forced on him he gave over the business care of the monastery to others, and continued his life of meditation and education. He was a born teacher; few could resist his subtle persuasiveness. Osbern, a young rebel monk of Bec, became his ardent disciple, and when the young man died, Anselm wrote to Gaudulf (who built Rochester Castle and the Tower of London): "Wherever Osbern is, his soul is my soul; farewell, farewell, I pray, I pray, I pray, remember me, and forget not the soul of Osbern, my beloved; and if that seems too much for you, then forget me and remember Osbern."

We have seen that Lanfranc did not scruple to forge false documents when they were needed to prove a case in accordance with his designs. But we are told that Anselm never went to a law court except to stop any sharp practices being played by his own side: whereas he went to sleep, or read the Scriptures or philosophy, if the opponents followed such doubtful courses. There one has the difference between the two men. It was not that Anselm lacked brains: he could seize hold of the vital points in a case as quickly as the lawyer Lanfranc; only Anselm could not be bothered with the twistings and turnings of worldly craftsmen, when there was the whole realm of spiritual and moral subtleties to turn round and round in his philosophical mind. He was a spiritualist because he frankly found the spirit more interesting than matter.

Soon after 1078, when he became Abbot of Bec,

Anselm visited England, and stayed at Canterbury, where his friend Lanfranc had been archbishop for eight years. The new Cathedral was just finished, and Anselm lived in Christ Church as a member of the monastery, for the monks admitted him as a brother of their house. Here he met Eadmer, who afterwards wrote his life. All the monastery was charmed by the grace and learning of Anselm's speech, both in public debate and in private discourse. It was during this visit that Lanfranc referred to him the question whether Archbishop Ælfheah had any right to the crown of martyrdom, for had he not died in a common struggle with drunken men? Was this a death in defence of any particle of the Christian faith? To which Anselm gave answer that Ælfheah had died in order that his dependants might be spared the payment of his ransom: since the welfare of the poor was a Christ-like act, therefore he who died for such an end was dying for the faith of Christ, and the murdered man deserved the glory of a saint. Lanfranc submitted to the judgment, as indeed he was always accustomed to follow the guidance of Anselm in a very intimate manner. It was during this same visit that Anselm found in his bed a golden ring, and thereupon Lanfranc predicted that his friend would follow him in the see of Canterbury.

The Abbot of Bec was now accounted the most holy man in the north of Europe, and his presence was in demand at the death-bed of every one great enough to hope for that honour and solace. Thus William the Conqueror sent for him as he lay expecting death at Rouen. When Anselm arrived the Duke felt better and began to hope for recovery, and the man of religion was told to wait outside for a few days. As it happened, Anselm himself grew sick, and when the Conqueror died the abbot was not present to hear his last confessions, though he took part in the burial-service at Caen, which was rudely disturbed by a claimant of the land in which the body was being laid. When William Rufus posted to England to seize the crown on his father's death, after calling at Winchester to get possession of the royal treasury, he went straight to Canterbury to present to Lanfranc the letter which William the Conqueror had written asking the archbishop to crown Rufus as king: and the two left Canterbury together to journey to Westminster for the coronation ceremony.

Within two years of William the Conqueror's death Lanfranc had also died, and the revenues of the see of Canterbury were the spoils of the new king for several years. While no archbishop was appointed, William Rufus used the income for affairs of State or his private purposes. When the Council of State cravenly asked him to allow them to pray that he might see the sinfulness of this robbery of the Church, William replied: "Pray or not as you please; for I shall do as I like. All your prayers will be without effect on me." However, he suddenly grew perilously ill, and the man who a little before had sworn "by the holy face of Lucca, neither Anselm nor anyone else shall be archbishop at present except myself," now was in grovelling terror lest he should die with this insult to the Church on his conscience. The attendant bishops, seeing that the moment had come for turning the screw, demanded instant signs of repentance by the appointment of men to fill the offices of the Church which were vacant. They bethought them of Anselm, who happened to be again on a visit to England. When he arrived at the bedside of the king he received his confession and a pledge to do justice if he recovered, and the rest standing round, demanded an immediate fulfilment of his pledge by the choice of a successor to Lanfranc at Canterbury. William feebly pointed towards Anselm: "I choose that holy man." But Anselm had no ambition for the worldly troubles of such an office, and when his comrades tried to force him forward to receive the pastoral staff from the sick king's hand, Anselm refused to take it. He said he was old, that he was a foreigner, that he had no knowledge of affairs of State. Again they pushed him forward, and the staff of office was literally forced between his clenched fingers. Then he was almost dragged to the nearest church to be the object of some religious ceremonial. Anselm wrote to his brethren at Bec: "It was hard to tell whether a reasonable man was being dragged by a mob of madmen, or whether, rather, some men were seizing a fool."

William quickly recovered, and his generous promises very soon went for naught. However, the appointment of Anselm, for some reason or the other, he did not repeal, though the archbishop-elect was still reluctant, and met William at Rochester to lay down terms on which alone he would even now consent to receive the see: the lands of the archbishopric of Canterbury which had been filched away by William or other royal thieves must be restored without any dispute, and the king must take the advice of the archbishop in all spiritual matters, and Anselm, in return, would acknowledge William as his temporal lord; finally, of the present rival Popes, Anselm must be permitted to accept Urban. At last, after much bargaining, Anselm was enthroned in the Cathedral of Canterbury on September 5th, 1093. The popular joy was rudely disturbed by the appearance of Ralph Flambard, the royal money-extortioner, who served a writ on Anselm during the service, for some claim that his master had against the archbishop. On the following December 4th, Anselm was consecrated in the Cathedral by the Archbishop of York and almost all the bishops of the Canterbury province.

Things seemed to go smoothly at first, but it could not last for long. As Anselm had said when he tried to escape from this great office, the joining of himself with William Rufus in the government of the kingdom was "to yoke an untamed bull and an old and feeble sheep together." There could scarcely have been two men so different in their outlook on life as William and Anselm.

The archbishop demanded that Rufus should give the vacant abbeys back for the use of the Church; he pleaded with the king to help in driving out what this mystic considered the vices of the Court. The king laughed and sneered in his face: "What are the abbeys to you? Are they not mine? Shall you do as you please with your manors, and shall I not do as I please with my abbeys?" And Anselm answered: "They belong to God, and their revenues are for the support of His ministers and not for the waging of your wars."

So Rufus took steps to get rid of such a stubborn prelate. He offered the Pope a bribe if he would deprive Anselm, having failed to make Anselm renounce his allegiance to this same Pope—a position which for sheer topsy-turvy lack of logic it would be hard to beat. Then the papal legate arrived in England with the pall which Anselm had not yet received from Rome. William's aim was to get the legate, with his precious burden, into his power before Anselm could see him. Then the king could make terms for his own good and for the worsting of Anselm and his Church. At this moment there were two men squabbling for the right to be Pope of Rome: one was Clement, whom the Emperor favoured; the other, Urban, was the one generally accepted by the Church, and by Anselm, one of its most faithful sons. When the papal legate arrived in England he was rushed through Canterbury without the archbishop's knowledge, lest Anselm should get his ear before the king had his say. But Urban's messenger was a better man than Rufus at diplomacy. He got the king to publicly proclaim his master, Urban, the Pope; and then, when William proceeded to ask for the price, namely, the deposition of Anselm, the legate flatly refused. William therefore had the alternative of presenting the pall to the archbishop himself or allowing it to be presented by the legate of the man he had just acknowledged. The position was undignified, but inevitable. So the king sent for Anselm to come from Canterbury to Windsor to be reconciled with due formality. Anselm received a hint that if he would give the king a present of money, William would bestow the pall with his own hands. The archbishop refused, and the obstinate monarch had to go through the hollow reconciliation without the money to soften its submissiveness, and both the legate and Anselm refused to allow the pall of holy office to be presented by lay hands, whether the king was willing or not. So Anselm in triumph returned to Canterbury; and on the third Sunday after Trinity (June 10th, 1095) the legate entered that city in state, bearing the pall in a silver casket. The whole body of the clergy and monks of Canterbury, with a vast assembly of the citizens of all ages and both sexes, went to meet him; for the moment the men of Christ Church and of St Augustine walked together; and as the procession neared the Cathedral, Anselm, also, came to meet it, with his feet bare, but dressed with all the robes of his metropolitan office, and with all the bishops of his province in his train. The casket was placed on the altar; and the archbishop took from it the pall with his own hands, signifying that it came from the Pope's hands direct, without the intervention of any inferior. It was one of the triumphal moments in the ecclesiastical history of Canterbury, for the most headstrong of kings had thus been humiliated by the Church.

So complete was Anselm's triumph, that William gave into his charge the defence of the whole of Kent against the expected invasions by the rivals from Normandy. Anselm obeyed his instructions with the greatest zeal; and, for the moment, his civil duties were accounted greater than his ecclesiastical ones; for he refused to leave the city of Canterbury—whence he was controlling the operations—for a single day, even, when the legate asked him to visit him on business of the Church.

Then, during the year 1096, we find Anselm borrowing a hundred pounds from the monks of Christ Church, in order that he might give financial help to William, who was arranging to lease the Duchy of Normandy from his brother Henry, who was longing to set off to Palestine with the knights of Urban's Crusade. Doubtless the archbishop told himself that, by giving this money to the ungodly William, he was subscribing indirectly to a holy war, which happened to be a piece of conscience soothing which was true in this particular case. Anselm gave his manor of Peckham to the monks as security for the loan; and the monastery spent the rents in that great rebuilding of the choir of their Cathedral, as we shall see later.

Then Anselm asked the king's permission to set out on a journey to visit the Pope in Rome. He was refused. The third request was met with the threat that "if he goes, let him understand that I will take his archbishopric into my hands again, and never will I again receive him as primate." And Anselm replied, "It is good to obey God rather than man." There was further lengthy discussion and much losing of tempers, and it ended by William petulantly telling Anselm he might go, only not one fragment of the king's goods might he take with him. The archbishop replied with the brief statement that if his horses and clothes were the king's, then he would go naked and on foot, to which the king sent the shamefaced reply that he did not mean anything so discourteous as that, but he must leave the realm within eleven days. Thereupon the archbishop went to the king and asked him to receive his holy blessing before he set out, and in one of his softer moments the king bowed his head and received it; and Anselm set off for Canterbury to take leave of his fellow-monks and the people of his episcopal city. There was a mighty gathering of monks and clergy and people in the Cathedral on the day that he blessed the multitude, and took the staff and scrip of a pilgrim from off the altar, and set out on his journey to Rome, near the end of 1097. He spent Christmas at Cluny, and it was late spring when he arrived in Rome. Everybody was charmed by the sweetness and grace of his manners—even the Duke of Burgundy, who had intended to waylay him on the road and rob him of his reputed wealth, took the humble archbishop's kiss and blessing instead.

Anselm asked the Pope to take the archbishopric off his unwilling shoulders, for up in the delicious coolness of the Italian hills in summer-time, Anselm had been seized once more with the love of quiet contemption and study. But the Pope said, "No." Then William's own messenger arrived in Rome, and spread his money so wisely round the papal court that the threatened excommunication (if William would not take back Anselm) was delayed. Anselm saw the Pope was time-serving; but he was kept in Rome against his will, and treated as one of the ecclasiastical sights of the city. At last, there being a deadlock between unstable Pope and stubborn king, Anselm left Rome, and was living in France when a monk from Canterbury brought the news that William Rufus had been killed in the New Forest in the August of 1100.

His monks, and then the new king, Henry, begged Anselm to return; and in September he was back in Canterbury again, after three years' absence.

But there was very quickly a difficulty in the matter, for the king demanded, although with all courtesy, that the archbishop should do homage before he received the temporal possession of his see of Canterbury. Henry was a gentleman and a scholar and a man of grace: Anselm had no longer to do with a man like William, who would have found his fitting place on a western ranch rather than as a king. The contest was now between the firm principles of perhaps the most saintly of Canterbury's archbishops, and one of the most accomplished of England's kings. Anselm himself had apparently no strong objection to acknowledging the temporal power of the king; but unfortunately he had himself, while at Rome, sat on a papal council which forbade any cleric to admit the right of any temporal power over the Church. And the word of the Church was sacred to Anselm—whether it was common-sense or not. So he flatly refused to do homage to Henry for the manors belonging to the see of Canterbury. Then the matter was referred to Rome. The Pope, now Paschal, was diplomatically vague in his answer: he would not commit himself on paper, though he sent a verbal reply that so long as Henry chose good men for his bishops, so long would the Pope be conciliatory and lax concerning the matter of homage for the temporal possessions of the sees; and even the granting of the ecclesiastical ring and staff might be accepted from the king's hands. Anselm was in a predicament; he did not know whether a verbal reply was good enough against the solemn resolutions he had heard passed by the council in Rome. There was another temporary compromise while more messengers went to Rome.

Then in the Lent of 1103 Henry came to

Canterbury, where he had business to discuss concerning the Count of Flanders. He also discussed the situation once more concerning the investitures, for by this time the last messenger had returned saying that the verbal reply was a tale manufactured by the deceitful bishops who brought it, adding that the decrees of the Church were to be obeyed to the letter. There was a remarkable scene between the great secular statesman and the great spokesman of the Church: both were adamant; when suddenly the king dramatically begged the archbishop himself to go to Rome and put the case before the Pope. It was a strange thing to commit one's cause to the advocacy of one's opponent. At the next meeting of the great council of the realm the assembly of magnates added their requests to the same effect, and Anselm went back to Canterbury to make ready for his journey, and within four days he was off from Dover.

When he arrived in Rome things were quickly put into terse language without beating about the bush. Henry's spokesman—not Anselm, for the king after all did not trust the whole case to him—finished his speech with these words: "Know all men present that not to save his kingdom will King Henry lose the investiture of the churches." The papal reply was equally to the point: "Before God, not for the safety of his head will Pope Paschal give it up to him." However, these fine heroics were mainly for stage effect, and no serious breach happened, although neither side would give way.

Nevertheless, the deadlock was so serious that Anselm would not go back to Canterbury until the wrong—as he understood it—had been put right. At last, after two years of this passive struggle (during which Henry looked after the property of the see with discretion, giving Anselm all that was necessary for his own personal use) Anselm suddenly announced that he was about to excommunicate the king as a punishment for his obstinacy. Henry coaxed and pleaded in every possible way; but Anselm was one of those few people who are not won over by sweet words. Then the papal messengers arrived with permission to withdraw all the excommunications levied against those who had submitted to the king in the matter of investitures and homage. It left the subject still open in principle, it only forgave past offenders. So Anselm returned to Canterbury, whither he had written to the monks of Christ Church, but a little while before, commanding that the breaking of the canon enforcing celibacy without fail should be followed by the deprivation or excommunication of the offending clergy. On his arrival in the summer of 1106 Anselm was received with a great welcome, the queen coming to meet him and travelling before him to prepare his way.

The matter of investiture was at last settled at a great council held the following year in London, the terms being those which Henry and Anselm had agreed to when they met in France in 1105, which terms had since received the papal approval which the archbishop required as part of the bargain. But Anselm was not present at the debate, though he was there when the compromise was published. After all the struggle the king gave up his right to present the ring and staff to a bishop-elect; that is, he gave up all pretence to confer the sacred offices, while the Pope allowed the bishops to do homage to the Crown for the grant of the temporal estates of their sees. It was a common-sense decision, and they probably all wondered why they had not agreed without so much commotion. But as a matter of fact it was really Henry who had won; for he still had the right to select whom he chose for the office of bishop.

Then Anselm got back to his work of managing his

province of Canterbury, and reforming the English Church. On August 11th there was a great consecration service in the Cathedral, when Anselm laid his hands on five bishops. But the archbishop was getting old, and with age it would seem that he became a little harsher and more peremptory in his methods. He had a violent struggle with the Archbishops of York to compel them to acknowledge the dominion of Canterbury, which had been discussed at such length in Lanfranc's time. His last letter was one in almost violent terms, suspending Thomas, who was at that time the archbishop of the northern province; and he continued a stern, relentless enforcement of the canon of clerical celibacy.

On April 21st 1109 he died, with a half-wish on his lips that he might be spared to finish a problem which filled his mind, a problem which he said he did not quite know who else could solve when he was gone. The worthy archbishop's doubt has been amply justified—no one has yet solved the riddle. The problem was—the origin of the soul!

They buried him in the nave; and afterwards his body was placed at the base of that south-east tower which still bears his name, and still stands over his remains. A few words which he himself wrote in a letter to Gundulf, his friend at Rochester, would seem to sum up Anselm better than any amount of mere biography: "Let no threats, no promise, no cunning wring from you either homage or oath or bond of fealty. If any should ask of you these things, give this for your answer; 'I am a Christian, I am a monk, I am a bishop, therefore would I keep faith with everyone to whom I owe it.'" There is just a touch of stubborn pigheadedness in that avowal; and there was just that trait of narrowness in the big brain of St Anselm.

We are now ready to consider the material changes

which were effected in the Cathedral Church during the period of Anselm, or at least begun under his supervision. The immediate charge of the work was probably under that famous prior of Christ Church, Ernulf, who had followed Lanfranc to Canterbury, after sitting at his feet at Bec. William of Malmesbury has recorded that this Ernulf was a Frenchman, but the Rochester annals claim him as an Englishman. Anyhow, his career was in England, and was a credit to whichever race can best claim him. Lanfranc advised him to come to Canterbury because there had been some disturbances in the monastery of St Lucian of Beauvais, whither Ernulf had gone, and (said Lanfranc) he might not be able to save his soul in that unruly place. He therefore came, and was a monk of Canterbury during the whole time of Lanfranc, and was made prior of Christ Church by Anselm, and afterwards (to finish the outline of his life) he became Abbot of Peterborough, and (in 1114) Bishop of Rochester. The last office was sorely against his will, according to the chroniclers, and he had to be taken, with much reluctance, to his old home of Canterbury in order to be consecrated to his new bishopric.

If it be true that he was at Canterbury during the whole ("toto tempore") of Lanfranc's archbishopric, then, of course, he must have seen, and perhaps overlooked, the great building operations of the new and first Norman church which we have already considered in the last chapter. He must have been a builder of some experience, for he took the responsibility of continuing the works during Anselm's exile.

Any precise description of the building done under Ernulf will be found in the next chapter, where it can be more conveniently and satisfactorily discussed as it stood when the rebuilding was completed in 1130; for Ernulf's work was carried on by the next prior, Conrad, whose name, indeed, has been linked in history to this new part of the Cathedral. Suffice it to say here that Ernulf, "having taken down the eastern part of the church which Lanfranc had built, he rebuilt it with such splendour that nothing could be seen in England of such brilliancy as the colour of its windows, or the shining of its marble floor, or the many-coloured frescoes." It was merely the choir of Lanfranc's church which was touched during this rebuilding by Ernulf; and Lanfranc's nave remained standing until it was pulled down two hundred years or so later, by Prior Chillenden, when he built the nave we now possess in main outline.

The records of the building operations of Anselm's time have been summed up by Professor Willis in the following abstract of the account recorded by Eadmer, the friend of Anselm: "His [*i.e.* Ernulf's] works at Canterbury, however, originated with Anselm, for that prelate allowed the monks to manage their own affairs, and gave them for priors Ernulf and then Conrad, both monks of their own monastery. And thus it happened that in addition to the general prosperity and good order of their property, which resulted from this freedom, they were enabled to enlarge their church, by all that part which stretches from the great tower to the east; for which work Anselm himself provided. For when Duke Robert of Normandy undertook his Crusade [A.D. 1096], great riches were extracted from the English by his brother King Henry to supply him with funds; and the archbishop, being compelled to contribute, drew out a large sum from the treasury of the church of Canterbury. And to make amends straightway granted to the said church the revenues of his manor of Peckham for seven years; the whole of which were expended upon the new work."

CHAPTER IX

The Growth of the Ecclesiastical Power

THE onlooker at the end of the reign of Henry I. might well have been excused if he had decided that the power of the Church of England was melting away under the strong hands of the Norman kings. Anselm and the king had come to close grips, and although it was called a compromise when they came to terms, yet Henry seemed to have all the substance of victory and Anselm mainly the shadow. But, in fact, the church had won: and if we wish to understand the supreme triumph of Thomas Becket's canonisation fifty years later, then we must endeavour to grasp the process of ecclesiastical growth which preceded it. It was a growth intimately linked with, and pictorially expressed by, the enlargement of Canterbury cathedral and the monastery building and its archiepiscopal palace, which became so energetic under Lanfranc and Anselm, and was continued under their immediate successors, who will be treated of in this chapter.

The moment had come in the history of the Church of Rome when it claimed a far greater dominion than it had hitherto dared to demand. Not to go into earlier phases, the policy of Hildebrand, who became the famous Pope Gregory VII., was nothing less than an attempt to rank higher than the Emperors of Rome, and become the supreme lord of the world. The power of the Church was to be universal, and since the

Popes of Rome spoke with the voice of God, therefore theirs was to be the highest authority on earth. When Hildebrand, as the man behind the commands of Pope Alexander II., gained the papal blessing for William the Conqueror's raid on England, the autocratic Norman duke was granting a far-reaching claim on the part of the Roman bishop. It is a little doubtful whether William went so far as to promise that he would hold England, if he conquered it, as a fee of St Peter; but, in any case, the Norman army started out with the holy banner of Rome at its head; and this pirates' raid was, by the blessing of the Church, turned into a holy war.

We have seen how, under Lanfranc and Anselm, the Church of England had struggled, with apparent unsuccess, to free itself from the strong grip which the Norman kings, spite of their promises, kept over the ecclesiastical rulers at home, and how the monarchs so boldly defied the jurisdiction of the Popes when legates and bulls arrived from Rome. But irresistibly, if rather silently, the power of the Church and of its Popes was growing greater and greater. Keeping to the case of England, the Church had now its separate courts of law; whereas, in the time of the Saxon rule, the law of the Church and the law of the layman were administered in large part together. It was a dangerous experiment, their allowing the ecclesiastics separate courts of their own, though the kings would have scored heavily if the Church had not been strong enough to stand isolated. But if the Norman kings were reckoning on isolation being a weakness, they mistook their problem: for standing alone, divided by hard lines from the rest of the people, the Church was stronger than ever.

The revival of the monasteries played a great part in this growth of ecclesiastical power. There was, at this time, a new movement of reform. The missionaries of Cluny had arrived in England in the reign of William I., and there they had established almost forty houses within thirty or so years. The Cistercian Order of monks first arrived in 1128, they became still richer than the Cluniacs before they had been here long. These monkish Orders, with their strong rules of caste, were repeated pictures, scattered over England, of the individuality and power of the great Church of Rome, to whom they professed obedience more humbly than to either king or bishop. And the independence of the monasteries had, at first, the effect of supporting the freedom of the bishops in their struggle with the royal power. With these few sentences of general introduction we can now return to the particular part of the Church which is the subject of this book, and in close connection with its history and its ecclesiastics we shall be able to trace the growth of its Church in power—a more satisfactory proof than by any number of generalised statements of principles.

When Anselm died in 1109, Ralph, the Bishop of Rochester, became the acting administrator of the province of Canterbury, and used the revenue for the good of the see. This continued until 1114. The fact is itself a proof of the strength of the Church, when we remember how the last king had kept the archbishopric vacant in order that he might seize the income himself, which at that time was apparently a legal right as between a king and the vacant see. In a few years' time the charter of King Stephen formally acknowledged the new precedent which was practised in the action of Ralph which we have just stated.

In the year 1114 Bishop Ralph was ordered by the king to attend his council at Windsor, with the prior and some of the monks of the Cathedral monastery of Christ Church, in order that an archbishop should be chosen. The choice fell on Ralph himself, partly because he had been a monk in his earlier days, partly

NORMAN TOWER, CANTERBURY CATHEDRAL

because he had now ceased to live as one, since he had been driven out of his abbey by the violence of a Norman baron. Such was the compromise between the party which thought all bishops should be monks, and the party which thought all bishops should be secular clergy. But it is not necessary to consider the reign of Ralph in detail, suffice it to say that he was on all points tenacious of the privileges of the Church in general, and of Canterbury in particular, without lapse. It is recorded that when at some great ceremony he observed that Henry was wearing the crown, which the archbishop had not put on with his own hands, the scandalised cleric indignantly asked who had dared to encroach on his sole right of placing the crown on the king's head. It turned out that it was the king himself who had ventured to crown himself in a moment of absent-mindedness, and he said he would be quite pleased to have it off and put on again with full ceremonies, if the archbishop desired it; and Ralph said that such was his pleasure, and so it was done all over again. It all seems rather tiresome to-day.

Ralph died in 1122 and was buried in his Cathedral; and William of Corbeuil, a secular priest, was chosen to succeed him. The appointment was made at a great council at Gloucester; and the prior and a few of the monks of Canterbury Cathedral, who had come to take their part in the election, said they desired to select one of their own fellow-monks of Christ Church, and ask the king which of them he liked best. But the bishops present at the council were nearly all seculars, and advised the king to choose a secular for the archbishopric. The king took their advice, and after a two days' argument, the prior and his brethren were given the choice of four secular priests, and told the king would appoint the man they chose. It was William, and he got their votes because he was a member of the Order of the Augustine Canons, which was a good way to a monk, and, at least, all they could do under the circumstances. William was consecrated at Canterbury, in February 1123, by the bishops of his own province; for the Archbishop of York, Thurstan, was at this time stubbornly raising again the old question of the independence of York from the supremacy of Canterbury; so William refused to be consecrated by a man who would not acknowledge that the archbishop of the southern province was primate over all England. This Thurstan was a lasting trouble to William, and they were both a trouble to each other. When William started off to Rome to fetch his pall of office immediately after his consecration, Thurstan set out in pursuit, and, what was more to the point, got there first, and so filled the mind of the Pope with prejudices that it began to look doubtful whether William would be recognised at all. Every pretext was found for asserting the illegality of his election to the archbishopric. The reasons are interesting, for they show the theoretical ecclesiastic claims of the period. First, said the Pope, the election had been in a royal court "where the judgment could be death"—and the Church did not admit the shedding of blood; secondly, the chapter of Canterbury had not given its free consent; thirdly, William was not a monk, and by the canons of St Augustine no secular priest could become an archbishop; lastly, he had not been consecrated by the Archbishop of York. Not one of these rules was followed by custom in England, or ever had been admitted, probably; but the assertion is another example of the firmer claims of the papacy. But by liberal bribes of money and royal persuasion (in the words of the "Anglo-Saxon Chronicle," "that overcame Rome which overcomes all the world—that is gold and silver. And the Pope was satisfied") the Pope gave way, and William started home again with his pall; but the question of the position of the Archbishop of York was left to be decided by a papal legate, who was to follow the two claimants to England, and hold a council before which their arguments could be placed.

The reception of this legate in England was very remarkable, and an ample testimony to the rapid rise in the power of the Papacy. In the words of the "Saxon Chronicle" once more: "The Pope sent from Rome to this land a cardinal named John of Crema. He first came to the king in Normandy, and the king received him with great worship; commending him to the archbishop William of Canterbury; and he conducted him to Canterbury where he was received with great worship and a great procession; and he sang the high mass on Easter day at Christ's altar." This taking of the place and office of the archbishop was in itself an acknowledgment of the papal supremacy over the primate of England; and William the Conqueror would have resented it, in all probability. The monks of Christ's Church were openly glad that a secular archbishop had received this insult. Then the legate set out from Canterbury on a tour round the religious houses of all England; "and everywhere he was received with worship, and all gave him great and noble gifts." When the council was held it decided nothing about the relations of York to Canterbury, but chiefly concerned itself with issuing fresh canons against the clergy who still persisted in the state of wedlock. The chronicler Gervase, in his "Actus Pontificum," writes of the terrible indignity the whole of the ecclesiastics and nobles of England suffered in thus sitting under the presidency of a papal legate of Rome.

So off the two archbishops started once more for Rome. But this time William scored, for there was a new Pope, who made the Archbishop of Canterbury the papal legate in England. It was a crafty move; for it made the king and Church of England acknowledge the papal power by admitting a legate to the realm, and it soothed their pride by choosing as this legate the head of the national Church. Of course there was no further doubt as to the supremacy of Canterbury over York, so long as the holder of the former province was the holder of the legate's commission. We shall see the result of this commission of William's later, when it became the permanent right of all Archbishops of Canterbury from the time of Stephen Langton.

Things now went fairly smoothly, and the strengthened archbishop attempted once more to deal with the rebellious married clergy. At a council in London, all the bishops agreed to a judgment that every married priest should lose his church if he had not put away his wife by the next St Andrew's Day. But the story, as it is told in the "Saxon Chronicle," is too terse and humorous not to be given in full: "Then soon [1129], by the king's counsel and by his leave, the Archbishop of Canterbury sent over all England, and bade the bishops and abbots and archdeacons, and all the priors, monks, and canons that were in all the cells in England, and after all who had to preserve and watch over Christianity, that they should all come to London at Michaelmas, and should then speak of all God's rights. When they came thither, the meeting began on Monday, and held on to the Friday. When it all came forth, it was all about archdeacons' wives and about priests' wives, that they should leave them by St Andrew's mass [Nov. 30th]; and he who would not do that, should forgo his church and his house and his home, and never more have any calling thereto. This ordained the archbishop William of Canterbury and all the suffragan bishops who were then in England; and the king gave them all leave to go home; and so they went home, and all the decrees stood for naught: all held their wives by the king's leave, as they did before."

During all this time, during the terms of the Archbishops Anselm, Ralph, and William, the great rebuilding of the choir of Canterbury Cathedral had been proceeding, and in the year 1130 it was consecrated with gorgeous ceremonials. Gervase tells us: "This church of Canterbury, which had been refounded and completed by Lanfranc, and enlarged by Anselm, was dedicated with great honour and liberality on the fourth of May. At this dedication there was present Henry, King of the English, who presented to this church, as a dowry, the church of St Martin's of Dover, which the ancient king of Kent, Wihtredus, had founded. There were also present David, king of Scotland and all the bishops of England. Never had there been such a dedication on this earth since the dedication of the Temple of Solomon."

This is a fitting moment to consider the great building of Christ Church as it thus stood complete at a famous period of its history, for it was in this church, as it was dedicated in 1130, that Becket was murdered forty years later. At this period, the nave was the work of Lanfranc, and the choir was the one which had been built under Anselm and his two successors. This church has been described as a whole by Gervase (who wrote during the years 1188-1210), but who knew it as it had been before it was destroyed by the great fire of 1174; and this description we shall find it profitable to follow in detail, for it will help to give us the true atmosphere of the church, with its crowd of saintly relics and their shrines, and the reverence which was paid to them.

Gervase's description of Lanfranc's nave we have

already repeated in the chapter on that archbishop's work and period; we will now translate the description of the choir, which was added to that nave between 1093 and 1130. The two descriptions, read together, will revive for us the Cathedral in which some of the greatest events of its history were enacted. When Gervase wrote, the choir had disappeared in the fire of 1174; but he had been in Canterbury since 1163, as a monk of Christ Church; so the old choir must have been very familiar to him. So it must be remembered that we are reading the words of an intimate contemporary observer, one of the well-known characters of the town, who lived there most of his days, until his death about 1210.

"Now that the choir of Conrad," writes Gervase, "once so gloriously built, has piteously been consumed by fire in our own days, therefore must I endeavour to describe it, however simple and nerveless may be my pen, lest the memory of so great a man and so famous a work be lost for ever. Although it is not my purpose to describe the mere stones of the building, yet it will not be possible to show the places of the Saints and their tombs in the church, without first describing the building in which they were arranged under the eyes and with the co-operation of the chronicler Eadmer.

"Let us therefore begin with the aforesaid Great Tower which stands in the centre of the church, and let us proceed eastwards. The east piers of the tower stood out from the solid mass in semicircular relief. From here, down the choir stretched a line of eight pillars on each side of it, almost equidistant from each other: and then came six in a semicircle, arranged from the ninth pillar on the south side to the ninth on the north side [forming an apse at the east end of the choir]. . . . Arches were turned from pillar to pillar; and above these the solid wall was set with small blank [*obscuris*] windows. Above the wall was the passage which is called triforium, and then the upper windows; this was the continuation of the interior wall. On this rested the roof and ceiling, ornamented with excellent paintings. At the bases of the pillars was a wall of marble slabs which surrounded the choir and presbytery, this dividing the body of the church from its sides, which are called aisles [*alæ*]. This wall [or screen, as it would be called now] inclosed the choir of the monks, the presbytery, the High Altar, dedicated in the name of Jesus Christ, and the altars of St Dunstan and St Alphage with their holy bodies.

"Above the wall [*i.e.* screen], in the apse behind and opposite to the altar, was the patriarchal chair formed out of a single stone; in which, following the custom of the Church, on high festivals the archbishops were wont to sit during the solemn mass until the time of the consecration of the holy elements, whereupon they descended to the altar of Christ by eight steps. From the choir up to the presbytery there were three steps; from the pavement of the presbytery up to the altar three steps; up to the patriarchal seat there were eight steps. At the eastern horns of the altar were two wooden columns, gracefully ornamented with gold and silver, which carried a great beam, of which the ends rested on the capitals of two of the pillars. This beam, decorated with gold, was carried across the church, above the altar; and bore on it the image of the Lord and the images of St Dunstan and St Alphage; also seven chests worked over with gold and silver and filled with the relics of many of the saints. Between the two wooden columns there was a gilded cross surrounded by a row of sixty transparent crystals. Under this altar of Christ there was, in the crypt beneath, an altar of the Holy Virgin, to whom the whole of the crypt was dedicated. And this crypt was in length and breadth of almost exactly the same size as the choir above it. From the middle of the choir there hung a gilded crown carrying twenty-four candles. And such was the position of the choir and presbytery."

Having thus described the core of the Cathedral, Gervase now turns to the outer aisles and chapels which encircled the choir. "The exterior wall of the aisles was of this fashion: beginning from the martyrium of Saint Thomas, that is to say, from the transept of Lanfranc's church, and going eastwards as far as the higher transept, there are only three windows in that wall. From the fifth pillar of the choir there sprang an arch over to the wall; and there the north transept is built: and its breadth is the distance between the fifth and the seventh pillar; for opposite the seventh pillar, as from the fifth, there sprang a wall northwards, completing the north transept with two apsidal ends. In the south apse was the altar of St Stephen, and in the crypt beneath it was the altar of St Nicholas. In the north apse was the altar of St Martin, and under this, in turn, was the altar of St Mary Magdalene. Before the altar of St Martin lay the bodies of two archbishops; on the right Wulfhelm and on the left Lyfing. Likewise before the altar of St Stephen there were two others; on the left Athelheard, and on the right the venerable Cuthbert. This last it was who, with great wisdom, won for Christ Church the right of free burial. For it had been the custom that not only the archbishops but all those who died in the city should be carried to the church of SS. Peter and Paul outside the city and there buried in the ancient place; for in that time they held that the city was a place for the living and not for the dead. But the blessed Cuthbert grieved to think that after his death he would be torn from the church and the society of the sons whom he had loved during his life with such affection: so he petitioned the great pontiff at Rome and obtained for Christ Church the right of free burial. We are given to believe, that he was the first, by the grace of God and the authority of the great pontiff and the permission of the king of England, to be buried in Christ Church, and all the archbishops after him have been likewise buried here except one only named Jaenberht.

"From this apse of St Stephen, the aforesaid wall, on its way east, had a window opposite the side of the High Altar [which was in the choir]. Then came a high tower arising outside the aforesaid wall, which was named the tower of St Andrew, because there was an altar dedicated to that Saint in it; and under it, in the crypt, was the altar of the Innocents. From this tower the wall went in a slight curve, with a window in it, until it reached the next chapel, which was built at the east end of the church opposite the high chair of the archbishops: but since there will be many things to say concerning this chapel, it will be better to wait at its entrance, until the south wall is described until it reaches this same chapel.

"This south side of the Cathedral, beginning at the apse of St Michael in the transept of Lanfranc's church, has three windows before it reaches the upper [*i.e.* the south-east] transept. This transept, like its companion one, had two apses on its east side. In the south apse was the altar of St Gregory, where lay the bodies of two archbishops; on the south, St Brecgwin, and on the north, St Plegmund; and under it, in the crypt, was the altar of St Audoen, archbishop of Rouen. In the other [*i.e.* the north] apse was the altar of St John the Evangelist, where two archbishops were buried; on the right, Æthelgar, and on the left, Ælfric; under which last, in the crypt, was the altar of St Paulinus where archbishop Sigeric was buried. Under the altar of St Audoen, almost in the middle of the pavement, was the altar of St Catherine.

The outer wall of the Cathedral continuing eastwards from this transept, had a window opposite the High Altar, and then came a high tower in which was an altar to the apostles Peter and Paul. But St Anselm,

NORMAN TOWER, CANTERBURY CATHEDRAL

having been translated thither to this spot and placed behind the altar, gave his name to the altar and to the tower. From this tower the wall continues a little further and has a window in its curve; and then arrives at the above-mentioned chapel of the Holy Trinity, built at the east end of the church. Here an arch springs from each wall, both south and north, and completes the circumference.

"This chapel extends to the east beyond the main wall of the church, but joined to it: and has the altar of the Holy Trinity, where the blessed martyr Thomas celebrated his first mass on the day of his consecration [as archbishop]. In this chapel, both before his exile and afterwards, he was accustomed to celebrate mass, to attend the services and to pray frequently. Behind the altar were buried two archbishops, on the right St Oda, and on the left St Wilfrid archbishop of York: on the south side, against the wall, was the venerable Lanfranc; and on the north side was Theobald. In the crypt beneath were two altars: that on the south was of St Augustine, the apostle of the English; the northern one was that of St John the Baptist. By the south wall lay the archbishop Æthelred; and by the north wall lay Eadsige. In the middle of this chapel rose a column which bore the arches and vaulting from all sides. At the base of this column, on its east side, was laid that deed of martyrdom on the 3 Kal. of January, of which the seal had been struck on the previous day by those four notaries of the Devil. This is the place, I mean, where the most blessed martyr Thomas was buried on the day following his martyrdom."

Without the careful survey of the details thus recorded by the monkish chronicler, Gervase, it would be difficult to realise the real meaning of this great Cathedral, namely, a storehouse of the relics of saints and holy men, and a place where they could be met in prayer and supplication. So this lengthy translation of the old chronicle has been given almost in full. When the reader comes to survey the modern church, he will be continually reminded that, in main form, it is still the same building which Gervase surveyed at the end of the 1100-century. The chief change to note will be the addition to the east end, of which we shall follow the building in a later chapter, still under the guidance of the monk Gervase. So far, in 1130, we have reached the third great period in the history of the Cathedral: there was first the Saxon church, which was destroyed by the fire of 1067; then came Lanfranc's church; then the new choir, which we have just surveyed, of Anselm and his successors. Of this a large part stands with its very stones to-day, as we shall find in our modern itinerary in a later chapter. We have given the complete picture in the words of the old surveyor, in order that we may the better understand what is left.

Each addition has seen the enlargement of the choir, as the collection of holy relics grew larger. The Saxon choir was a mere apsidal recess, in all probability; Lanfranc's choir was larger; Anselm's extended beyond that again, and finally we shall see the bones of Becket demanding the last great extension of all, which makes it the largest choir in England.

Such was the church which was dedicated in the great service conducted by Archbishop William in 1130. It was not the only experience that William had of extensive building operations; for he had received a grant of Rochester Castle from King Henry, and had built that great keep which is still standing in part. This was, perhaps, an act of sensible forethought on William's side; for he may have seen troublesome days ahead when Henry was dead and his daughter, Matilda, might have to fight for her throne. To support this daughter, William had already taken the oath of allegiance to her as his future queen. When Henry died, William may have had every intention of keeping his promise, and when Stephen landed at Dover to claim the crown, he found Canterbury fortified and in the hands of ths soldiers of Robert, Earl of Gloucester, Matilda's half-brother.

The city refused to admit Stephen; and he had to leave it untouched, and passed on to London. But the lord of Canterbury soon saw that it would be wiser to break his oath and go over to Stephen; especially when he heard that the new king was prepared to give numberless liberties to the Church. So William crowned Stephen at Westminster, and behaved like the discreet, timid man he was.

The struggles and jealousies between the Cathedral and the abbey of St Augustine were at this time in full flood, and there was much appealing to the king and the Pope to support one side or the other. But the details it will be more convenient to keep to a separate section on the history of the abbey.

William died at Canterbury in 1136, within a year of Stephen's crowning, and the historians who favoured Matilda were careful to point out with glee that such was a fitting end for a man who had broken his oath, overlooking, in their mediæval piety, that death happens to the most faithful of men. He hastened his death by hurrying to Dover to protect the secular canons of Merton, who had been endowed with the church of St Martin's in the former town; but when they had arrived to take possession the monks of Christ Church had put in a claim that this church in Dover belonged to them, and that the archbishop had nothing to do with it, in spite of the fact that Henry, the king, had refounded it in honour of the great dedication service of 1130, which we have noticed; and when Henry had gone on to present it as an addition to the estates of the archbishopric, the monks made their claim. They also saw their chance to get some revenge for being compelled to accept a secular priest as archbishop, instead of a monk like themselves; so they demanded that the refounded church in Dover should be placed under the control of Benedictine monks, instead of secular canons. The story is a good example of the friction

THE BAPTISTRY, CANTERBURY CATHEDRAL

between the two branches of the Church; and it is the more suggestive in that it had now come between the secular archbishop and the monkish chapter of his own cathedral. The archbishop had set his heart on the secular canons, and he ordered the Bishops of Rochester and St David's to introduce them into their new home. But the monks sent a fiery champion, a monk named Jeremiah, to state their case; he called on the bishops, in the name of Rome, to desist. But the bishops replied by referring to William's orders, and calling him "archiepiscopus et vester dominus." However, Jeremiah thoroughly scared them by his threat of appealing to the Pope, and the bishops said rather meekly, "There is not one of us who desires to see the face of Rome on account of this matter; so we will return to our lord archbishop and tell him what we have done, and what we have heard." Whereupon the archbishop, says the chronicle, was greatly moved in spirit and died in a few days: "and when he was dead, the monastery of Canterbury sent twelve monks to take possession of the house at Dover and make William of Longaville the prior."

There was over a year's vacancy before the see of Canterbury was filled again; then, after being summoned before the king and the papal legate, the prior and monks of the Cathedral monastery chose Theobald, Abbot of Bec, for their archbishop; and Gervase tells us that their choice was "consecrated in Canterbury before the High Altar of Christ, on the eighth day of January, by Alberic, bishop of Ostia and legate of the chair of the Apostle, almost all the bishops of England being present and assisting in the service. And in a few days the legate went over the sea . . . and in the same month Theobald also went over the sea to Rome to fetch his pall." All this was a great disappointment to Henry, Bishop of Winchester, King Stephen's brother, who longed for the see of Canterbury himself. But Henry was too powerful a noble to have this ecclesiastical honour added to his possessions, so Stephen opposed the wish, and got his way, as we have seen. Nevertheless, Henry scored when the Pope appointed him the papal legate for England, thus passing over the late precedent which united that office with the see of Canterbury. But Theobald was not a hasty man and said little, and waited his time. Things were in an unsettled state, as they always were under the rule of Stephen; but the archbishop considered that he was right in acknowledging the monarch who had been accepted by the Pope; so he was on the side of Stephen officially, though privately he seems to have considered that the rival claimant, the Empress Matilda, would have made the better ruler. But with the civil wars of this reign we have nothing to do, except so far as they concern the history of Canterbury. When Stephen was seized by his rivals and imprisoned at Bristol, Theobald journeyed thither apparently to ask his permission to acknowledge Matilda as queen. Whatever happened there, he certainly was openly on the side of the Empress in the middle of 1141, but again changed sides when Stephen came up top once more in the hurly-burly which they were pleased to call the government of England at this time. And at the next Christmas, Stephen and his queen arrived in Canterbury and were both crowned by Theobald in the Cathedral.

But Theobald, who was a sound ecclesiastic and apparently a man of deep religious convictions as his essential characteristic, must have been rather out of keeping with his fellow-bishops. The chief of these, Henry, Bishop of Winchester, possessed about six castles, which may have been of more practical use than a firm faith or theological learning in Stephen's days; but Theobald did not think of the Church as an institution maintained by force of arms. Likewise

Roger, Bishop of Salisbury, and his family had in their hands many powerful sees and offices; and they, also, were fortifying every castle they could seize or build as new.

Such was the clerical atmosphere in which Theobald tried to develop the intellectual and spiritual growth of the Church. His mind was inclined to precise definitions of law, and he founded in Canterbury a school of civil law, and gathered round him, in his palace, a group of students who became famous in later life as ecclesiastics and statesmen. Of these the one that most attracts our interest here is that Thomas of London, sometimes called Becket, who arrived in Canterbury about 1143. About the same time, Theobald persuaded Vacarius of Mantua, a famous lawyer, to come to England and deliver a course of lectures in his new school; and once again it looked as though Canterbury might take the prominent position in teaching that Augustine had from the first days designed, when he brought manuscripts from Rome to deposit in the libraries of the new monasteries he had founded in his cathedral city and outside its walls. As one of the students in this legal school, Thomas Becket has a more intimate claim to be part of the history of this city than would even be granted by his official position as its chief ecclasiastical lord. His training in the laws of the Church and the practical politics of the world took place mainly in the palace of the archbishops, as a listener at the lectures, and the confidential secretary of Theobald. When Thomas himself became archbishop in later years, he was but doing the work he had helped his predecessor to do many years before.

The Archbishop Theobald was especially in need of intimate counsellors in his own palace; for, more and more, the archbishops were being isolated from their adjacent monastery of Christ Church, of which they had once been the recognised heads. We have seen how this isolating process had been hastened by the action of Lanfranc. Theobald himself had acknowledged that the monks had the right to exclude his archdeacon from their Chapter House; and if he was requested to attend to give his advice, he was not entitled to vote. That Becket, Theobald's chief confidant, should not be a monk of the monastery was a typical example of the new state of affairs. The palace and the house of monks were distinct places. At this time the two came to the point of enmity even more bitter than had been the case in the previous holder of the see.

The leader of the opposition party in the monastery was the same Jeremiah who had acted before in the case of the house at Dover. Theobald had himself appointed him as the prior, and since the election had entrusted him with the whole affairs of the house. But there arose a quarrel between them, and Theobald turned the prior out of his post. Therepon Jeremiah set out for Rome and put his case before Pope Innocent, with the result that he came back to Canterbury with papal letters ordering his restoration. To which Theobald, "moved with great bitterness, turned away his favour from the monastery," and retaliated with the declaration that never again, so long as Jeremiah remained in the house, would their archbishop perform the rites of Holy Sacrament in their church. This threat brought the rebellious monk to his knees, for he feared that his fellows would turn on him if the threat was carried out. So he resigned his post, and withdrew to the neighbouring house of St Augustine, where he died and was buried. Jeremiah was the more anxious to retire from the contest, because Theobald had been to Rome and had won his suit against the other rebellious house of St Augustine. Further, the authority of the legate, Henry of Winchester, had expired with the death (1143) of the pope who commissioned him; so Theobald had no ecclesiastical superior in England—a great addition to his strength, of course.

The Popes of Rome were now taking an autocratic line with the King of England. The claims of Hildebrand as Pope Gregory VII., to be the ruler of the world, had been more patiently accepted by the aforesaid world than might have been expected when that somewhat ambitious theory was first propounded. We are now nearing the high-water mark of papal power over Christendom, when the Popes of Rome almost succeeded in establishing a substantial kingdom upon earth, which would have overridden the inferior jurisdictions of the mundane kings and princes and barons.

There were already little indications of the way the wind was blowing. For example, the king's chosen man for the Archbishopric of York was ejected from his see; and in revenge Stephen refused to give the ordinary permission for Theobald to leave England as a delegate at the Council of Reims in 1148. But Theobald, "fearing God more than he feared the king," says Gervase, crossed the Channel in a cockleshell of a boat, without the necessary permission, and in spite of the fact that Stephen was having all the ports carefully guarded to seize him if he made the attempt. The king had told the archbishop that if he went he must consider himself banished from the kingdom, and his estates confiscated. The Pope retaliated by a threat to excommunicate Stephen, to which the king defiantly answered by a formal banishment and confiscation against the archbishop. So when the latter came back to England he was almost immediately compelled to fly from Canterbury again. The Pope, hearing the news, published an interdict on the whole country; but since almost all the rest of the Church in England stood by the king, it was only obeyed in Kent, and even there the prior of St Augustine and a few of his brethren disobeyed it also. Then there was peace patched up between the king and Theobald, and the latter was conducted by the Royal Commissioners to Canterbury with honour and rejoicing. His first act was to excommunicate the rebellious monks of St Augustine who had disobeyed the interdict, and with them, also, all who had received the sacraments at their hands. So two of the monks set off post haste to Rome to get the Pope to protect them from the archbishop's thunders; but the Pope refused to see them, and told them to return and obey the archbishop in all things. They returned humbled to Canterbury, where Theobald deposed their prior and suspended the rest, for a period, from the exercise of their holy offices.

At this period Queen Matilda, Stephen's wife, lived much at Canterbury in or near St Augustine's Abbey, and since the Augustine monks were at this time under Theobald's excommunication, she was wont to send for the Christ Church monks to conduct service for her at St Augustine's Church. Her necessity for being in the neighbourhood at all was that she was very anxious to hasten the building of Faversham Abbey, which she and Stephen had founded near by. This queen was a conciliating link between the archbishop and her husband, and she had probably patched up the last peace.

Then came renewed trouble with both St Augustine's and the monks of Christ Church. Apparently in 1151 Hugo the abbot had died, and Theobald did not approve of the choice of Silvester, the prior, to fill the vacant post. He was the monks' own choice, and they had received from Stephen the privilege of free election; so Theobald said if he gave him the blessing of consecration it must be done in the Cathedral; but

Silvester said it was against the privilege of his abbey to be compelled to attend in Christ Church. So he went to Rome to maintain his argument, and came back with the Pope's orders that the archbishop must give way. He professed to be about to obey the papal instruction, and set out for the ceremony at the abbey, when—probably by arrangement—the prior of Christ Church placed himself in front of the procession, declaring that it was a violation of the privileges of his priory that the ceremony should take place beyond its walls. So once again the suit was taken to Rome; again the verdict was in favour of St Augustine's; and the archbishop had to administer the blessing in the church of the rebellious monastery.

The other squabble was with the monks of Christ Church. One effect of the wild days of Stephen's reign seems to have been that the monastery of Christ Church found itself in a very straitened financial position. Apparently, they put this down to the numberless poverty-stricken people who had applied to the monastery for relief when the Civil War brought famine in its train. So the prior went to the archbishop and asked him to take into his charge the estates of the monastery, and defend them from the robbers by the special strength which he held from God; he was to keep these lands, under his control, so long as England was in a disturbed state; giving, meanwhile, to the monastery sufficient for the necessaries of life. The archbishop at first blankly refused to undertake the trust, but under pressure he agreed. As might naturally have been expected by the monks, the only way to make two ends meet was to lower the expenses until they balanced with the revenue. To cut a fairly long story short, the monks said the archbishop was using the revenue of the monastery for the upkeep of his own palace. The monks put the case in a self-obliterating way, saying that they were now compelled to turn the stranger and the poor away from their doors, unaided. So they demanded their property back again into their own keeping. There was a wordy war and much straight speaking on both sides. At last Theobald ordered the doors of the monastery to be shut, and set guards at them, and two monks who

RUINED ARCH—GARDEN

had been sent to negotiate with the Pope, he put in prison: and the prior was deposed and sent to the Abbey of Gloucester, where the abbot was instructed to keep him under control. Finally Theobald restored the estates after holding them four or five months.

The death of Stephen, and the accession of the strong Henry II. in 1154, together made England a comparatively peaceful place once more; and Theobald was able to settle down until his death into the more humdrum life of a reformer of his province. One of his last requests was that Henry would come to see him; or at least that he would give Thomas Becket leave to visit Canterbury: but the king seemed not to have been able to spare time for either of these favours. Faithful to his reputation of being a charitable man, Theobald left his goods to the poor, and died in the April of 1161, and was buried in his Cathedral.

There was an interval of a few years, and then the most famous of all the ecclesiastical lords of Canterbury was placed on the archiepiscopal throne. He will demand a chapter to himself. On his fame depends most of the fame of Canterbury Cathedral, and if we wish to understand its place in mediæval history, we shall have to understand Thomas Becket, who is one of the keys of history, and certainly the chief key to the gates of Canterbury.

CHAPTER X

Thomas Becket

THERE could be little doubt that if Becket desired to be Archbishop of Canterbury he would get his wish: for his power was almost supreme. In the words of the chronicler, Gervase, when he has recorded the death of Theobald, he leads up to the new man by these words: "There was in these days a man, Thomas, Archdeacon of Canterbury, and the most powerful chancellor of the king's in all England; he was glorious in the eyes of all men, famous for his wisdom, admired by all for the dignity of his soul, awesome to his enemies, at once the friend of the king and the second in the kingdom, and the guide and almost guardian of the king." Whether he was worthy of such a flourish of trumpets on his entry is a matter of opinion, perhaps. But his life was big enough to show a good many different phases of thought and action, and differing judgments thereon.

We must first sketch his earlier career, for he was about twenty-five before he appeared on the stage of Canterbury. His birthplace was off Cheapside in London; the date somewhere between 1115 and 1120, probably 1118. His father was Gilbert Becket, one of the aristocratic merchants who at that time were a recognised class, and then in control of the government of the city. The family was Norman and the father had been in earlier days a merchant of Rouen; and in London he had been one of the portreeves. His mother was of the burger class of

Caen. His education at first was in the Priory of Merton in Surrey, then in London, and this was followed by a course in Paris until his twenty-second year. The prosperous father had passed through financial misfortunes, and Thomas had to set about making a living. He seems to have been appointed a kind of estate agent to a young aristocrat, whom he had played with as a boy; and this master was followed by another, a relation of the Beckets, who was Sheriff of London.

It was in 1143 at the latest that he drifted down to Canterbury and got into the household of Theobald, the archbishop, and became his confidential clerk, and a student in the school of law attached to the palace. That is the latest date, but he probably went earlier, for in this year mentioned he went to Rome in the archbishop's train. He became so intimate with his new master that he had twice to leave his post because of the violent jealousy of Roger Pont l'Evêque, another of Theobald's confidants. Then, in order to improve his skill in the law of the Church, he spent a whole year at Bologna and Auxerre, engrossed by its study. He travelled with Theobald to Rome in 1143, and in 1148 he took his place in the cockle-shell boat which carried the archbishop secretly across the Channel in defiance of the king's forbidding. All this time Becket seems to have been planning his life for a career in the Church, and in 1143 he was presented to the livings of St Mary-le-Strand in London, which then stood where Somerset House is now (the newer church now stands in the middle of the main thoroughfare outside), and of Otford, where the archbishops had a palace in Kent. The latter place was to remain closely connected with Becket, for here he afterwards did work in creating a water-supply, an act of public administration which grew in the local legend until it has assumed the story of a miraculous flow of water appearing when the holy man, as archbishop, struck the ground with his staff, whereupon opened up the spring of St Thomas's Well near the palace. The palace is in ruins now, but the spring still comes from the ground, and there are still those who believe that its water has supernatural powers of healing.

Then Becket, hovering still half-way between the heavens and the earth, in the state of minor orders, was given a prebend's stall in St Paul's Cathedral in London, and then another stall in Lincoln Cathedral; and when his admiring master, Theobald, made him Archdeacon of Canterbury in 1154, Becket was well on the way to ecclesiastical power and worldly wealth.

But there came a sudden change in his career. Becket was one of those men of colossal energy and determination to succeed, who are fitted equally for any sphere, who dominate any order or class. The petty details of circumstances are only rather trivial things when measured against the hugh bulk of their ambitions. This is by no means an accusation of any purely selfish aim. Personal ambition is so easily blended with the belief that its success is good for the world at large. The difference of detail between a career in the Church or a career in the State offices was a little matter to a man like Becket. So it happened that Henry II. made him Chancellor of England in 1155. This appointment was made in the year following Henry's accession to the throne, and he had probably had Becket in his mind for some time, at least since the day when Theobald, the archbishop, had refused to crown Eustace, Stephen's son, in 1152; for it was an open secret that Becket had been the chief advocate of this refusal, and Henry was naturally grateful that his path to the throne had been thus kept open. This repudiation of Eustace had taken place in a council held at London, and

Theobald had been obliged to hurry back to Canterbury, whence, after seeing to the business of the monastery, he had fled across the sea to Flanders.

Becket, as chancellor, was immediately at the head of affairs in England, and it seemed that Henry could not do without his advice for a moment; and, quite apart from business, the brilliant chancellor was clearly the best of companions. The chroniclers of this period are continually using such terms as "by the great help of Thomas the chancellor," or "by the industry of Thomas the chancellor," in their records of the chief domestic and foreign affairs which they relate. Thus, in 1156 Becket was touring Aquitaine and Gascony with Henry, demanding homage and hostages. In 1158 he was charged with the duty of heading an embassy to the Court of France. When the French nobles saw the splendour of Becket's train of knights, they were amazed; and with the king, Louis VII., they said, "If this man be only chancellor of England, what must be the glory of the king himself." The progress of the chancellor was a triumph of display; which must surely have had a deeper basis in Becket's nature than a mere diplomatic scheme to impress his French opponents. We must remember these things in order that we may better appreciate the dramatic change to Thomas the Saint. In 1159 Becket was in France, at the head of seven hundred knights, the finest body of men, said his rivals, that they had ever seen in the field. Becket had not the technicalities of feudal etiquette so firmly fixed in his mind as his master, and when the latter hesitated to wage war against his suzerain, Louis of France, Becket had no such nice scruples; and we find him on the Norman border with his knights, at the head of their raids into French territory, fighting himself hand to hand with the enemy.

In 1162 Becket negotiated with the barons the

recognition of Henry II.'s son as the heir to the crown. The young prince had been given into the chancellor's charge some time before, and, if anything, the splendour of his tutor's household must have surprised his father's Court. A large income from both his ecclesiastical offices and his legal office as chancellor, with all its perquisites, combined with the skill of his avoidance of envy or malice, made Becket a triumph of success. In the career of a layman he had everything in his grasp. One might have imagined that he had dismissed the Church from his mind, not only because of his worldly display and courtier-like habits, but because he did not hesitate to strike blows against the ecclesiastical power if his secular master's needs called for it to be done. Thus, when Henry marched against Toulouse (probably by Becket's persuasion), the taxation to meet the expenses was levied on the Church more heavily than on the lay wealth. In later years, his enemies turned this against Becket, probably with justice, and said that "having the sword of State in his hand, he did drive it into the bosom of the mother Church, thus robbing her of the thousands which were spent in this war against Toulouse." This may have been fair criticism when Becket was posing as a Churchman of the strictest sect, but it was not very effective criticism against the chancellor when he was in the field at the head of every fight. There was little trace of the ecclesiastic in the Becket of this period.

When Becket came to England in 1152, Gervase records the facts as following: "King Henry being full of business across the sea, sent that admirable chancellor, Thomas, to England, that he might deal with the affairs of the kingdom; but his first object was that Becket might be chosen as Archbishop of Canterbury." He goes on to tell how three bishops, an abbot, and the justiciar, Richard de Lucy, were sent to Canterbury, on the king's behalf, bearing a message to the monks that a few of them were to come to London with their prior, there to join with the bishops and clergy in choosing a primate of all England. They all met with the nobles of the realm, and, "after much discussion as to the manner of the election, William, the prior of Christ Church and his fellow-deputy monks, having first invoked the blessing of the Holy Ghost, chose Thomas, the King's chancellor, in the name ot the Holy Trinity." Becket hesitated; for he saw critical difficulties ahead. He was a man who insisted on all, if he made a demand; and he must have known that as head of the Church of England he would have to ask the king, his dear friend, for many rights and much obedience that would not be readily granted. But he was persuaded to make the great experiment; and the election was formally completed. "And when the election was accomplished, as the archbishop-elect was on his way to Canterbury to be consecrated, a vision of the night appeared to him in the form of a venerable man bearing ten talents. And Becket immediately appointed masters over himself who would correct him if he exceeded his duty in any particular."

Becket was not even yet a fully-fledged priest; technically, he was still only in "minor orders." So the first matter was to get him ordained as a priest, and this ceremony was performed in Canterbury Cathedral on Sunday, the second of June 1162; and the following day he was consecrated archbishop by Henry Bishop of Winchester, with the aid of almost all the bishops of the province.

The mental change in this man, outwardly at least, was drastic. The splendid, gay, courtier statesman became the severe Churchman. He had once, a little while ago, been prepared to crush the Church if it stood in the path of the State; and now he was to apply exactly the same principle exactly in the reverse order. Henry got a dispensation from the Pope which allowed Becket to continue to hold the great seal pertaining to the chancellorship. He refused; and this was the first sign of the rigid change he intended to make in his work and life. But, rather strangely, he kept the archdeaconry of Canterbury in his hands, until Henry made him resign it in 1163. Becket, or Thomas, as he may now more usually be called, henceforth apparently lived the life of an ascetic, though the style of his household was still on a handsome scale; but, if the general testimony be right, then the master of this household did not share in its luxuries.

The refusal to retain the chancellorship probably upset Henry's definite plans; if his closest confidant could be Archbishop of Canterbury, then the supremacy of the Church over the State, which was threatening every secular ruler in Christendom, might be tactfully avoided in England. If Becket had retained his lay office, he would have admitted his intention of fitting his ecclesiastical policy within the bounds of the king's policy. But the decided refusal told the king what he must expect. He had soon very positive grounds for knowing what the archhishop's new policy was likely to be; for an order was quickly published forbidding any clerk in the service of the Crown to hold an ecclesiastical benefice. Henry had good reason if he received the news with a cynical smile, for Thomas Becket had himself held these double privilege throughout his career as chancellor.

Even then there might have been no serious breach between king and archbishop. But the matter grew serious when Thomas interfered in a pure matter of taxation, concerning the use and collection of the sheriff's dues in their counties. It had no direct bearing on the rights of the Church; and Thomas seems to have been the only one who made any objection to the proposed change; but he did it with such determination that Henry gave way. The result was that Thomas had the opportunity of posing as a disinterested defender of the national rights, and Henry was made to appear in the light of having attempted a tyranny. In an angry mood of defeat Henry next heard that the archbishop had excommunicated one of the royal tenants-in-chief without the customary notice to the king.

But the great fight between the two champions of the Church and the lay State was on a matter of general principle, which spread over almost the whole field of the national government. It is not a matter which can be considered here in detail, nor is there any need that it should be so discussed in a history of Canterbury. But it is necessary to realise the broad issue, for it was this dispute which directly led to the murder of Thomas, and the greatness of Canterbury Cathedral and the fame of its town.

The Church of Rome had announced its claim to overrule all power and dominion of earthly princes. Such was the doctrine of Hildebrand, Pope Gregory VII., in William the Conqueror's time. But the earthly kings were strong, and the heavenly Popes had a certain worldly discretion in their behaviour; so there were still many gaps in the perfect working of the papal theory. But, nevertheless, it had been growing in strength, and in England, under such a weak king as Stephen, it had distinctly taken long steps forward since the days when Lanfranc suited his policy to the desires of William, or since Anselm fought so patiently against the later Norman kings. Henry II. did not dare to treat the Church as Rufus had treated it; and the Church had never made such wide-reaching claims as it did in Archbishop Thomas's time.

The great fight in England began in this manner.

Henry discovered that since the beginning of his reign over one hundred murders had been committed by clerks in Holy Orders, besides many other less serious crimes. One case in particular attracted his attention: a canon of Bedford murdered a knight, and then escaped all punishment by swearing in a bishop's court that he was innocent. A system of justice which allowed a man to judge himself by his own oath was obviously ineffective. So Henry had him summoned before a royal court. The canon refused, with gratuitous insults thrown in. The king swore "by the eyes of God" that the canon should appear: the archbishop replied with the haughtiest theories of Rome, "A layman cannot be judge of the deeds of a priest of God."

Such was the pass to which the power of the Church had come; for Henry had to swallow his pride, and allow the canon to defy his officers of justice. It was obvious to anyone but a bigot that such a state of affairs must be changed by a compromise of some sort. And Thomas and Henry were particularly bad subjects for compromises. As Gervase says, "Hence, between himself [Becket] and the king the discord continued and increased more and more every day." The king told the bishops that they must solemnly promise to obey the customs of his grandfather. The bishops promised with some ambiguous phrase about "saving the rights of our order," which amounted to begging the whole question. Then Henry seized some of the archbishop's castles, which he had never given up since his chancellor days, and took his son Henry out of Thomas's charge. At last, on the pressing of the Pope, Becket offered to give the required promises, with the added words, "in good faith without guile and according to law." Then he repented of his surrender, but coolly offered to make the necessary public avowal, remarking, "It is my lord's [presumably the Pope] will that I forswear myself: so I must take the risk of perjury now, and do penance for it afterwards." If this was sound ecclesiastical morality, then it is clear that we must judge Thomas Becket by some principles which we do not apply in ordinary history. He was either an unscrupulous scoundrel, or he really believed that the law of his Church raised him far above all earthly codes. That latter is a possible state of mind which the reader must endeavour to understand if he desires to take a further interest in the history of a Cathedral which became chiefly famous as the tomb of this man, who was, to put it candidly, made a saint for thinking like that, and for being murdered in defence of his thoughts.

So the customs were put into writing and are known as the Constitutions of Clarendon. It was concerning these that Becket made his stand against the claims of the king. When these Constitutions were drawn up in the form of sixteen statements, which Henry maintained as stating the acknowledged law of the relations between Church and Crown, Thomas flatly refused—in spite of all his solemn promises—to sign or recognise a single one of them. Reading them to-day, no reasonable mind can hold that these demands of the Crown were beyond what was absolutely necessary if the king was to be responsible for law and order. Here are some of the chief clauses: If a priest was accused of crime, it was for the royal justices to say whether the case should be tried in a lay or an ecclesiastical court of law, and if it was sent to the ecclesiastical court, then the king's justices should appoint an officer to watch the proceedings, and if the accused was found guilty, he was to be handed over to the lay officers for punishment; no tenant-in-chief of the Crown should be excommunicated or his land placed under an interdict without the consent of the king; before consecration the holder of an ecclesiastical office should do homage and fealty to the king as to his liege lord for life and limb and earthly honour, saving the rights of his order.

But if such clauses seem perfectly reasonable to-day, it does not follow that they were equally reasonable to the mind of a churchman of Thomas Becket's

DOOR LEADING FROM CLOISTER INTO MARTYRDOM

day. The great question as to whether the Holy Church of Rome was or was not superior to the government of the earthly kings had still to be decided. Thomas thought undoubtedly that he had as much right to maintain the final supremacy of the Church as Henry had to say that the Crown was the final court of appeal. To say that the Crown of the king was of more authority than the Cross of the Church would then have been begging the whole question at stake. That was the point at issue between Henry and Thomas. We shall never understand their struggle unless we get back into the mediæval atmosphere ; we must try to grasp the train of thought that passed through the minds of the archbishop and his monks and clerks as they debated the question within the walls of the close of Canterbury Cathedral. Within those walls they considered that they were the representatives of a power which was far above the authority of any power that the king could claim over them. They held that Canterbury Cathedral was as much the seat of earthly authority as was Westminster Palace, indeed, Thomas and his church were now almost claiming that their was the dominant power.

We shall better grasp the contemporary thought if we read the case as it was recorded, a few years afterwards, by Roger of Howden, remembering that he was on the side of the Church.

"In the same year [1163] a great dispute arose between the King of England and Thomas, Archbishop of Canterbury, concerning the ecclesiastical dignities, which this King of England was endeavouring to disturb and lower in the sight of all, whereas the archbishop did attempt, by every possible means, to preserve the power and dignity of the Church untouched. For it was the king's wish that if any priests, deacons, sub-deacons, or other officers of the Church should be arrested for the commission of theft, or murder, or felony, or arson, or the like crimes, then they should be taken before lay judges and punished as if they were laymen. But the Archbishop of Canterbury replied to this, that if a clerk in holy orders or any other officers of the Church should be charged with any such offence, then he ought to be tried by his fellow-clergy and an ecclesiastical court, and if he be convicted, then he should be deprived of his holy orders, and if he should then offend again, he should be judged by the officers of the Crown, for he would not then be in the dominion of the Church, having been thus deprived of his holy office."

We have already seen how Thomas conducted himself up to the time when he repudiated the first vague promise he had given. In the words of Roger Howden: "The archbishop repented that he had made this concession to the king and wished to withdraw from his agreement, for he saw that in so conceding he had greatly sinned and would sin no longer. Thereupon the king's anger was fiercely roused against him, and he did threaten death and exile against the archbishop and his people; whereupon the bishops of Salisbury and Norwich and also the earls of Leicester and of Cornwall, and two templars, went to the archbishop, and, throwing themselves in tears at his feet, did beg him for the dignity of the king to go to him and declare before the people that he had acknowledged these laws. The archbishop, being conquered by the entreaties of such great men, did go to the king, and before the clergy and the people he said that he acknowledged these laws which the king claimed to be the laws of his grandfather."

When Thomas received a copy of these Constitutions of Clarendon, Roger of Howden records the words which he spoke, as he turned from the king, who had himself handed him the copy, to the clergy who were standing around: "Be of firm courage, my brethren; for by means of these writings we shall be able to know the evil desires of the king, and against them ought we to be on our guard. Whereupon he withdrew himself from the Council, and could by no means recover the favour of the king." Here we have the declaration of war. Thomas, feeling that he had put himself in an unfortunately delicate position by the breaking of his solemn promise, by his own will and act suspended himself from the duties of his office until he had received the opinion and commands of the Pope. He made more than one attempt to escape from England, secretly, but was unsuccessful.

Then Henry took action, and Thomas was summoned to appear to answer a claim of John the Marshall to a piece of land then in the possession of the See of Canterbury. Thomas refused, partly because he was sick, he said, partly because he said the case should be tried in his own court. Henry then ordered Thomas to be tried for contempt before the council of the realm summoned to meet at Northampton. There, writes Roger of Howden, "he inflicted great annoyance upon Thomas, the Archbishop of Canterbury. For in the first place, the king put his own horses in the quarters where the archbishop had taken his lodgings; and on this the latter sent word to the king that he would not come to Court until his lodgings had been cleared of the king's horses and men. On the day following the Council, Archbishop Thomas came to the king's court and sought his leave to cross over the sea immediately to the Pope Alexander, who was then lingering in France; but he was unable to obtain it. For the king replied: 'You shall first answer to me for the wrong which you have done to John the Marshall in your court.'" To which Thomas replied with an accus.tion that it was the Marshall who was in the wrong; and the king, without regarding the reply, swore that he would have justice, and the archbishop was fined five hundred pounds, and compelled to admit the judgment and give security for its payment.

"And the archbishop returned to his lodgings, where he sickened of a severe illness, brought on by the indignation and humiliation which he had suffered.

When the king heard this, that he might the more afflict him, he sent messengers to him, commanding him to appear on the following day, in order that he might give an account of those offices which he held before his consecration as archbishop." But Thomas knew that if he went he would be sentenced to a long term of banishment, so he sought for excuses.

One after another demand was made by Henry, concerning funds which Thomas had administered as chancellor; now it was the rent of some manor; now money lent by the king for the archbishop's use during the war before Toulouse. Thomas replied that the sums had been already properly spent and accounted for; and that, in any case, he had been indemnified against all claims when he was appointed archbishop, which was true, probably. Then he heard that even his life would be in danger when he appeared in Court. So, on the following day, after a consultation with his friends as to the proper course to take, he first celebrated the mass in honour of St Stephen, which contained the following significant words in its services: "For princes did sit in judgment over me, and did speak against me." Then he commended his cause to God, and set out for the Court in full robes, with the cross in his hand. "Immediately upon this a great crowd did assemble that they might see the end of the affair. And the archbishop carried the cross in his right hand, and in his left were the reins of the horse whereon he rode. When he came to the Court of the king, he dismounted, and, still holding his cross, he entered the king's house; and he entered the outer chamber alone, still bearing the cross; but none of his followers followed him; and when he had entered he found many people there, and he sat himself among them. But the king remained in his private room with his confidential friends."

Now began a series of negotiations between the king in his room and the archbishop in the public court. Henry sent out bishops to persuade him to lay down his cross; for even the autocratic Henry feared to lay hands on Thomas while he held the sacred emblem. But at last, losing all patience, he ordered his barons to pass judgment on this rebel who refused to submit himself for trial. So judgment was passed, and two of the earls went to the outer court to tell Thomas what they had done: "Listen to the judgment which has been pronounced on you." To which the archbishop replied: "In the name of Almighty God and on pain of excommunication, I forbid you to pass judgment on me this day, for I have appealed to my lord the Pope." While the earls were carrying this defiant message to the king the archbishop left the council chamber and also the palace, amid loud shouts of "Where goest thou, traitor? stay and hear your sentence." When he reached the outer gate he found it locked, and for a moment it seemed that he had been trapped; but one of the servants found the key and the royal guards did not dare to interfere, so he went through without another word. He adjourned to the house of some regular canons, where he entertained all the poor who were waiting at the gate by inviting them to dine with him, and rested before the high altar, as the place of greatest security from an attack by his enemy.

While it was yet half dark he set out secretly, as the king and his companions were at supper, and reached the coast in disguise. Apparently he must have passed through Canterbury, for he eventually embarked at Sandwich, and landed in Flanders and went on into France. Before he reached the court of the French King, emissaries had arrived from Henry begging Louis not to receive Thomas, and to use his influence with the Pope to reject him also. But the effect was to make Louis all the keener to aid the fugitive priest. Another embassy to the Pope direct had as little effect. Henry's messengers then suggested that the Pope should send legates to England to hear the whole case, and judge it. But the Pope did not consent, for, says Roger of Howden, "he knew that the King of England was strong in word and in deed, and also that legates were wont to be corrupted very easily, since they loved gold and silver more than justice and equity." So the embassy left unsatisfied.

Four days later Thomas himself arrived, and placed the Constitutions of Clarendon before him: surrendered his ring of office as token of his confession of failure to uphold his holy rights against the king. But Alexander gave him back his ring; and judged that while six of the Constitutions were possible, yet, on the whole, they could not be acknowledged. But the Pope was in a delicate position himself; for he was, like Thomas, an exile, having been driven out of Rome by a rival Pope, who was supported by the Emperor. So when Henry declared all the estates of the See of Canterbury confiscated, and all the relations and followers of the archbishop banished, Alexander asked Thomas to take it as quietly as possible, and see how things worked out.

But in the beginning of 1166, Thomas was told he could do what he thought necessary; and after two unanswered letters to Henry, Thomas sent a third which threatened to excommunicate him. But Henry had already announced what he would do in such a case; for he had issued some months before an order which ran: "If so be that any person be found bearing letters from our lord and Pope or from the archbishop of Canterbury, containing an interdict relating to England, then let him be arrested and without delay tried as a traitor to the king and the realm . . . And further, if any bishop, priest, abbot, monk, clerk, or layman, shall observe any sentence of interdict, let him be banished from the kingdom without delay, and all his kindred . . . and let their chuttels and possessions be seized into the king's hand." That was terse and much to the point; so it was little wonder Thomas and the Pope had hesitated so long; and that Thomas, even now, when he had threatened, hesitated to carry out his threat, and seized the excuse of the king's sudden and severe illness for further delay, and only excommunicated seven of the royal counsellors instead.

In the May of 1166 we even find Thomas writing to Henry with a mixture of affection and timid beseeching and stubborn determination. He says: "I have desired greatly to see your face and to speak with you, much on my own account, but still more on yours . . . that you might recall the service which I devoutedly rendered to you, so far as my conscience allowed me . . . that I might move you to take pity on me when I am driven thus to live as a beggar among strangers, although, thanks be to God," Thomas adds a little proudly, "I have enough and to spare of food." Then, after a long letter advising the king to do justice to the Church, the archbishop closes: "Permit me freely to return to my See, and then am I ready to serve you loyally as my dear lord and king, in whatsoever way I can, saving the honour of God, and of the Church of Rome and of my order. And if so be you will do otherwise, then know most certainly that you will feel the divine anger and vengeance."

But Henry was obdurate; and since Thomas was being sheltered in a Cistercian abbey, he declared that, in revenge, he would expel every member of that order from his dominions, if they did not turn his enemy out of their house. And out he had to go. Then we find him endeavouring to rouse his bishops to fight his battles. "My dearly beloved brethren, why do you not rise with me against my enemies." Considering that Thomas was hiding away in France, the question has its humour side. At last, in the first month of 1169, Thomas appeared unexpectedly at a royal council at Montmiral, where, flinging himself at Henry's feet, he said he was ready to be reconciled on any reasonable terms, "The whole case between us, my lord, I commit to your arbitration, saving the honour of God." When he heard that last phrase, Henry drove him away with insults. And Becket hurled the thunder of excommunication against two of the bishops of his province who had taken the king's side ; and against six persons who had taken possession of property which belonged to the Church. There arose temporary friction between Louis of France (who was present at this interview) and Thomas ; and for several days the former ceased to visit the archbishop or to send him supplies. But they were soon reconciled.

But everyone, except Becket, wanted peace almost at any price. Thus, we find the bishops of the province of Canterbury writing, "Our holy Mother, the Church, has been set between the hammer and the anvil ; unless, indeed, the mercy of God shall be shown to her, then will she bear the blow of that hammer. . . . In things of earth as in spiritual things, the church of Canterbury is sadly impoverished. Like a ship upon the sea, without her pilot, is she buffeted on every side by the fury of the winds ; and by the king's will her shepherd is forbidden to live within the borders of his own land. In his wisdom, he has exposed both himself and us to the bitterness of pains and penalties, heedless that it would not take from his real strength if he used conciliatory measures. Although we indeed sympathise with him in his troubles, yet has he proved ungrateful towards us and ceases not to persecute us, although we suffer with him. . . . If the evils that would come upon the Church, did not influence his judgment, then, at least, he should have held back from opposing the king because of all the riches and honour which this sovereign had heaped upon him." There is not much concealment about the frank worldly outlook of this letter; it is a candid invitation to weigh the king's gifts against spiritual convictions. And the Pope was pressing for peace, on his side. Becket met the papal legates near Gisors, in Normandy; and the legates talked much about the "mighty power of the King of England, the necessities of the Church, the wickedness of the times, the love and kindness which the King of England had shown him and the honour in which he had held him. They also mentioned the injuries which the king had complained of suffering at his hands, and amongst other things, that Becket had urged the king of the Franks to wage war upon him. And the legates asked how they might appease the king's indignation." Becket made an answer to all these arguments, and professed to show their hollowness, but he said he was willing to do everything that would bring peace, "saving always the honour of God, the liberties of the church, his own dignity, and the possessions of the churches." It was the old phrase, which had ended all attempts to reach terms of peace. Then the legates tried to persuade him, if he would not formally accept the Constitutions of Clarendon, yet at least that he would discreetly look the other way, as it were, and return to his see on the tacit understanding that he would say nothing one way or the other. To this suggestion Becket answered that rather than give the king such a moral victory, he would remain in exile for ever, or die if need be, in defence of what he held to be just, for, he said; "there is a God who forbids the priesthood to be silent in such a matter; and who has prepared a hell as the portion of those who thus play false with their beliefs, a hell where there will be no doubt as to their punishments."

But in spite of all this brave show, Thomas sent a message to the king at Montmartre, in November, 1169, begging that he and his friends, might go back to England and take possession once more of their lands and goods. Henry by this time was beginning to waver, and offered a verbal promise; but Becket demanded securities and the kiss of peace, but the kiss Henry would not give, though he offered a thousand marks to help toward the expenses of the return. Then it came out that Henry was arranging that the Archbishop of York should soon perform the coronation of his eldest son, in order to secure the succession. This was an open defiance of the privileges of the Archbishop of Canterbury. In spite of the prohibitions of both Thomas and the Pope this coronation took place. But Henry was rather afraid that he had overstepped his power, and when he and Becket met in France shortly afterwards they patched up a peace. Becket asked whether he might punish the Archbishop of York and the other bishops who had insulted the dignity of Canterbury by taking part in this coronation, and Henry said he might excommunicate them if he desired. Then there was some rather elaborate by-play, during which Becket got down from his horse and kissed the king's feet, and Henry, in return, raised Thomas into his saddle with the words that "it was proper that the lower should serve the higher."

It was agreed that Henry and Thomas should return

to England together, although the latter had with him letters from the Pope suspending the Archbishop of York and his assistants. Then Henry drew back and made excuses. So it ended in Becket going alone. The Archbishop of York and his fellow-bishops were plotting to avoid their suspension, and they were hovering in the neighbourhood of the port in the hopes of seizing Becket's papers when he landed. But apparently Becket sent them on in front, and the papal orders were delivered to the Archbishop of York and the bishops of London and Salisbury when they were lodging in Canterbury itself. Then they set off to await Becket's arrival at Dover, where they expected him to land, but he appeared at Sandwich instead; and the men of the town armed themselves in readiness, lest it should be necessary to defend their lord Thomas; and the burgesses of Dover did likewise. Some knights set out to do battle with them, but the opponents were held back by the advice of John of Oxford, whom the king had sent to conduct Thomas to England.

Then the demand was made on behalf of the king that Thomas should forgive his ecclesiastical enemies; but Thomas said that Henry had no right to be angry with what he had himself assented should be done. And Becket set out for his city, and entered Canterbury amid the rejoicings and joyous tears of the people and the clergy and monks of the town. Once more messengers arrived demanding the forgiveness of the offending bishops. But Becket's answer made them go forth hurling wild threats against him.

Thomas Becket made up his mind to visit the young Henry, but a message came to meet him when he got as far as London, and he returned to Canterbury. There he had to submit to a virtual boycott: "Whoever showed to him or to his household a cheerful countenance was held to be a public enemy. However, all these things were endured by this man of God with great patience; and he kept himself to his own household, edifying them all with his conversation and with words of exhortation; and once more the archbishop took his seat in his cathedral, fearlessly awaiting the hour at which he should receive from God the crown of martyrdom. For being warned by many beforehand he knew that his life would be short and that death was at the gate. . . . In his discourses to his brethren, the monks of Christ Church, he would say: 'I have come to die among you,' and then at other times he would say: 'In this church there are martyrs, and in a short time God will increase the number of them."'

Besides his ecclesiastical enemies of York and elsewhere Becket had temporal matters to deal with concerning the estates of the See which had been seized during his exile. No further off than Saltwood, near Folkestone and Hythe, he found his castle in the possession of one of the De Brocs, who had made it little better than a robbers' fortress. It was on the Christmas day of 1170 that he publicly excommunicated these thieves after he had preached on the text "Peace on Earth."

But by this time words had fallen from Henry's lips in Normandy, whither the rival bishops had gone to carry their complaints against Thomas. Mad with anger at the interminable length of this stubborn quarrel, Henry burst forth with scornful words of reproach that "he was miserable indeed since he had nurtured so many ignoble men around him, for no one of them was willing to avenge so many injuries." Henry had all his life been subject to these violent outbursts of anger: he probably never really intended to suggest that Thomas should be slain: and the archbishop was probably wrong in thinking that his life, under ordinary circumstances, was in danger, or had been in danger on the day when he went to the council of Northampton with the cross in his hands to protect him against violence. But, as fate would have it, there were four knights who took the king at his literal word. Reginald Fitzurse, William de Tracy, Richard le Breton, and Hugh de Morville, were the names of these four men, who have made themselves immortal in history by their evil deed. There are some whose only hope of immortality is their wickedness; it being often an easier path to fame than by the way of virtue. These knights set off at once for England when they heard their master's words, although an attempt was made to stop them when the reason of their departure was guessed. They landed at Dover and proceeded to Saltwood Castle, where they passed a sleepless night with De Broc, the robber landlord. Then on to Canterbury, on the 29th of December: and their first visit seems to have been a call at the Abbey of St Augustine. Then they presented themselves at the private chamber of the archbishop without any greetings, and announced that "We have come from beyond the seas, bearing orders from the king": and Becket asked, "Do you wish to speak to me in public or in private?" And they answered, "As you please." So Becket asked his servants to withdraw for a short time. But having listened to their speech, he then said: "I wish these things to be heard by others"; so he sent for the monks and the clergy. Then followed a violent dispute. The archbishop said it was the Pope, not himself, who had suspended the bishops. He called upon Fitzurse to bear witness that he had been present when the king gave his consent to the punishment of the bishops. But he denied it; and the knights left the chamber telling the monks that they would be held responsible for the custody of the archbishop. Then Becket followed them to the door and called after them: "Know ye that I did not come here that I might take refuge in flight, and I scorn your threats."

To which they made answer: "They will be more than threats."

The knights, having gone out of the palace, then came back with the followers whom they had left outside while they were speaking to the archbishop, and these they armed. While this was happening, the monks persuaded Becket to come into the church, where it was the time for vespers; they had rather to drag him than lead him; and he had got no further than the steps leading up from the north-west transept to the choir, when the four knights rushed along the cloisters and entered the Cathedral by the door through which Becket had just passed on his way from the Palace. The archbishop's attendants had wanted to fasten this door; but Becket forbade them, saying: "The house of God must be shut to no man." So the monks, all except three, fled to hide themselves in the dark depths of the Cathedral when they heard the armed men approaching.

Not seeing their prey in the dark, the first of the knights called out: "Where is the traitor?" and receiving no answer, he repeated: "Where is the Archbishop?" Whereupon Becket, coming again down the steps he had ascended, answered: "Here am I." The accounts differ as to the exact words, but the substance is the same. Then he seems to have singled out Reginald Fitzurse, for he tossed at him the bitter reproach. "Many are the benefits I have done you, Reginald, and now you come against me with arms." But Fitzurse seized the archbishop's pall, and apparently they all tried to get him to leave the church. But Becket would not move; he forbade them in the name of God to do any wrong to his people under penalty of his curse. Roger of Howden has given the words which passed: "In the spirit of his frenzy, one of these fell knights made answer to him, 'You shall die now, for it is impossible to let you live any longer.' And the archbishop answered him, no less steadfast in his words than in his soul, 'Then am I ready to die for my God and for the defence of justice and the liberty of the church: but if you demand my life, then, in the name of God and under pain of excommunication, do I forbid you to touch any other, whether he be monk or priest or layman, whether great or of no account.'"

It was after these words that the knights made their effort to save themselves from the sin of sacrilege by dragging their prey from the sacred building, that they might do their murder beyond the walls. Becket was now alone but for only one remaining companion, Edward Grim, who still stood by his side, holding the cross before his master. A desperate struggle now began, and the archbishop and his friend were able to resist the dragging of the four knights and the traitor priest, Hugh of Horsea, who had joined them. In this darkened church, with its terrified monks hiding in trembling silence in the black depths behind, the most famous moment of its history was now at the moment of its accomplishment.

When they saw that Thomas could not be moved, the knights determined to slay him where he stood: they drew their swords, and when the archbishop saw their purpose, he gathered himself together for his end, and awaited the blow with his face covered, saying: "To my God and the blessed Mary, to the guardian Saints of this Church, and to St Denys do I commend my soul and the Church's cause." Then the first blow was struck; but it fell mainly on the arm of Grim, who raised it to save his master's head. The arm was almost severed, and Grim apparently let fall the cross, and Becket took it up into his own hands, and stood silent and bowed. A second and third crashing blow on the head brought Thomas to his knees, and his last words, as he turned towards the altar of St Benedict, were to murmur: "For the name of Jesus and the de-

THE MARTYRDOM, CANTERBURY CATHEDRAL

fence of the Church, I am ready to die." To share the responsibility for the deed, each of the knights struck a blow on the fallen head; and it is said that Hugh the priest scattered the brains of the archbishop on the pavement.

It was no time to tarry, for the murderers feared the people were gathering to the rescue. "Let us begone," one of them muttered, "he is dead"; and they made their escape through the cloisters, whither they had come, and reached their companions who were waiting with their horses outside, or plundering the palace, while the murder was being done. But the people of the city were gathering together and the murderers fled.

The monks gradually came forth from their hiding places, and the body of Becket was raised and borne, with the scattered brains and the spilt blood, to a place before the high altar, where it lay all night "with closed eyes and pressed lips and rigid limbs," until the morning at early dawn, when, so the old chroniclers tell, the dead man raised his hand in blessing on the monks who were watching around. In the morning the monks, fearing that there would be further violence and desecration, and that the body might even be taken from them, therefore hastened to bury the remains of their master in the crypt. There could be no full religious service in the church, for it had been desecrated by the spilling of blood; and the door was shut against any celebration of the mass until it had been reconsecrated a year later by the writ of the Pope. They took from off the corpse the archiepiscopal robes, and left him in the simple habit of a monk, and so he was buried.

The murderers fled to Knaresborough in Yorkshire, which was the manor of Hugh de Morville; and Roger of Howden tells us that they became despised of the people, and even the dogs would not eat the food which was left from their table. After a little time they went to seek pardon from the Pope, and at his command they did penance by setting out for Jerusalem and eventually were buried before the doors of the Temple there.

The death of Thomas Becket by this outrageous violence, with every touch of audacity that could have been imagined, roused a storm of protest throughout the civilised world. We find King Louis of France writing to the Pope: "Let there be some surpassing retribution for such a crime. May the sword of Peter be unsheathed to avenge the martyr of Canterbury; for the universal Church does cry aloud that his blood demands vengeance for all the Church, rather than for himself alone." While William, the archbishop of Sens, wrote in a similar strain: "A wild boar from the woods has destroyed the vineyard of the Lord of Sabbaoth and a single wild beast has pastured thereon. The Church universal . . . weeping and repulsed, cries aloud to the ears of the Lord of Hosts, 'Avenge, O Lord, the blood of thy servant and martyr, the archbishop of Canterbury, who has been slain, nay, indeed, crucified, for the liberties of the church. . . . For another Herod, of the seed of Canaan and not of Judah, the offspring of vipers, sending his lictors from his side, has not been struck with horror that he has scarred with deep wounds the symbol of the passion of our Lord, which he bore on his head. . . . For what place is safe, if the raving of a tyrant can thus stain the Holy of Holies with blood."

This is the kind of cry that went up in demanding vengeance on Henry of England, for his part, direct or indirect, in the great crime. We must remember the position: the Church of Rome was near the extremity of its claim to overrule the world, above the heads of all temporal kings and rulers. And here something has happened which is a terrific blow to that theory of ecclesiastical supremacy. An archbishop of the Church has been murdered in his own Cathedral, admittedly by the servants of the king with whom he has been quarrelling for so long. If this is to pass unpunished, then not only is the Church torn down from her supremacy, but she is even beneath the the right to the protection of the most ordinary earthly justice.

Even if Henry had desired to resist the torrent, he would have been swept away. For that unrestrained thing, public opinion, was whole-hearted on the side of the victim, and this public opinion took the form of a greedy acquiescence in, and a vigorous multiplication of the miraculous tales which almost at once gathered round the tomb and relics of Thomas Becket. Whether the monks of Christ Church were shrewd and worldly enough to see their chance, or whether they were all earnest believers in the signs of saintly power which were said to have been manifested at Becket's tomb, however that may be, this burial place was quickly one of the most revered spots in Christendom. One startling recovery from illness or bad luck followed another, until the sick and the unfortunate of every land that acknowledge allegiance to the Christian creed turned to Canterbury as the surest hope of restoration and happiness. And thus Canterbury became great because Thomas Becket had been done to death within its Cathedral walls. The extraordinary development of the habit of journeying to Becket's tomb — the Canterbury pilgrimages—and the effect this had on the revenue and glory of the great church, all this will be left for another place, when we can think of it at its full flood. We have told the tale of Thomas Becket at some length because, whether he was a great man or not, whether his cause was right or wrong, whether his death was noble or insignificant, certainly it

CLOISTER AND GARDEN, AND BELL, HARRY TOWER

was the foundation of the fame of the Canterbury Cathedral as we must visualise it at the height of its glory. As we have said before, this Cathedral was a storehouse of holy relics, and infinitely the greatest of these relics was the body of St Thomas of Canterbury. For it was only a few years later, in 1173, that the Pope, yielding to a great cry from every side, canonised Thomas Becket as a saint, an unusually rapid rise to sancity, which in most cases needs a longer silence before the saintly character pushes its way through the human covering which is most obvious to the contemporary generation.

It was in the following year, July 12, 1174, that King Henry II. did penance at the tomb of St Thomas for the unwilling part he had taken in his death. Roger of Howden thus tells the story: "Henry set out on a pilgrimage to the tomb of Saint Thomas the Martyr, Archbishop of Canterbury. As soon as he approached the city, within sight of the Cathedral in which lay the body of the blessed martyr, he dismounted from his horse, and having taken off his shoes, with bare feet and clad in woollen garments, he walked three miles to the tomb of the blessed martyr, with such meekness and repentance that in very deed it may be held to have been the work of Him who looketh down on the earth and maketh it to tremble. To those who beheld them, his footsteps seemed to be covered with blood, and so it really was; for his tender feet were cut by the hard stones, and a quantity of blood flowed from them to the ground. When he arrived at the tomb, it was a reverent sight to see his grief, and his sobs and tears, and how he submitted himself to the discipline of the bishops and many of the priests and monks." Another account, that of Gervase, tells us that this discipline took the form of being scourged by all the bishops and abbots present, and by some at least of the monks. To continue

Roger's account: "Here also, assisted by the prayers of many holy men, he passed the night before the sepulchre of the blessed martyr, praying, fasting and lamenting. As for the gifts and revenues which he bestowed on this church, for the remission of his sins, they can never be forgotten. On the morning of the following day, after hearing mass, he departed for London." Another account tells us that when he first arrived at the church, Henry knelt at the door in prayer, then continued until he reached the place where the archbishop fell under the blows of the knights, and here he wept and kissed the spot, and then proceeded to the tomb where he again prayed. Then, before the scourging began, Gilbert Foliot, the Bishop of London, standing beside the king, addressed the audience, confessing the king's penitence for the words which he had so hastily spoken, which had put it into the minds of the knights to do the deed; but he declared that Henry had never for one moment intended them to do what they did. He then made a formal pronouncement that Henry had restored all the privileges and property of the see of Canterbury, and had again taken into his favour all the friends of the archbishop who had been despoiled with him. It was then that the penance by scourging began, as Roger has told us already. There is the further addition to the story that there were eighty ecclesiastics present, and each bishop gave five blows and each monk gave three.

Then the miracle which struck the popular fancy so vividly happened when the king arrived in London, for, on the Wednesday following the scene of penance in Canterbury Cathedral, messengers reached Henry's Court at Westminster, with the news that the King of Scotland had been vanquished in battle, almost at the very hour that Henry had lain under the lash before Becket's tomb. It pleased his people to think that

Henry's submission had been graciously received by Heaven and rewarded by a victory over William the Lion of Scotland.

Before these events a successor had been appointed to fill Thomas's place as archbishop. But there was an interval of over two years before this was done. After such an act there was hesitation on both sides. Henry did not want to put anyone in office who would in any way continue the wearisome struggle, now that Thomas was dead; the monks of Christ Church, on the other hand, seemed determined that the successor should not surrender any of the position which Thomas Becket had gained with his blood. In the June of 1173 the king and the Pope were urging that there should be no longer any delay. In part, the delay had been because it was still a little vague whether the monastery had the complete control of the election, or whether the Crown and the bishops could influence the choice. It ended once more in an uncertain compromise; for when the monks were summoned to Westminster to perform the election, they put forward two candidates, both of whom were members of their order (for they insisted that this should be so); but one of whom, Odo, then prior, they preferred. But the bishops' party desired Richard, then the prior of Dover, but formerly, all his life almost, a monk of Christ Church; and as the bishops had clearly the king on their side in this choice, Richard was chosen, and the king's justiciar later on gave assent on his master's behalf. When Richard took the oath of fealty to the Crown the old phrase, "saving his order," was added; so the theoretical position had not become clearer than it was in the Becket days, while there was a tactful silence as to the matter of the Constitutions of Clarendon, for nothing was said about "the customs of the realm" which Henry had demanded should be accepted on oath by Thomas Becket. The election was, indeed, a drawn battle.

Richard went back to Canterbury to be consecrated; but the young Henry (who had been crowned already during his father's life) suddenly interfered and forbad the ceremony on the ground that his assent had not been given to the election. So off Richard, and the other partner to the suit, posted to Rome to satisfy the Papal Court, and it was not until April 1174 that the Pope himself consecrated Richard at Anagni and gave him the pall. And the archbishop started off for England, and it was on September 3rd that he reached London, on his way, and there received the news that his cathedral had been terribly damaged by fire on the 5th day of that month. It was in this fire that Conrad's choir was almost swept away; and when Richard was enthroned in his Cathedral on the 5th of October, he must have stood in the midst of a heap of charred ruins.

Gervase, who was an eyewitness of the fire, and a monk of Christ Church, has left on record the scenes. It is worth retelling in a literal translation of his words.

"In the year of the gospel, by the grace of God, one thousand, one hundred and seventy-four, according to the just but hidden will of God, the choir of Christ Church was consumed by fire, that glorious choir which had been finished by the careful industry of Conrad, the prior; in the forty-fourth year since its dedication, did this happen. And thus was the manner of its burning and its rebuilding.

"In the above mentioned year, on the ninth of September, about the hour of nine, during a south wind which surpassed in its fury all human experience, a fire broke out before the gate of the church, just beyond the walls of the monastery; and by this fire three cottages were destroyed. While the citizens were gathering together and beating out this fire, the cinders and sparks were carried by the wind to the roof of the church choir, and by the fury of the wind were driven between the joists of lead and reached the half-decayed beams of wood, and in a short time the increasing heat attacked the rotten rafters. From thence it spread to the greater beams and their supports, and no one noticed what was happening or helped to stop it, for the elaborately painted ceiling on the lower side, and the lead sheeting above, prevented the fire between from being observed. In the meantime, the three cottages having been destroyed, all the crowd quieted down and went home to their own affairs. Only Christ Church, all the while, was being consumed by the fire which had not been discovered; and the beams and braces went on burning until the flames rose to the slopes of the roof, and the sheets of lead began to melt. Then the roary wind, as its entrance holes increased, fanned the fury of the fire, till at last the flames burst forth to sight, and a cry arose in the churchyard below: 'Look, look, the church is on fire.' Then the citizens and the monks ran together, they drew water, they worked with their hatchets, they ascended the ladders, longing to save Christ Church, which already was beyond their help. They reached the roof, but there was naught there but black smoke and raging flames; and they who had come sought their safety and turned back again.

"By this time the fire had severed the beams from their binding pegs, and the half burnt timbers fell down on the choir below, on to the seats of the monks, and there, being a great mass of woodwork, caught fire in turn, and so the mischief grew worse and worse, . . . and the flames, increased by this mass of wood, rose upwards of fifteen cubits, and scorched and burned the walls, above all damaging the columns of the church. Then the people ran to the ornaments of the church and pulled down the hangings and curtains, some with the desire to save them, but others because they hoped to steal them. The chests containing the relics were thrown down from the beam above on to the pavement beneath, and the relics were scattered; however, the monks gathered them together and they saved them from the fire. But there were some inflamed by a wilder and diabolical desire, who did not fear to seize the things which belonged to the church. And thus was the House of God, once a delightful paradise of delicious things, now reduced to a despicable heap of ashes, made a wilderness and thrown open to the ravages of the weather. While the people marvelled much at the long-suffering of God, and maddened with grief, they tore their hair and beat their heads and hands against the walls and pavement of the church, cursing the Lord and His saints who were the guardians of this church. Many of them, both laymen and monks, would far rather have died than that this church of God should have perished so miserably. Not only was the choir consumed by this fire, but also the infirmary with the chapel of St Mary, and several other offices of the house, and many of the ornaments of the church were reduced to cinders."

The monks hastily put up an altar in the nave of the Cathedral, where the daily services could be performed; and the bodies of St Dunstan and St Alphage, apparently then considered the greatest treasures of the church, were reverently moved from their buried tombs in the choir, and reinterred before the temporary high altar in the nave; and so the church remained for five years. But with the death of Becket and the destruction of the Norman choir of Conrad we reach the end of a great chapter in the history of Canterbury Cathedral; and we will leave the story of the rebuilding to be told in another chapter.

CHAPTER XI

The Monks of Christ Church

THE murder of Thomas Becket was the turning point in the history of Canterbury. Henceforth it is one of the most famous towns in mediæval Christendom. Let us first see how Becket's immediate successors took their place in the history of the national Church, where he had cut such a striking figure. It is by no means easy to determine whether the death of the archbishop made the Church stronger than it had been before in its struggle with the Crown. Did Rome really gain by the murder of her high priest in Canterbury Cathedral? That the monks of Christ Church gained, and this very fully, there is no doubt of course. The death of Becket was as the gaining of a veritable gold mine of material wealth and ecclesiastical reputation.

Henry had bought his peace with the Church of Rome by a variety of acts and promises. He had promised to go to the Crusades for three years, and to keep a regiment of Knights Templars in the field for a whole year. Such were some of his bids for restoration to the favour of the Church. But in spite of all his penances and abasements, he maintained his position with fair success. While he had to leave to the clerical courts the punishment of the greater crimes of priests—such as murder and all felonies except high treason—yet the lesser crimes were punished in the lay courts, where also were heard all suits concerning the rights of property, even when that property was so eminently clerical as the right of presentation to a living. On the other hand the Church had the whole law of marriages and wills to itself, and these were a source of great profit. The Constitutions of Clarendon debate had ended fairly evenly, is perhaps the right verdict, and this in spite of the fact that Henry formally surrendered the Constitutions altogether. But Henry quickly showed that he was not going to cringe at the stool of St Peter just because a few of his knights had got out of hand for a time. The papal legate was a subject of scant ceremony in England at times. There is one scene recorded of the year 1176, when, at a great council, the Archbishop of York tried to push his way into the superior seat placed for the Archbishop of Canterbury: it was the old-standing feud between the two archbishoprics. The partisans of the two priests took to the floor with clubs and fists, and the papal legate was seen running about the chapel in despair, crying that "he had no authority in England." Perhaps he was stating a greater truth than he imagined; and it is significant that he should have said it so soon after the royal penance at Becket's tomb. Shortly after, when another legate landed in England, on his way to Scotland, Henry sent two bishops to meet him, with the pertinent question, "By whose authority did he dare to enter this kingdom without permission of its king?"

Archbishop Richard, whether from compulsion or by conviction, was not unwilling to allow the king to exercise his rights or claims over the Church, and he had plenty of enemies who accused him of being a traitor to his religion. Although Richard was a monk, and from the end of his schoolboy days a brother of Christ Church, yet he was rather a man of the world after all.

When he did show vigour in defence of the rights

of his Church, it was in a matter where he, at the same time, was attacking the privileges of the Popes of Rome. For the old-standing quarrel with the abbots and monks of St Augustine's Abbey had another outburst of flame at this time. When Roger, the abbot-elect of St Augustine's, came to the archbishop in 1177, and asked for his benediction, it was granted to him on the condition that he would profess the fullest and frankest submission, as abbot, to the supremacy of the Archbishop of Canterbury as his clerical overlord. Roger refused any such absolute submission, though he offered something going very far towards acknowledgment of the archbishop, if he might add the mental reservation, "saving the privileges of his order." This Richard would not accept; so Roger went off to Rome to get an order from the Pope overriding the archbishop's decision. He was successful, and even more than that, for he gained new privileges which encroached on the archbishop's rights. As an added insult, the papal letters in his possession allowed the necessary benediction of the abbot to be performed by the Bishop of Worcester. This brought Richard to a more conciliatory state of mind, and he hastened round to St Augustine's Abbey with a body of his priests and also laymen, and sent in a message that he was ready to pronounce the benediction himself. But the abbot, in his turn, was haughty; and he had purposely left the precincts in order that he might not be driven to receive Richard's advances. Richard appealed to the Pope, and he was ordered to appear at Rome in person. He started, but apparently never meant to go all the way, for he had the good wishes of the king in his favour, and no intention of really giving way in the matter; for the struggle of the abbeys to throw off the supremacy of the archbishops and their suffragans was now clearly linked with the attempt of the Popes to deal directly with the great monastic houses without any intermediate jurisdiction on the part of the State and its officers. In spite of all the pretensions of Rome, the archbishops of Canterbury were still appointed with the approval of the Crown, and still were unable to do much without the king's consent. So that the direct submission of the great Abbot of St Augustine's to the Pope, and the rejection of the privileges of the archbishop over him, would have been a triumph for the Pope over the king. But if Richard would not appear before the papal court, Roger did, and the problem was solved by his obtaining his blessing from the Pope himself; but the words were these: "Brother, we place on you the hand of benediction, saving the right and dignity of the church of Canterbury." But when he followed thus up by a letter to the archbishop, ordering him to give the benediction in future without requiring from the abbots any profession of submission, Richard stoutly fought the instruction and declared that the charters on which the abbey based its claims were forgeries, a contention which he successfully proved. One of the documents produced was a tattered and corrected deed, without a seal, which the monks said was the original charter of Ethelbert; and another professed to be the deed of St Augustine, but this looked much more recent. So in 1183 the king was able to wring from the abbey an agreement by which it lost many of its privileges. It was by actions of this nature that Richard gained the reputation, in monkish records, of being a traitor to the Church and the servant of the lay Crown.

It was on the 23rd of August 1179 that Archbishop Richard received one of Canterbury's most famous guests. This was King Louis VII. of France, the man who had ruled his land for over forty years, and had befriended Thomas Becket during his exile. Louis was now in trouble. His young son, Philip Augustus, now almost fifteen years old, had been seized with sudden illness, brought on, it was said, by a night of wandering, lost in a forest during a hunting expedition in the woods of Compiègne. The anxious father bethought himself of the tomb of his old friend, St Thomas, now the greatest wonder-working shrine in all Europe. But there was a difficulty in going to worship and beseech at its altar, for Canterbury was in the domain of a king who was one of Louis's most dangerous rivals. Louis was advised by his courtiers that it would be indiscreet to place himself in Henry's power. But he took the risk, and Henry rewarded his confidence with the frankest generosity, for the English king travelled to Dover to meet Louis on his arrival. The act was probably rendered significant to the mediæval mind by the occurrence of an eclipse of the moon almost at the moment of meeting. The two kings were received in Canterbury with great honour and rejoicing, by the archbishop and his bishops, the monks, and a great gathering of the nobles of England. Louis had brought with him the Earl of Flanders, and Baldwin, Earl of Guisnes, Henry, the Duke of Louvaine, and other great barons of France. Roger of Howden has described what happened: "On the day following the reception at Dover, that is to say on the vigil of St Bartholomew the Apostle, Henry escorted Louis to the tomb of Saint Thomas the Martyr, at Canterbury. And upon his arrival, Louis, King of the Franks, offered upon the tomb a golden cup of great size and of immense value; further he also dedicated, for the use of the monks of the church, a hundred tuns of wine to be delivered to them each year, for ever, at Poissy, in France, at the absolute expense of the King of France. Again, he granted to them that all their goods or material which they henceforth purchased in France for their own use, should be free of all tolls and customs duties. All these grants and privileges he caused to be included in the terms of the charter which they received from the hands of Hugh de Pudsey, chancellor of the King of France, the son of the Bishop of Durham. On the third day after these events, the King of France and the people who were with him returned to Dover, still escorted by the King of England, and on the following day, the King of France recrossed the sea to Flanders.

OLD DOORWAY, CANTERBURY GARDEN

. . . In the meantime, his son Philip, by the merits and prayers of the blessed Saint Thomas, the Martyr, was restored to his former health."

The whole story is typical of the importance to which Christ Church of Canterbury had now attained, and of the main cause of this story, namely, the miraculous power of the relics of St Thomas over the mediæval mind.

In 1184 Archbishop Richard died at Halling, in Kent, as he was travelling to Rochester; and his body was brought to Canterbury and buried in the north aisle of the Cathedral, in the oratory of the Holy Mary. As he had slept at the village of Wrotham the night before his sudden seizure, the story goes that a terrible form had appeared to him in a dream, demanding, "Who art thou?" and when the archbishop did not reply, the vision supplied the answer in the words: "Thou art he who has dissipated the goods of the Church which had been entrusted to thy care; and now I will drive you also from off the earth." The story was probably told by the monkish chroniclers, with a certain malicious insinuation, as a revenge for the way in which, according to them, Richard had failed to maintain the privileges of their order. Only a little time before his death he had particularly upset the dignity of the monks of Christ Church by appointing the new Bishop of Rochester without the consent of the monastery, which considered that the see of Rochester was in its gift. But the great struggle between the archbishops and Christ Church monks was to come in the time of Richard's successor, Baldwin.

The enormous treasures which were now pouring into the coffers of the monks of Christ Church, the offerings of the innumerable pilgrims at Becket's tomb, had now made that monastery an object of envious interest. The greatest men of the time were pilgrims to the shrine: for example, only in this year of Archbishop Richard's death, Count Theobald, the uncle of the King of France, had visited the tomb; and he is but a sign of the times. Another example from the same year is Henry, Duke of Saxony, who also paid homage before the saint's resting-place. While the monks were more envied, they were also, on their side, more haughty in their claims. They now regarded themselves as quite independent of the archbishop, who, they declared, had no control over their revenues. Indeed, he was in a sense their servant, for they declared more firmly than ever before, that the right of electing the archbishop was vested in themselves, and beyond the power of the suffragan bishops of the province of Canterbury. It was over the election of this next archbishop that the fight was to be so fierce.

The monks had already nominated the Abbot of Battle and four others, whom they were ready to elect as the archbishop, but the king had refused to listen to any of these as possible; and before the council had assembled in London, he had sent for the monks to visit him at Windsor, where he begged them to have a conference with the bishops and come to some mutual understanding. The conference had come off, but it had only ended in stubborn claims; and the king then went to the bishops, asking them to give way. But they only took a higher ground than ever, and declared flatly that the archbishop should be chosen by the bishops of his province. And so the thing was tossed backwards and forwards.

"By command of our lord the king," wrote Roger of Howden, "the bishops of England and the monks of Canterbury met in the king's presence in London, in order that they might choose an archbishop of Canterbury; and there being a continuation of the dispute, Gilbert, the bishop of London, who, according to the ancient right of his see, had the first vote in the election, made his choice of Baldwin, the bishop of Worcester, as archbishop of Canterbury: upon which all the other bishops assented to that choice. The monks of the church of Canterbury, being alone opposed to this selection, rose up and departed to make an appeal to our lord the Pope: while the bishops presented their chosen man to the king; and the king received him with the kiss of peace and love; and his example was followed by his sons Richard, Geoffrey, and John."

The prior came back to London at the request of the king, and he had to listen to a mixture of blandishments and threats, none of which had any effect in shaking his persistent demand that the king himself should go down to Canterbury and tell the monks, with his own lips, that he intended to respect their privileges, and that the election by the bishops was squashed. So, as Roger of Howden tells us, "Our lord the king came to Canterbury, in order that he might put an end to the anger of the monks, and holding a conference with them, he prevailed upon them to elect Baldwin, which they accordingly did."

Gervase of Canterbury has recorded the somewhat remarkable series of events which occupied the king's visit. Henry went first to the tomb of St Thomas, where he humbly worshipped, and then proceeded unattended to the chapter-house of the monks, where the whole monastery had assembled, whom he addressed as: "My lords, I have come as you desired, to testify to you, in the name of God, my dearest lords, that I will never cease to defend your rights"; and he ended his speech on bended knees and with tears. And the prior answered: "Truly indeed was this matter done in a way other than was proper, as you have admitted; therefore were we grieved in our hearts. But never did we desire to attempt anything against your honour by what we have said or done. It was the dignity of our church which was at stake, as it has been from immemorial times. So we now accept this man who has been elected, only asking, in all humility, that, so far as you are able, you will respect the form of our rights." Apparently, when the king got back to town he tried to wriggle out of the promise he had made to declare that the election by the bishops was invalid; but the prior, when he heard this statement, was so overcome that he fainted on the spot, and the king rushed forward in alarm, thinking he was dead and that there would be another clerical murder to his credit. So, throwing water over the face of the unconscious prior, he said, "Oh my lord prior, take comfort, take comfort: I did but speak in fun. I will do what you wish, and more." And according to his word, Henry declared that the election by the bishops was null and void; and Baldwin on his part refused to accept any election unless it was made by the monks of Christ Church. So with these formal declarations of their rights and privileges, the prior arose and said: "'In the name of the Holy Trinity, we have chosen that venerable man, the Lord Baldwin, bishop of Worcester, to be the father and pastor over the church of Canterbury': and the monks then gathered around and led the newly elected one into their church, singing and praising God." It is interesting to note, as a sign of the triumph of the monastery, that it was the monks, as well as the king, who sent messengers to Rome asking for the pall on behalf of the new bishop.

Within a few weeks of this final election the Patriarch of Jerusalem, Heraclius, arrived in Canterbury, on his way to persuade Henry to go on a crusade to rescue the Holy City from its enemies. Baldwin the Leper, the present King of Jerusalem, was a first cousin of Henry II., and his embassy was made up of great personages, such as the Grand-Masters of the Templars and the Hospitallers (though the Grand-Master of the former had died on the journey). Canterbury citizens must have seen brave sights on the days of their sojourn in the town. This was in 1185, and we shall see its sequel later, in 1190, when the Archbishop of Canterbury himself set off for Palestine as a soldier of the Cross. But there are many important events to relate before that departure, and the chief of all, the great struggle between the archbishop and the monks of Christ Church.

We have seen that although the monasteries had acquiesced in his appointment, and had given it a formal ratification, yet Baldwin was not the real choice of the monks. Since the earliest days of the foundation of the Church in England (as elsewhere) there had been a conflict of interests between the monasteries and the bishops. The gradual tendency had been in the direction of the freeing of the monkish houses from the jurisdiction and control of the bishops, and towards placing the abbeys and priories of the monks under the direct hand of the Pope of Rome. We have seen this tendency manifesting itself in the struggles between the Archbishop of Canterbury and St Augustine's Abbey just ouside their Cathedral walls.

In the case of the monastery of Christ Church there was an added complication: for these monks, after all, had a double rôle. Their house was something besides a monkish colony; for they were also the chapter of the Cathedral, and the governing council of this church, which was, strictly speaking, the chapel of the monastery. They were thus struggling as monks, to be free from archiepiscopal jurisdiction; while as the chapter they were demanding the initial control of electing the archbishop after their own choice.

From the days of Lanfranc until the present Baldwin, all the Archbishops of Canterbury except two (William of Corbeuil and the great Becket) had been themselves monks; and, during all this time, the monastic chapter had been gradually increasing its independence. We have seen how Lanfranc had divided the estates of the monastery from the estates of the archiepiscopal see. Anselm had given more complete power of management, such as the right to hold their manorial courts on their estates; more important still, as it turned out, he had assigned to the monastery the whole of the offerings collected at the high altar, and the Christmas and Easter offerings from the manors. In short, Anselm in form resigned almost every interest which the archbishop had in the revenue of the monastery, although he was himself officially the Abbot of Christ Church. However, he had no intention of resigning the practical control, and his object had been solely to prevent the estates falling into the hands of the king during royal quarrels with the archbishop, quarrels which led to exile and the seizing of the archbishop's estates.

The final act of renunciation by the archbishops was performed when Richard allowed the monastery to retain all the wealth of offerings which came to the tomb of St Thomas. At the time of Baldwin's succession, the matter of these offerings became every day of greater importance. It is true that Baldwin was now himself a monk ; but he had at first been a secular, and had become a monk of the Cistercian Abbey of Ford, in Devonshire, out of real conviction that the monkish rule was the true way of salvation. He was, in short, a monk not only by profession, but also by vivid conversion ; and he had the ardour of the new faith. He was of humble birth, and this, added to his new religious ideas, made him easily shocked at the great extravagances and luxurious life that he beheld in the monastery of Christ Church at his period. In the words of Dr Stubbs,[1] "the hospitality of the convent became famous in all the Western Church, from the crowds of pilgrims who returned from the shrine of the martyr. The internal expenditure was also immense. The refectory was the scene of the most abundant and tasteful feasting.

[1] Introduction to "Epistolæ Cantuarienses: the Letters of the Prior and Convent of Christ Church, Canterbury"; the Chronicle and Memorials of Great Britain and Ireland, the Rolls Series.

Seventeen dishes were served up at the prior's table. The servants and equipages of a hundred and forty brethren were numerous and splendid. The monastery had become a little town, in which the prior was supreme both temporally and spiritually."

The battle opened rather suddenly when Baldwin celebrated the first anniversary of his election by ordering that the monastery should no longer receive the annual gifts which were made by the manors at Christmas and Easter. The monkish historian of the day, Gervase, puts this action down to the poisoning of the archbishop's mind by "certain secular priests" who were around him, pouring into his ears malicious tales about the monks. Then Baldwin took another step: he seized the revenues of three churches which had formerly been devoted to the use of the monastery, and especially allotted to the almonry. Baldwin had already taken the precaution of begging a letter from the Pope sanctioning this reappropriation of property: this was very necessary, for the Pope had already approved of the earlier transfer to the monastery. With this authority the archbishop acted with rather boisterous energy: "the manors and rents which had been assigned of old for the provisioning of the monastery, he passed to the custody of his secular priests and his laymen. Thus, stricken down, the monks were driven to appeal to the apostolic chair . . . but the archbishop would not desist either for their prayers or their appeal: and manors which he had not seized before the appeal, he now took into his possession." In other words, he seized the whole estates of Christ Church, as his defiant answer to their appeal to Rome.

But both sides gave way from this extreme position, on the mediation of three abbots who came to make peace. The archbishop restored the estates, and the monks withdrew their appeal to Rome. This still left Baldwin in possession of the annual gifts and the three churches, for they naturally remained with him when the monks withdrew the appeal which they had raised specifically on that point. But, even then, one of the monks refused to admit this point, and himself maintained the case before the court at Rome. But there was a practical peace for the moment.

In the May of 1186, Henry himself arrived in Canterbury, and Baldwin got his approval of a series of rearrangements of posts, which would get his troublesome rivals out of the way and also reward his friends. So, at a council held at Eynsham, in the presence of the king, Alan, the troublesome prior of Christ Church, was made abbot of Tewkesbury, and Honorius, the cellarer of Christ Church, was made prior in his place. There was probably quiet chuckling on both sides over this latter appointment, for Baldwin thought Honorius was likely to be an easy tool in his hands, while the monks had quite another opinion of his possible merits : and events proved that they had good cause for their decision.

Baldwin's next step was more dramatic than anything that had happened so far, for he declared that he was about to found a new church in the immediate neighbourhood of Canterbury ; and he held letters from the Pope giving his approval, and also sanctioning a new distribution of the gifts received at the altars in the Cathedral : henceforth, only one-quarter of these was to go unreservedly to the monks ; the remainder was to be equally distributed between the poor, the upkeep of the fabric of the Cathedral, and the archbishop, who could use his share as he thought fit.

Of course, the monks put the worst possible construction on this plan of a new church. Gervase wrote that the archbishop designed, not only to seize the churches and the gifts, for "he was meditating how he could overturn the whole state and tranquillity of Canterbury Cathedral," and this by the building "of a marvellous new church in honour of the holy martyr Thomas," which was to be placed in the charge of a house of secular canons, just outside the town. If this was what he really intended, then this was striking at the very root of the power of Christ Church, for that monastery held the most valuable monopoly then existing in the whole ecclesiastical sphere, or, perhaps, any other sphere. The right to receive the gifts of the pilgrims to St Thomas's shrine was the source of the unique supremacy of these monks. To build another church to St Thomas the Martyr in their neighbourhood would have been much the same as granting Acts to two different water-companies to supply the same town; and in this case, it was a matter of trying to smash a company already in possession.

The king gave his consent to the scheme, and Baldwin came down to Canterbury to arrange for the installation of his new canons, as a temporary place, in the parish church of St Stephen at Hakington, now to be found just a little north of the railway station. According to the account of Gervase, the house was to be a substantial endowment of the archbishop's friends; the king and the bishops of the province of Canterbury were to be made the possessors of prebends (that is, shares of the estates of the house), but each of these was to appoint his own prebendary and vicar and allot the necessary revenue to them. Then, further, "every one who held a church in the gift of the archbishop or of the monks was to be inscribed as a canon of the church of Hakington." If this was not the beginning of a new cathedral, it was very like it; and the monks apparently thought that the time had come to do something drastic to stop this reckless archbishop.

So they dragged in the supernatural, and the de-

CANTERBURY CATHEDRAL, DARK ENTRANCE

parted St Thomas appears on the scene, and warned the monks of their danger. If we are to believe Gervase, the monks were wholly ignorant so far of what was proceeding, and their first intimation was by a vision which appeared on St Catherine's night to a young monk of the house, brother Andrew John by name. And the vision said to him, "Andrew John," and he replied, "What would you have me do, O lord!" for he then saw that it was St Thomas. And the martyred saint answered; "Arise and follow me"; and he led him out of the dormitory into the choir of the Cathedral, where they beheld the monks gathered together with sorrowful countenances. When the young monk was about to take his accustomed place in the congregation, then the phantom of Thomas Becket took his hand, saying, "Follow me still," and they proceeded to the tower adjoining the choir. And the vision showed the monk a great wheel of flame "Lo! this is the wheel of St Catherine: it is the work of your archbishop." Then they saw the phantom of Baldwin approaching them, and St Thomas drew back on one side a short distance. The visionary Baldwin then chose two of three swords of bent shape, and then sent a messenger calling the prior to come to him; and when he came, with five or six other monks, the vision of Baldwin spoke again, saying, "It is my wish to destroy this new cathedral which you are building [that is, the one which was replacing the burned choir of Conrad], and for that end have I made this wheel; but now I am unable to turn it without your help. Therefore push it round, and destroy all this work." So the prior and the five others put their shoulders to the wheel and pushed, and they were not able to move it. And Baldwin, when he saw this, said, "There are too few; go, fetch other monks." And two more came; and they also were unable to move the wheel.

Therefore Baldwin cried out indignantly, "Go, call the whole monastery"; but only two more would come. But now the young monk turned trembling to St Thomas. "Have pity, have pity, O my lord, for if the whole monastery should come and the wheel should move, then will all this new building be destroyed, and then will the whole monastery be overthrown." And Becket replied, "Do not fear: it will not move"; and he drew forth a sword of great size and splendour, and on it were written letters of gold; and when the young monk looked around, lo! the Archbishop Baldwin and all those who were with him had vanished. Then Becket turned to the monk and said, "Andrew, read what is written on this sword"; and he read the words to himself in silence. But St Thomas spoke again, "Not so, but read it with your voice, also." So the monk read the inscription aloud, "This is the sword of the blessed apostle, Peter." Then the saint spoke again, saying to the monk: "Take this sword to the prior, and tell him from me that with it he may break the wheel in pieces." When the monk had taken the sword into his hands he awoke, and knew it was all a dream; and the next day he turned it all over in his mind without saying anything to anyone. Then at night, the vision of Becket appeared once more, saying, "Why have you not done what I ordered you to do?" And the third night it was all repeated much as before; only this time there was the added threat of the saint that if the prior did not do as he was instructed, then would St Thomas strike him with the sword which he had refused to use on the accursed wheel of St Catherine. The monk, sorely perplexed, still feared that the prior would laugh at his story if he told of his vision, yet on the other hand he feared to offend the holy martyr by keeping silence. So he told the tale to the prior Honorius, who was astounded at the events, and knew not what they could portend.

Then another monk of the house had a vision, as he slept during matins; and he saw the Archbishop Baldwin come to remove the body of St Thomas Becket from its tomb; and when he had raised it out of its coffin, Baldwin attempted to cut off the head. The horrified monk attempted to interfere, but Baldwin was continuing with his work of desecration, when suddenly his mitre was swept off his head, and the body of the dead archbishop remained untouched: the monk then awoke, and when he told his brethren there was great astonishment.

The modern reader will perhaps brush all such tales on one side as impossible superstitions; but it is imperative to remember that it was on the basis of such impossible idle fancies as these that the mediæval affairs of Canterbury were often conducted. And even if the whole matter were a deliberate concoction of the monks and a plot to turn the popular sentiment in their favour, it is equally interesting and of historical importance to know that it was by such kind of tales that their object could be gained. Whether the visions were realities or not—and there is no reason to believe that they were not perfectly real to the monks who dreamed them—their recital as facts is part of the scientific history of Canterbury Cathedral.

Filled with such terrible tales as these, it is not surprising to learn from the chroniclers that the monastery received with consternation the news that the villain of the piece, Archbishop Baldwin, was coming to visit his Cathedral. But by this time the monks had put an interpretation on the events of the dreams, and they said it was clear that the wheel of St Catherine personified the new cathedral which Baldwin was threatening to build, while the sword of Peter was meant to suggest that an appeal should be made to

St Peter's representative, the Pope of Rome. Gervase, the actual historian of these events, was himself one of the deputation which the monastery sent to the archbishop to inform him of an intention to carry the case to Rome. But Baldwin asked the deputation to tell him why he had not the right to build a church on his own lands, and the answer was brief: "Because your land is our land, and all your rights are ours also, and all these things belong not to you, but to the whole Church of Christ." "Very well, so be it," replied the archbishop, "I accept your decision to appeal, and if necessary I will go myself to answer it." So it was a declaration of war to the end.

Three days after Baldwin arrived at Canterbury, and Prior Honorius sent a body of monks to St Stephen's Church to protest when the archbishop began to install his new canons. Baldwin promptly replied by suspending the monks from their right to officiate at the services of the cathedral, and then took his new canons to St Stephen's. "Nothing could stop him in his mad career," says the chronicle, "neither the appeal of the monks, nor the cry of the people or the priests, nor the cursing of the poor." And that same day he also suspended the prior from his office, and shut the doors of the monastery, and no monk could go out without his permission. Prior Honorius fled to Rome, and Baldwin set out to keep his Christmas at his palace of Otford, thus meaning to punish the Canterbury monastery for its riotous behaviour. It so happened that two papal legates were then due at Canterbury, on an embassy from Rome to Ireland. When they found that there was no archbishop to take precedence of them, they made the most of their opportunity on the occasion of their solemn reception in the Cathedral on Christmas Day. Never before had it been permitted, says Gervase, that such should enter the province of Canterbury, nay, the Cathedral itself, with their upright crosses before them and wearing their mitres.

The matter soon became a European quarrel, for Henry was probably behind Baldwin, and was using him as a weapon to strike against the Pope of Rome, who on his side was using the monks here and elsewhere as a convenient buffer against the power of the national kings and the lay State which they represented. The King of France (who perhaps thought he owed his life to the intercession of St Thomas when Louis, his father, had gone to the holy tomb) and the Earl of Flanders and the whole order of the monks of Cluny took the part of Christ Church, while Henry the Lion and the King and Queen of Sicily, with all the Cistercian houses throughout Christendom, were on the side of Baldwin. The Church in England was torn asunder on the subject, though the bishops were mostly on the side of the archbishop, likewise was the College of the Cardinals in Rome. But the Pope himself, now Urban III., was the great stay of the monkish party, and the bitterest of Baldwin's enemies.

Then Baldwin took the practical, businesslike step of collecting the rents of the monastery's estates, a proceeding which met with the opposition of the monks, although, after all, the archbishop had only appointed three of their own house to receive and administer the revenue. Even this point he surrendered; and since the king happened to be passing through Canterbury at this time on his way to the Continent, he begged him to use his influence with the monks and bring them to terms. "I will send to them as many and whatever messengers the archbishop desires," replied Henry. So the Bishops of Norwich and Worcester, and Hugh of Nuant (which last was one of the two legates who had worn their mitres so indiscreetly, as we have just seen), went to the monastery and asked the monks to agree to a friendly conference to make terms of peace.

After a second day's discussion, the monastery refused to consider any compromise; and the announcement was received with the usual mediæval tears on both sides of the assembly.

Then the sub-prior went to visit the king at Chilham; and, if Gervase gives the true account, Henry was much impressed by the firm bearing and elegant speech of the sub-prior, and by the unity of the whole monastery; and he sent him back to Canterbury greatly consoled.

Then Henry himself arrived at Canterbury on the Ash Wednesday of 1187. He had with him a great train of nobles and churchmen and abbots, and there was an immense gathering of the people, for there were persistent rumours that anything might happen. The critical meeting was held in the chapter-house, whither the king proceeded with the archbishop, great care being taken that no one should be present who had no right there. There were called thither two bishops, Hubert Walter and another, and the sub-prior and a few monks whom he wished to have with him. Meanwhile, the monks were praying in the Cathedral, while their sub-prior was fighting their battles in the chapter-house; and Gervase recalls how once the people had fought while Moses prayed, but now, he adds, the positions are reversed, for the leader does the fighting while his followers pray.

The king took the chair as it were, and did his best to bring the parties together. Apparently the two parties retired to different halls, the king acting as the go-between and bearer of their respective messages. He first asked the monks if they would withdraw their appeal to Rome, and decide the dispute in a conference at home. They said "No," nothing could be decided without the approval of their prior, who was on his way to Rome. Having failed on these lines, the king returned to the archbishop and asked whether he would not take off his interdict forbidding the monks to perform the offices of the divine services. The archbishop said he would do so if the monks would confess their faults and ask pardon in the presence of witnesses, either before priests and laymen, or at least in their chapter-house before a bishop and the abbots. This offer the monks refused, on the ground that it was contrary to the rules of their Order that any stranger should be present at a meeting of the chapter ; otherwise, they said, they were each willing to give the desired statement. But as the archbishop stood firm on the matter of witnesses, there was a complete deadlock ; the conference broke up, and the king went on his way to Dover. But the archbishop, before he left, granted a general absolution.

Then, soon after returning to Canterbury, Baldwin chose a new place for the building of his contemplated great church, this time laying the foundation in a field opposite the church of St Dunstan, on the London road, outside the west wall of the city.

By this time Honorius, the prior, had reached the papal Court, and a letter came from the Pope to Baldwin, ordering him to declare the suspension of the monks to have been an illegal act ; and the three abbots of Battle, Feversham, and St Augustine's (all neighbouring potentates of the archbishop's) were directed, by another letter, to see that the ruling was carried into effect.

This was to pour the final insult on the archbishop's head ; for the right of the abbeys to equality with the bishoprics in their relations with Rome was one of the main points in their rivalry ; and here was a judgment of Rome to be enforced by men whom Baldwin considered his theoretical inferiors. The Pope followed this up by declaring that all the gifts made at the altars of the Cathedral belonged to the monastery of Christ Church, and not to the archbishop. When the monks sent one of their brethren to deliver the Pope's letter to the archbishop, the latter was in residence at his palace of Otford, and the monk was instructed to ask with all humility that Baldwin would return to Canterbury, there to consecrate the chrism (the holy oil), instead of performing the ceremony in London, as it was suspected he contemplated doing. The archbishop flatly refused; high words passed between them; and the next day Baldwin performed the rite in St Paul's Cathedral in London. Further, he took no steps to obey the Pope's instructions.

But it is unnecessary to follow in all its details this struggle against the building of a new church in Canterbury. After stubborn defiance on both sides, Baldwin was eventually beaten, but that was only after several intervals of triumph. The whole situation had its humour. When Baldwin began a temporary new church of wood, the Pope wrote forbidding it, and Baldwin's reply was immediately to start one of stone. So long as Urban was alive, there was bitter war; then, when Pope Gregory succeeded, the archbishop found a more kindly superior; but when Clement followed Gregory as Pope, in December 1187, the persecution began again. Anyhow, the upshot of the whole affair was that the threatened church was never built in Canterbury; and Richard Cœur de Lion, who succeeded his father on the throne in 1189, came to Canterbury and helped to patch up a peace: his interest had been quickeneed in the case by a present of five hundred pounds from the monks. It was quite time to interfere, for matters had gone so far that there was fear of physical violence; and the unhappy subprior who was trying to weather the storm had to fly from the city and seek refuge in Arras and advice from the papal legate. At Richard's first arbitration meeting there was a violent row, and the king threatened to use any measures he pleased against the monks. Then the archbishop bethought him of the plan of torturing the monks; and between November 11th and the 14th the monastery of Christ Church was besieged by armed men, who cut off all provisions, and insulted the monks and the pilgrims, both men and women, who attempted to reach the tomb of St Thomas; and, as a minor torment, a continual din of singing and dancing was kept up, night and day. Then a rumour reached the monks that the king's officers were coming down from London to turn them out neck and crop; and the secular priests were going about, boasting that within a few days there would be seculars in the Cathedral of Canterbury instead of regular monks. The officers duly arrived; the monks collapsed in their opposition; and, accepting the king's terms, they were released from the siege.

On November 27th, the king, Richard, arrived in Canterbury, and was received in state by the bishops and the monks, with music and singing. There were gathered in the city at this time, to meet Richard, a vast number of nobles and Church dignitaries, and "a multitude of the people." The King of Scotland and his brother David were amongst the crowd of celebrities present. The following day, the king sent the Archbishop of Rouen and certain other bishops to both the Archbishop of Canterbury and to the monks, with the question whether they had in any degree changed their minds concerning the disputes between them. According to Gervase, the reply of Baldwin was as usual—"in few words and those ambiguous." The monks said they could not think of a settlement so long as the archbishop forced Roger Norreys on them as prior, and so long as he proceeded with the building of his new church, which the monks call a chapel (*capella*). After interminable discussions and arguments, these two points were agreed to by the archbishop, and the monks threw themselves on his good will for all the rest that was between them.

There was a dramatic final scene in the chapter-house; late one afternoon, when a fog came on and made it darker than usual, and the king himself could scarcely be seen, for all his brilliant robes. Then the Archbishop of Rouen arose, and, speaking with great emotion, said that at last "the dayspring from on high hath visited us"; that this long quarrel between the lord bishop and the monks of Christ had found a satisfactory conclusion. But when he gave the words of the judgment, the monks and their friends were filled with astonishment, for it seemed to them all a complete victory for the archbishop. This judgment ran: "We have decided that the archbishop can build his chapel wheresoever he pleases, and can appoint the prior. Let the monastery seek his pardon and let him put his anger on one side." What could they reply to this? They were in fear of being slain or driven out of their house, and yet if they gave way might not God demand an account at their hands? When the Archbishop of Rouen had finished his speech, the monks were commanded to come forward into the middle of the hall; and there they stood, not knowing what to say or do. Then cries arose, from those around, that the monks ought to go down on their knees; and so they did. At last one of the older of them found his tongue, and said, "If in anything we have offended you, O holy father [this to Baldwin] we ask your pardon, and that you will preserve the laws of the Church as they are and ought to be observed." To which Baldwin replied: "I will pardon you all, except only the prior, who by his own actions suspended the holy services of my church"; and all the monks remained on their knees, begging pardon for their sub-prior also. But the archbishop answered that if he wished to be forgiven, let him come on his knees with the rest of them; and if, he added, he on his side forgave them everything, then they, too, on their side, must freely forgive everything from the depths of their hearts. Then did the Archbishop of Rouen rise again from his chair and pronounce the final, formal reconciliation: "Since these long-drawn discords are now, by the council of the king and the bishops, and with the consent of the Lord Archbishop of Canterbury and the monks, all settled, namely, that the prior is to be withdrawn and that the chapel is to be destroyed; therefore let us now go into the Cathedral where we may sing and praise God; and then will the archbishop give to his reconciled sons the kiss of peace. And so it was all done." The next day, further, Baldwin attended the meeting of the chapter and restored the manors to the monastery, and said that he had already discharged the prior they found so obnoxious, and that it was his desire on all other points that the rightful privileges of the monastery should be preserved.

But there is an unexpected postscript to the story. After the above terms had been settled, the papal legate, who was waiting at Dover, was admitted to the city; but there was first a long discussion whether this should be done or not, some of the bishops being on the side of receiving him, and the others demanding that he should be turned out of the country with all speed. It was finally decided to follow the advice of those who were in agreement with the king and Baldwin, namely, to receive the legate with all honour, but to get him sent over the sea again as quickly as possible. So, on this understanding, the Pope's ambassador was received by the bishops and the monks of Christ Church; and he was lodged at the expense of the archbishop and surrounded by his servants, in order to prevent the monks getting at the legate and talking him over to their side. But in spite of the precautions a secret meeting was held, and the legate and the monks condoled with each other on having been tricked in the past negotiations. But the legate had no good advice to offer them except to follow the obvious method of making the best they could of the circumstances, and having uttered this not very profound piece of wisdom, he blessed them and set off again for Dover under the escort of the clerks of

OLD BRIDGE ACROSS THE STOUR

the archbishop's household. But that was only the tale which was announced for the public use, for one valuable thing he left behind with the monks: this was a deed declaring that the monks had been coerced by fear into agreeing to the above settlement; that, therefore, the arrangement was of no lawful effect. This document was quietly hidden away until the time came when it could be produced with the greatest effect, and for the moment the matter dropped.

William, the King of the Scots, was present in Canterbury at this time in order that he might do homage to Richard for his possessions in England, and, in return for this and a release from all homage for the kingdom of Scotland, William paid Richard ten thousand marks sterling.

It was a busy time in Canterbury, for on the very day in which the charter was signed with the Scottish king, Hugh, the Bishop of Durham, and Hubert, the Bishop of Salisbury arrived in the city that they might appeal to the papal legate (who was then in residence here, as we have seen) to annul the election of the Archbishop of York, on the ground that they had not been present when the choice was made. Bucard, the treasurer of York Minster, also appeared before the legate, bearing the same request, which he drove home with the additional information that the new archbishop, Geoffrey, was "a murderer, born in adultery, and the son of a harlot." However, Roger of Howden tells us that " although all these allegations were made against him, this legate, Cardinal John of Anagni, confirmed the election.

Then the king dispersed various honours and wealth to his brother and mother, and set out from Canterbury, on the 5th day of December, to go to Dover, where a fleet lay ready to carry him over to Calais, on his way to the Crusades; and in a few days the legate followed him, having dealt with the monks as we have seen.

In the following February, Baldwin, who had been arranging to build his new church for secular canons at Lambeth, since he could not force it on Canterbury, himself set out for the East on the Holy Crusade. It was on the 24th day of this month that he knelt before the High Altar of his Cathedral, and took the final vows as a soldier of the Cross, and passed on to Dover, where he left England for the last time. Before leaving his city he had read his appeal to the Papal Court of Rome against all oppression;

and this he did in the presence of the monks, the clergy, and the people. The monks had one letter from their archbishop, telling of his arrival at Acre; and in that place he died, much troubled in spirit by the riotous excesses of the holy army of Crusaders: he

OLD WINDMILL NEAR CANTERBURY—TO BE DEMOLISHED VERY SOON

was apparently disappointed because he found it so difficult to worship a god of peace with arms in the hands.

We have lingered over the details of this prelate's term of office, because they give a very useful picture of the relations between the monks and archbishops and kings as they concern the town and church of

Canterbury. These details, if rather petty squabbles in themselves, yet will help the traveller to realise that this city had that intimate personal life which cannot be expressed in the vast generalities of history. Real life is very often petty.

The man who was to succeed Baldwin was with him in Palestine when the latter died : this Hubert Walter was most active both as a military administrator and as a spiritual leader. He was one of the first pilgrims that the Turks allowed to enter the Sepulchre, and when Richard started for Europe, Hubert was left as the leader of the army on its return to Sicily. But before continuing the story of the general history of Canterbery Cathedral, we must devote a chapter to the vast architectural operations which had been proceeding at the Cathedral since the choir was destroyed in 1174 by the great fire.

CHAPTER XII

The Early English Choir of the Cathedral: The Shrine of St Thomas

WE have considered, as the main theme of the last chapter, the political and ecclesiastical claims of the monks of Christ Church. In the present, we propose to examine in detail those great building operations which were the chief material manifestation of their power, as it was expressed in their great church. It happens that a contemporary historian, Gervase, whom we have so often quoted, has left one of the most remarkably intimate descriptions that remains to us of mediæval building. It is so valuable, both for its architectural information as well as for its insight into the monkish mind and atmosphere, that we propose to give a translation of this record almost in full. It would be useless to attempt modern exposition when we have the original at hand.

In previous chapters we have quoted from Eadmer and Gervase, both monks of Christ Church themselves, giving details of the Cathedral as it had stood in the Saxon, and then in the Norman period, as it was rebuilt by Lanfranc and Anselm and their assistants. We now proceed to give Gervase's account of the rebuilding of the choir in the years which followed the great fire of 1174.

The keynote of this new choir, the ultimate reason for its existence, was that Christ Church might have a fitting shrine for the relics of St Thomas, the most revered body in all Christendom; just as the monks had manifested their ecclesiastical pretensions by the struggle with Baldwin which we have described in the last chapter, so now they manifested their spiritual pride by the great choir which they now began to build. As a matter of fact; this new architectural work was at once the expression of their material and their spiritual wealth; for it was mainly erected out of the vast offerings which were presented at the tomb of St Thomas, by the innumerable pilgrims who came to pray before it. So we must read Gervase's words as the record of the glorification of St Thomas the Martyr.

Let us first fully realise that the nave of Lanfranc's building was still standing; and the account which now follows is concerned only with the rebuilding of the choir, which took the place of the choir of Conrad, which had been begun under Anslem and completed about 1130, and destroyed by the fire of 1174. It is necessary to get that firmly fixed in the mind, even at the cost of some repetition. And now to Gervase.[1] We take up his words at the point where he describes how the services of the Cathedral were transferred before a temporary altar erected in the Lanfranc nave which had not been touched by the fire. Here they were conducted for five years and seven months, while the rebuilding was proceeding, and until it was sufficiently advanced to allow the services to be again performed in the new choir, although it was not yet finished.

[1] The original Latin chronicle is printed, with an introduction by Dr Stubbs, in the Rolls Series of the "Chronicles and Memorials of Great Britain and Ireland," in the two volumes entitled, "The Historical Works of Gervase of Canterbury," vol. i. pp. 19-29. But both these volumes of Gervase's works are of interest throughout for the student of the history of Canterbury.

"And the monks existed in tears and sorrow for five years in the nave of their church, separated from the people by a little wall.

"The brethren, in the meantime, took advice as to how the burnt church could be restored, but they could not reach any satisfactory conclusion . . . They sent, therefore, for both French and English craftsmen; but they differed in their advice. Some of them said they could repair the columns without danger to the walls above them: but the others replied that the whole church must come down if the monks wished to be safe. If this latter was true, then the monks were filled with grief; and it was little wonder; for they could scarcely hope that such a mighty work could be carried out by any human skill in their own time. However, among the craftsmen there was a certain man of Sens, William by name; one who was of great energy, and a most skilful worker in both wood and stone. So they sent away the rest and engaged him, on account of his sparkling genius and his great reputation for work. And to him, and to the providence of God, the work was committed. Then for many days he lived with the monks, carefully surveying the walls above and below, within and without; but he did not reveal all that it would be necessary to do, lest the monks might be overwhelmed when they were in so fearful a state of mind. But he never ceased to prepare, either himself or by the use of others, those things which were necessary for the work, and when he saw that the monks were somewhat consoled, then he confessed that if they wished to have a safe and irreproachable building, the damaged pillars and all the work above them should be pulled down. And convinced by this reasoning, they consented; for they desired to have the work as he promised it, and also to have it perfectly secure. So they consented with patience, if not willingly, to the pulling down of the damaged choir.

"Therefore he set himself to the work of bringing stone from over the sea. He designed, with great ingenuity, machines for loading and unloading ships, and for moving cement and stone. He produced moulds for shaping the blocks of stone for the use of the sculptors he had collected; and other things of this kind he carefully got ready. Then they pulled down the damaged choir; and this was all that was done during the first year's work. . . .

"In the following year, between the feast of St Bertin and the winter, he raised four pillars, two on each side; and when the winter was over, he added two more; and thus there were three in all, on each side: over these, towards the outer walls of the aisles, he built arches and a vault, that is three keystones' bosses (*claves*) on each side. . . . With these operations, the second year passed. The third year, he added two more pillars on each side, of which the two last he adorned with marble columns; and since it was there that the choir and the transepts met, therefore he made these greater piers. And having completed the keystones and the vaulting, he put many marble columns in the triforium between the great tower and the aforesaid transepts. And over this triforium he built another, of different materials, and also the upper windows. . . . Then he added the three keystones of the great vault, from the great tower as far as the transepts. All which things did seem to us, and to all who saw them, beyond compare and most worthy of praise. Then did we rejoice that the beginning was so glorious, and hoped with confidence for the end, and took steps to hasten the work. And thus was the third year finished and the fourth commenced.

"In that summer of this fourth year, ten pillars were raised, five on each side, beginning at the transepts, and the first pairs he adorned with marble columns, and made them great piers, to match the two other piers over against them. And over these ten pillars he built arches and vaulting. Having finished the triforium and the upper windows on both sides, he was about to get ready scaffolding, at the beginning of the fifth year, for the turning of the great vault, when suddenly the beams broke beneath his feet, and he fell, amid a confusion of stones and timber, to the ground from the capitals of the upper vault, that is, a distance of fifty feet. Thus, sorely bruised by the timber and the stones, he became useless to himself and for his work, but no one except himself was injured. Against the master alone did the vengeance of God, or the envy of the Devil, thus rage. Being thus hurt he remained in bed for a time under the care of doctors, but found that his hope of recovery was vain. So finding the winter approaching, and that it was necessary to finish the upper vault, he therefore entrusted the work to a certain industrious and skilful monk, who was the overseer of the masons; and there was much envy and malice on that account, because thus a younger man was made to appear wiser than more powerful and richer men. But it was the master himself who gave the first orders, as he lay in his bed. And thus they made the great span (ciborium) between the four principal pillars; and there, in the keystone of this ciborium, the choir and the transepts seemed to meet. The two spans of the vault, on either side of this great vault, were finished before the winter, when persistent and heavy rains stopped most of the work. And so the fourth year was finished and the fifth began. Then the master, feeling that by no act or care of doctors could he ever recover his strength, gave up his work, and crossed the sea to his own home in France. To him succeeded another, also William by name, but this latter an Englishman, of small stature, but skilled and honest in many kinds of work. During the summer of the fifth year he finished the transepts on both sides, that is, on the south and on the north, and also the great span of the roof over the high altar, which the rains of the previous year had stopped, when all was prepared. Further than this, at the east end he laid the foundations for that enlargement of the church which was to become the chapel of St Thomas, an entirely new building. For that spot was chosen, namely the chapel of the Holy Trinity, where he [St Thomas] first celebrated mass, where he was accustomed to bend in prayer and weeping; and because he had been buried so many years in the crypt beneath, where God for his sake had made so many miracles take place, where the poor and the rich, kings and nobles, had worshipped him, and the sound of his praise had gone forth over the whole earth. It was on account of these foundations that the master William began to dig in the cemetery of the monks, and he was then obliged to disturb the bones of many holy monks. These were carefully gathered together, and placed in a large trench, which was between the chapel and the infirmary, on the south side of the latter. When he had made a firm foundation, in stone and cement, for the outer walls, he then raised the walls of this crypt as high as the bases of the windows. And in these works the fifth year and the beginning of the sixth were passed.

"At this beginning of the sixth year after the fire, the monks were seized with a desire to have the choir ready for entering it at the coming Easter; and when the master perceived this he set vigorously to work, in order that he might satisfy the desire of the monastery. He therefore built the wall round the choir and presbytery with the greatest haste; and he erected three altars in the presbytery. He carefully prepared a resting place for St Dunstan and St Alphage. A wooden wall for keeping out the weather was placed between the penultimate pillars at the east end, and in this wall there were three windows with glass. The monks wished to light the Easter candles in their choir, although it was only finished with the greatest labour. Since everything could not be carried out as was fitting in the holy season of Easter, when so much had to be done, it became necessary that St Dunstan and St Alphage, the holy fathers and patrons and fellow exiles [in the nave] with the monks, should be moved before that day into the new choir. So the prior, Allan, taking with him nine monks of the church, whom he trusted, entered the tomb of the saints by night, so that there might be an absence of any crowd or other obstruction, and he ordered the stones before the relics to be removed. So the monks and their attendants, following the commands of the prior, took down the stonework, and opening the stone coffins of the saints, they bore the relics to the vestiarium. Then, having taken off the cloths in which they were wrapped, now largely consumed by age and decay, they placed the bodies in finer palls and bound them with linen. And, thus prepared, the saints were borne to these altars and placed in wood coffins covered within and without with lead. The coffins, thus covered with lead, and strongly bound with iron bands, were placed in stone chests, and closed up by molten lead. Also the queen Ediva, who had been placed under the altar of the Holy Cross at the time of the fire, was likewise carried to the vestiarium, which things were done on the night before the fifth feria before the holy Easter, that is, the sixteenth kal. of May. On the following day, when this moving (translatio) of the saints came to the knowledge of the whole monastery, they were much astonished that it had been done without their consent; for they had decided that the translation of the saints should be done with such great solemnities as were worthy of them. They therefore summoned the prior and those monks who had been with him, into the presence of the venerable Richard, Archbishop of Canterbury, to answer for the injury done to himself and to the holy patrons of the church by such presumption. And the matter went so far that the prior and those who were with him were compelled to resign their offices. But the archbishop, and other men of influence having intervened, and full and humble apology having been made, the monastery was filled with goodwill again; and peace having been made between the prior and the monastery, the services were performed in the chapter house, for the altar for the monks in the nave of the church had been taken down to prepare for the following Easter feast. At the sixth hour of the day, the archbishop, with his cope and mitre, walked before the monks, who were adorned according to the custom of the church, with albs, and led them to the newly-lit Easter candle; and, having blessed it, he approached the new choir singing the hymn 'Inventor rutili.' Then, when he reached the door of the church, which opened into the martyrium of St Thomas, he received from the hand of a monk the pyx with the Eucharist which was wont to be hung over the High Altar; and this the archbishop reverently took, and carried it even to the High Altar of the new choir. Thus did our Lord Jesus Christ go before us into Galilee, that is, in our removal to the new church. Then were the other solemn offices of that day solemnly and devoutly celebrated; and thereupon, when these were finished, the Pontiff, standing at the altar with the infula upon him, as the bells rang out, began to sing the 'Te Deum laudamus'; and the monks, taking up the song with great gladness of heart, praised God, with jubilant voice and the sweetest tears, for all His goodness to them."

This entry into the new choir, incomplete though it

FALSTAFF INN

still was, took place on the 19th of April, 1180. It must not be confused with the great day when the translation of the body of St Thomas from his burial-place in the old crypt to the new Trinity Chapel above took place in 1220, when the whole of the great choir was finished. So far, St Thomas's body had not been touched or even the church above him. We shall now see how this covering was removed with the rest of the damaged building.

"In this same summer, of the sixth year, the outer wall (around the chapel of St Thomas) already begun before the winter, was raised as high as the turning of the vaulting. The master had also begun a tower on the eastern side, half outside the circuit of the walls, and of this tower, the lower vault had been finished before the winter came on. The chapel of St Thomas itself was then levelled to the ground; until this moment it had remained untouched on account of the reverence felt towards St Thomas, who was buried in the crypt. The bodies of the saints which were in the upper part were translated elsewhere . . . and this having been first done, the chapel was levelled to the ground; but St Thomas alone kept back his translation until the completion of the building of his chapel. For it was proper and clear to reason that such a translation should be done with due solemnity and publicity. So they built a temporary wooden chapel over the tomb. Outside this temporary chapel, having laid a foundation of stone and cement, they erected eight pillars of the new crypt, with their capitals. The master also wisely opened a passage from the old crypt into the new one. And all these things were done in the sixth year and the beginning of the seventh, but before I follow the works of the seventh year, it will be useful to go over once more certain things already mentioned, which have been treated too slightly, either from forgetfulness or on account of brevity.

"It has been said above that after the fire almost all the old parts of the choir were pulled down and then changed into a new and finer form. We must now state what were these differences. The pillars of both the old and the new choir are alike in width, but differ in length, for the new pillars are about twelve feet higher than the old. Again, the capitals in the old work were simple, in the new, they were subtle and elaborate. Formerly the circuit of the choir had twenty-two pillars, whereas now there are twenty-eight. Formerly the arches and all the other parts were simple and severe, being sculptured with an axe and not with the chisel, whereas now all the sculpture is fitting its position. Formerly there were no marble columns; now they are innumerable. Formerly the vaulting in the circuit around the choir was simple; now it is ribbed and bossed at the keystone. Formerly there was a wall set on pillars separating the transepts from the choir, whereas now there is no such separating, and there is one keystone placed in the middle of the great vault which rests on the four principal piers, and thus the transepts seem to meet, as it were. Formerly there was a wood roof, painted with excellent pictures; now the vault is of stone and light tufa and of handsome construction. Formerly there was only one triforium; now there are two in the choir and a third in the aisle. All which things will be better understood by examination than by any description, if one is willing to take the trouble. But this far it must be realised, that the new work is higher than the old to the extent that the upper windows, both of the main choir and of its aisles, are raised above the marble line.

"Lest at any future time anyone should be in doubt as to the reason why the breadth of the choir, as it stands as far as the tower, should be narrowed at the east end of the church, it may not be amiss to give these reasons. One of these is that the two towers of St Anselm and St Andrew, placed at equal distance on each side of the old church, would not allow the breadth of the choir to continue in the same line. The other reason is that it was decided that it was best to build the chapel of St Thomas at the end of the church, in the same position as the chapel of the Holy Trinity, and this latter was much narrower than the choir. So the master builder, not wishing to destroy the towers, and not being able to remove them whole, made the breadth of the choir, as far as the towers, in a straight line. But from that point, just avoiding the towers on each side (though still preserving the width of the passage beyond the choir, as far as he could, on account of the frequent processions which passed there), he contracted the building gradually, so that it might get narrower opposite the altar, in a fitting manner, and then, at the third pillar, he might narrow the building until it fitted the shape of the chapel of the Holy Trinity. Beyond this, four pillars at the same distance, but of different form, were erected on each side. After these came another four pillars arranged in a circle, and on these the building above was raised and gathered together to a finish. This is the manner of the placing of the pillars.

"As for the outer wall, it proceeds from the aforesaid towers, at first in a straight line; then it curves, and each wall meets in the round tower, and thus completes the building. But all these things are to be understood more obviously and pleasantly by the eyes, rather than words or writing. But thus much may be said, in order that the old work may be distinguished from the new.

"Now let us consider more carefully the quantity and kind of work done by our mason in the seventh year from the fire. In short, it was this: in this seventh year the new crypt was built with sufficient beauty, and over it were raised the outer walls of the aisles as far as the marble capitals, but neither the arches of the windows nor the inner pillars was the master builder able or desirous to complete, on account of the rainy season. And thus was the seventh year spent and the beginning of the eighth.

"In the eighth year the master placed eight interior pillars and turned the arches and vaults and the windows of the apse at the east end, and the tower he raised as high as the base of the highest windows under the vault.

"In the ninth year he ceased the work on account of the want of funds.

"In the tenth year the upper windows of the tower were finished, as well as the vault, and on the pillars were erected a lower and upper triforium, and the windows and the great vault; also the upper roof, and the roof of the aisles up to the place of the lead. The tower was finished, and many, many other things were done in this year. In this year Baldwin, Bishop of Worcester, was made ruler of the church of Canterbury, on the eighteenth kalend of January. He was enthroned there on the succeeding holy day of St Dunstan, the fourteenth kalend of June. How much evil and damage and adversities he brought on the church of Canterbury, will be told later to him who seeks the information."

The foregoing story, thus told by Gervase, the monk of Christ Church, is perhaps the most intimate piece of architectural biography that the mediæval historians have left us in consecutive form. It is still, after seven hundred years, a useful guide book for those who wish to inspect this cathedral as a historical monument. These words, written by a man who was present at the building, will help to make the church something more than a historical monument—which suggest something cold and dead —the words of Gervase will give it a breathing life.

But they are valuable for their mere architectural detail.

The whole story of this building under the two Williams, master builders, is the story of the glory of St Thomas the Martyr and the monks who possessed his shrine and ashes.

CHAPTER XIII

King John, the Pope, and Canterbury

WE have already discussed some of the events which were happening at Canterbury while the great rebuilding of the choir (recorded in the last chapter) was proceeding. We have seen how the archbishop was struggling with the monks of both the abbey of St Augustine and the priory of Christ Church; and behind, in the background, but approaching nearer, has been the figure of the Pope of Rome. We will now take up the story again at the moment when Archbishop Hubert Walter is about to take the place of his predecessor, Baldwin, who had died a Crusader in the East. The pretensions of Christ Church and the Pope, right or wrong, legal or illegal, whichever we consider them, will still be the main theme; only they will both take a more imposing form, they will both claim more than they have ever claimed before; and the Pope, at least, will get more.

The king being absent from England, there was a delay in the appointment of a new archbishop. For the moment the Christ Church monks were concerned defending the rights they claimed that a new bishop of Worcester could not be legally consecrated elsewhere than in their cathedral church; and it was further asserted that at the request of the monks of the cathedral, the Bishop of Rochester ought to come to Canterbury and take over the duties of the archbishop if he were absent for any reason. Anyhow, the bishop of Rochester obeyed the call of the monastery and came to Canterbury at the Easter season of 1191; and was lodged at St Geogory's under the hospitality of the canons there, "lest it might seem to ignorant persons that he was being entertained at the expense of the monks if he went to their house." This was followed by a meeting of bishops on the 4th of May; the usual compromise was made; and the legate of Rome consecrated the disputed bishops of Worcester, with words, "saving the rights of the bishops of Rochester and of London."

The next day, the legate, the new bishop and three clerks appeared at the chapter house of Christ Church and presented to the monks letters from Richard the King, to "his dear prior and all his chapter at Canterbury." He said he wished them to elect the bishop of Montreal as the next archbishop. But they had different views, and put off the matter by requesting further information. Indeed, the monks of Christ Church were in a lofty mood, and were "getting their own back," out of the dead Baldwin, all round. It was not a time to let bishops, dead or alive, have their way unchallenged, for in this very year the Bishop of Coventry had expelled the monks of his cathedral, and had put secular canons in their place. The Canterbury monks probably thought it well to be pugnacious and assertive. So, following their hesitation in obeying Richard's letter, they expelled their prior, Osbern, whom Baldwin had forced on them against their will, for they had regarded his appointment as a reward for his teachery in going over to Baldwin's side while the late quarrels were proceeding. So out went Osbern, in spite of the humble speech he made them, saying that never would he have accepted the post if he had thought it was against their will. But the revolutionaries had their way; Osbern was shut in the infirmary, and the sub-prior, Geoffrey, dragged into the prior's chair, sorely against his will.

Then, as the next triumph in their revolutionary career, letters arrived on May 28th, 1191 from the Pope ordering the final destruction of Baldwin's building operations at Hackington; and we may be sure that the monks did not interfere when, on the 20th of July, the aforesaid works were solemnly cursed; and the people of Canterbury present rushed in and reduced the place to ruins as quickly as possible.

The Pope's letter had given them a general cancelling of all the acts of Baldwin against their privileges; and it also revealed the secret letter which the legate, John of Anagni, had signed (as we have seen), to the effect that all their surrenders had been torn from them by fear of violence.

It was in the September of this year that Geoffrey, the Archbisbop of York, the half-brother of King Richard, was besieged in St Martin's Priory at Dover, and dragged therefrom, by command of Longchamp, the chancellor, who was governing the kingdom in Richard's absence. The rights of sanctuary were involved in this act; and the prior of Christ Church sent an indignant letter to the chancellor demanding that the archbishop should be set free. The reader will remember that this priory of St Martin was one of the possessions of the monastery at Canterbury: hence the interference. They got their way; for the chancellor apologised; and the archbishop was replaced in St Martin's Church; whence he came on to Canterbury, and then proceeded to London.

It was now Longchamp's turn to be besieged; and he had to defend himself against his avenging enemies by shutting himself within the walls of the Tower of London. There he had to come to abject terms, to surrender his office and his castle; and seeing the game was up, he came down to Canterbury, where he took the vows of pilgrimage and surrendered the legateship. Then he passed on to Dover, hoping to escape from the kingdom; and Roger of Howden prints for us a long letter of the Bishop of Coventry telling the tale of Longchamp's attempt to disguise himself as a woman.

It was now that a message arrived at Christ Church summoning the prior and some of the monks to London to elect their archbishop. They went, but refused to choose the Bishop of Montreal (Montis Regalis) as Richard had wished. However, the justices said the king's sealed letters must be obeyed: and December 2nd was fixed for the election to take place at Canterbury itself. But the prior and his brethren suspected that the bishops and the king's brother John, who was with them, might rush an election through against the will of the monastery; so they took advantage of the fact that the Archbishop of Rouen, and the bishops of Rochester and Bath and Coventry had arrived a few days before the appointed day; and suddenly announced to these prelates that the monks of Christ Church had chosen the Bishop of Bath as archbishop. And they carried him off to the cathedral and pushed him into the archiepiscopal chair. The poor Archbishop of Rouen, at his wits' end to know what to do, ran after them, "pale and trembling," and made a formal appeal against their decision. But the newly elected one, not unnaturally, said he was perfectly content to abide by the wishes of the monastery. Then he solved this most awkward problem by conveniently dying fifteen days after his election.

Richard by this time had changed his mind, and wrote home to his mother that his wish was that Hubert Walter, Bishop of Salisbury, should be elected to the vacant archbishopric: he was probably influenced in this choice by the fact that he (Richard) was a prisoner in Austria; and Hubert was one of the most likely men to get his ransom collected; and if he were made archbishop he would be the better able to tap the revenues of the Church. And, whatever was the motive, he had his way. The monks, on being summoned to the election, immediately, without waiting for the presence of the bishops, chose Hubert. When the Bishop of London met the prior next day, the former sarcastically observed that the monks had done wisely in choosing the bishops' own choice; to which the prior retorted curtly: "As for your election and your choice, we know nothing whatever." This was the most successful attempt at independence that the monastery of Christ Church had yet made; and the archdeacon of Canterbury appealed to Rome against the election, on the ground that the bishops had not been present. This happened in May, while Hubert was busy collecting the king's ransom.

Gervase tells in precise terms how he, himself, as sacristan, journeyed to Lewisham in order to deliver the cross to Hubert; and he gives his speech in full, with evident pride. On November 7th the archbishop arrived in Canterbury; and the formal ceremony took place, when the new archbishop, in his alb and mitre, followed by the procession of the monks, went with bare feet to the cathedral and received the pall from the hands of the legate; and then, accompanied by the other bishops, he was enthroned, and administered the mass. The bishops of London and Rochester had a quarrel as to whom should take the first place during the ceremonies; and they settled that they should each take precedence at different parts of the service. Then Hubert immediately went over to visit St Augustine's Abbey, where he was received with the kiss of peace and administered the mass. And in a few week's time he was made justiciar of the kingdom by order of Richard, who was still in prison.

The ransom was paid in part, and hostages given for the rest, and Richard was released and landed at Sandwich on March 12, 1194, and came to Canterbury the next day. Here, apparently, the Abbey of St Augustine tried to score off Christ Church by

VIEW ON RIVER STOUR—SHOWING WEST GATE

joining in the procession which led him to the cathedral; but he seems to have been careful to avoid offending the Christ Church brethren by paying any visits until he had called on them first. Then he set out from Canterbury the next day and met the archbishop near Rochester. When the great priestly statesman saw his master approaching, he ran to meet him with joyfulness, and the king leapt from his horse and fell on his knees before the archbishop, and the latter did the same; then they both rose and embraced each other with many tears. So all the due mediæval ceremonials were thus observed.

The Archbishop of Canterbury was, in a few months, when Richard went to France, left the supreme ruler of England, for he was both head of the Church and great justiciar of the realm. Hubert Walter was a remarkable man, placed in remarkable circumstances. He was the nephew, or at least the favourite pupil, of the great lawyer, Ranulf Glanvill, and his mind was full of exact thinking about constitutional matters. He was rather a statesman than a priest, though he was almost big enough to play both rôles well. As fate would have it, when he had to choose between the lay and the ecclesiastical profession, it was the former he resigned, but it was easier to cast off the justiciarship than the archbishopric. His chief skill was as a financial expert; in other words, he could raise money for Richard's endless military expenditure more easily than any other available man. Approaching the matter from the other side—the taxpayers' side—we have stated a good reason why he should not have been very popular.

There were many reasons why he was not congenial to his brother ecclesiastics; but we are now only concerned with his relations towards his fellow-clerics and the monks at Canterbury. The brethren of Christ Church, although they had elected him so readily, probably did so because they saw a chance of scoring off the bishops by putting an election through without their interference. But they could never have been much drawn towards Hubert, for he was a secular priest, whereas they were regular monks. We have already seen that the antagonism between the archbishops and the monastery of Christ Church had been growing more and more bitter of late, and this was mainly owing to the fact that the wealth of the offerings at Becket's shrine now gave the disputants something worth fighting about. It had got to the point when any archbishop would have serious friction with his chapter of the monks of Christ Church.

There is no reason to believe that Hubert behaved with any vicious desire to assail their privileges: he was too good a lawyer to disobey precedents if it could be possibly avoided. We have an example of the regularity of his administration when we read that in the December of 1195 the itinerant justices ("justitiæ qui vocantur errantes") arrived at Canterbury on their rounds. It was one of the first occasions when they had appeared under a precise warrant, and the organisation of this manner of justice—which remains to this day—may be safely ascribed to Hubert, for at this time he was in absolute control of the national administration. The chronicler, Gervase, definitely says that these justices were sent on their tour by the Archbishop of Canterbury. He adds that at Canterbury all criminals were submitted to the ordeal by water; if they belonged to the jurisdiction of the Crown they were dealt with by these administrators of the king; but if they were in the jurisdiction of the archbishop, they underwent the ordeal of water in the city ditch, at the spot where it passed the Westgate (which was specially in the domain of the archbishop). If, again, the prisoner was anyone in the jurisdiction of the monastery of Christ Church, then the ordeal also took place in the city ditch; but the officials of the prior and monastery were in charge of the proceedings in such cases. Thus the rights of any private owners seem to have been carefully respected by these royal justices sent round by Hubert's orders; that is, of course, assuming that he was as rigidly proper in the case of others as when his own jurisdiction was concerned. Gervase mentions one case by name, where Elfgarus Ledret, of Hollingbourne, was accused of stealing pitchforks, and other thefts; and when he appealed in the court of the monks to be tried by the ordeal of water, he was taken to the ditch and there successfully underwent the ordeal and was set free. The chronicler quotes the words of the royal charter which acknowledged this power of the monks: "We have confirmed that they have the same power over their men, both within and without the city, as our own officers might have. We do not wish that anyone should meddle in the affairs of these monks."

But there was soon to arise a situation where Hubert Wallter considered that the welfare of the State was at stake, and then he did not hesitate to throw ecclesiastical precedents to the winds. It happened thus: There was serious discontent amongst the artizan classes in London; or perhaps it is safer to say that the different parties in the trade guilds were engaged in rearranging their privileges. But the details of the case belong to the history of London, they only concern Canterbury in so far that the popular leader, one Fitz Osbert, or "William of the Beard" as he was called, after killing some of his opponents, took refuge in the turret of St Mary-le-Bow, that is, Bow Church, in Cheapside, which was one of the many possessions of the monastery of Christ Church of Canterbury. This Fitz Osbert refused to obey any messages from the archbishop asking him to come out of his fortress and sanctuary, when it was promised that he would be allowed to put himself under the jurisdiction of the ecclesiastical courts, where his life and limbs would at least be safe. So at last Hubert decided that he would order the rights of sanctuary to be broken; and he ordered the fugitives (for William had some friends with him) to be driven out of the church tower by fire. This was done; and the captured men were hanged.

The monastery of Christ Church was probably quite willing to seize the opportunity of getting in a blow at the archbishop, so the monks made a great outcry. In the words Roger of Wendover: "When the monks of Holy Trinity at Canterbury heard that their church at London, called St-Mary-at-Arches had been treated thus violently by order of their archbishop (who ought to have respected the rights of the Church fully, even though he was an officer of the king), then were they angry and their hearts were grieved at him; so that they were unable to treat any further with him on any subject in a peaceful manner."

Then the old trouble about Baldwin's proposed new church came up again: there was another long discussion whether it could be built at Lambeth, now that the Hackington building had ceased. After interminable arguments as to the advantages of secular canons over regular monks, and so on, Hubert, at his wits ends for a reply, rather tamely said he would pray that God would reveal his will in the matter to both the monks and himself. But the monks won; for in 1198, as we shall see, a letter came from the Pope ordering the archbishop to pull down the church at Lambeth which Baldwin had begun, and which Hubert was continuing. It is clear that the monks were getting stronger and stronger.

The real secret of the strength of Christ Church monastery was twofold; it possessed the most venerated relics of St Thomas the Martyr; it had behind it the power of the Pope of Rome. The quarrel about the Lambeth Church had been won by the monks in spite of the fact that the king interferred strongly on the archbishop's side: he wrote a letter to them even ordering them to disobey the papal instructions in the case; and when the monks would not give way, the royal justices informed them that the royal letter must be obeyed; and orders were given that the estates of the monastery should be seized by the king. The bishops and abbots tried to arbitrate between the violent opponents, but unsuccessfully; and the manors were forfeited. Then the monastery was ordered to show its treasures to a properly authorised royal messenger; but this step the king apparently did not approve. When the prior went to Rome to get the Pope's judgment, he came back with the letter to which we have referred above; accordingly Hubert gave orders that the church at Lambeth should be destroyed; and, on January 27, 1199, "it was levelled with the ground."

The Pope who ordered this to be done was, perhaps, the greatest of the successors of St Peter at Rome. He was Innocent III. who made greater claims on the obedience of Christendom than any pope who had gone before him. The history of England during the next few years turned round the monks of Christ Church: they were the central figures which Pope Innocent III. and King John of England pulled every way as best suited their respective plans. For Richard Cœur de Lion died in this year, 1199. He had not long before received a letter from the Pope lecturing him severely for his disrespect for the papal letters to the monks; but apparently without avail, for the monks soon wrote to Rome that their possessions had been seized a third time; and when they appealed to the archbishop to beg the king to withdraw his persecution, Hubert insulted the messenger, so they said, and he went on to the king to see if he would receive him more kindly. At this point Richard died.

All this quarrel, be it observed, was in defence of their right to possess the sole church which had any intimate connection with St Thomas, their precious monopoly.

In the year 1201, on Easter Day, John, "with glory and much magnificence, was crowned in the Church of Christ at Canterbury, by Hubert, its archbishop, by whose counsel the king was then mainly guided. And the queen was crowned at the same time with him. And in a few days he passed over the sea to hold a conference with the king of the French." In the following year John was again at Canterbury, and once more the crown was solemnly placed on his head by the archbishop. In those days of uncertain kingship, it was always well to emphasise such ceremonies as often as possible. John was at Canterbury in every year of his reign, except one.

In 1200 there had been a peace patched up between the archbishop and the monks; and, for some reason, they saw fit to agree that the former might rebuild his church at Lambeth, after all; but there were to be certain definite restrictions as to the sum of money he could assign from the archiepiscopal revenues for the maintenance of his new canons; these were not to exceed twenty in number; they were to be "regulars" of the Premonstratensian order; and no bishops might be consecrated in this church, or the chrism blessed therein. They may all seem very small points nowadays; nevertheless, these were the matters about which mediæval churchmen fought so desperately. It will be found that the eagerness of this defence of their privileges had usually a financial basis, and there we will leave it, with the remark that there were probably many saintly men in the church who cared little about money, but simple-minded men often make the best tools for craftier men to use.

At the Christmas of 1204 King John was the guest of the archbishop at Canterbury. In 1205 Hubert died, and, three days after, John arrived in the town, and conversed so graciously with the monks concerning the matter of a successor, that they were filled with hope that he would "rest in the bosom of the church." They might well have had immediate suspicions; for when John heard that the late archbishop had left to the church a present worth three hundred marks, "he quietly asked that he might see it; and, much astonished when he saw it, he ordered it to be carried to Winchester, and gave to the Bishop of Winchester what he had stolen from Canterbury." The next day he begged the monks not to make any election before the Feast of St Andrew (it was then the middle of July), and they agreed; whereupon John despatched ambassadors to Rome, and, hearing this, and not to be outdone, the monks sent off the sub-prior and some other brethren to defend their privileges, if need be, before the Pope. At least that was what they said, but as a matter of fact they had gathered together in secret meeting—to which not all the monks were admitted—and had really elected Reginald, the sub-prior, as archbishop, and sent him to Rome to be consecrated. When this move reached John's knowledge, by letters which he received from his own ambassadors, he was much astonished, and posted down again to Canterbury after the Feast of St Andrew; but the monastery flatly denied that it had made any election. To prove these words the monks promptly, at the king's wish, elected John de Grey, Bishop of Norwich, as archbishop, by the united counsel of the chapter and the consent of all: they led him into the cathedral in a choral procession, and, placing him in the archiepiscopal chair, they received the kiss of peace. John had been quite candid in pressing his choice, he said John de Grey "alone of all the prelates of England possessed his confidence."

But the monks who had gone to Rome to elect

Reginald were not inclined to sit down under this rebuff; they declared that they had not assented to it, and it had been carried by the violent interference of the king; therefore it was null and void.

Pope Innocent III. now appears as the chief character on the stage, and his theory of life, as he himself expressed it, will be the best introduction to his actions in the present affair. He had said: "The Creator has established in the firmament of the Church, two dignities; the greater, the papacy, which rules over the souls of men, as the sun rules over the day; the less, the royalty which rules over their bodies, as the moon over the night. The papacy takes its place before royalty, just as the sun takes precedence of the moon." Or again: "God has given to St Peter a mission to govern not only the Church universal, but the world. As all creatures in heaven and earth and under the earth must bend the knee before God, so must all obey His vicar, so that there shall be but one flock and one shepherd." This was the creed of existence which had been revolving in the papal mind since Hildebrand at least. But the latter was somewhat in advance of his time. So far as England was concerned, Hildebrand might have theorised how he pleased about the dignity of his office and the lordship of the world. For men like William the Conqueror had views of their own about such matters. With all his piety, the Conqueror could always reconcile it with a placid disregard of the Pope and his canons, when they interfered with the autocratic will of the Duke of Normandy. But the papacy had been gradually growing stronger all these years; and King John, the opponent of Innocent III., was not the man that his ancestor William had been. So the cards of this great game between king and pope were of a new deal, and the players were of different skill. The cards they played against each other bore on the face such figures as the monks of Christ Church, Canterbury, and edicts of excommunication and interdicts, and the execution of judgment on the goods and possessions of the Church and monasteries. And the prize for which they fought, king against pope, was the right to the supreme word in the government of the nation. In the case of John, he had probably no more lofty desire than to get a freer hand in controlling the great wealth of the Church, and perhaps a human objection to being dictated to by a Pope who wrote like this: "Individual kings have individual kingdoms, but Peter is over all the length and breadth of the world, for he is the vicar of Him whose is the earth and the fulness thereof, the round world and they that dwell therein. . . . Both kingdom and priesthood were instituted among the people of God; but while the priesthood was instituted by divine ordinance, the kingdom came into existence through the importunity of man."[1] Such words as these were likely to damage seriously the commercial value as well as the social advantages of kingship. One can scarcely blame John for being rather stubborn in his fight with the papacy.

We have arrived at the point in the affair where the Christ Church monks, with Reginald the sub-prior, at Rome, have repudiated the election of John de Grey. But by this time John had put his chosen candidate in possession of all the property belonging to the see of Canterbury. There was another addition to the confusion; for the bishops of the province of Canterbury sent off advocates to Rome in order to prove before the papal council that it was altogether irregular for an archbishop to be elected without their

[1] For an admirable summing up of the position of the mediæval Church of Rome see a brilliant chapter on "The Church in the Middle Ages," in "The History of Mediæval Civilisation," by M. Charles Seignobos (English translation, p. 86).

part in the election, which must be made by them acting with the monks of Christ Church. To which the monks replied that they were the sole electors, by ancient and approved custom, and by a special privilege granted to them by the Popes of Rome. After a long discussion, the Pope decided that the monks had the law on their side. This was really a declaration of the most extreme kind; for it was in fact a most serious blow against the control of the King of England over the Church. Hitherto, in spite of all theories about right of investiture, and so on, the Crown had really had the practical choice of the bishops, and on the whole they were a class that could be relied on to stand by the Crown if there was a struggle with Rome. For example, the bishops had deserted Anselm at some of the critical moments in his struggle with Henry; and again they had not supported Becket when he took up the defence of the Church against the State. The bishops were of the State rather than of Rome, so long as their election was in the hands of the king. But if an archbishop could be elected without the sanction of these State-appointed bishops, by a few monks of Christ Church, largely biassed in favour of the supremacy of the Pope, then there was no saying where the power of the Pope would end.

Innocent was now in a dilemma: some of the monks were demanding the immediate confirmation of the election of Reginald; others were proving by unending argument that this election of Reginald was void, for, these said, it had been made secretly at night when the larger and wiser part of the brethren were absent, and the king had not given his consent, all which formalities had, they said, been observed when John de Grey was chosen. They specially insisted that the king was not only agreeable, but actually present himself at the election. The Pope, unable to bring these conflicting parties together—perhaps not wishing to do so—cancelled both elections and ordered the monks to choose another man altogether.

This seemed to be quite a good solution. But

THE BELL HARRY TOWER, CANTERBURY CATHEDRAL, UNDER REPAIR, 1905

there was a hidden stumbling-block beneath the surface. The sixteen monks who had come to Rome to discuss the matter with the papal council, were authorised to decide on behalf of the monastery; and they had received, also, the promise of John that he would agree to any choice they made. But out of these sixteen professedly free men, twelve had pledged their word to John that they would consent to no other choice except of De Grey. When the Pope and the cardinals told the monks that they might make their choice freely if they chose an Englishman and a suitable man, they meant very plainly that Cardinal Stephen Langton, sitting before them in the council, was the man who should be chosen. When the twelve monks confessed their oath to John, the Pope, with gracious omnipotence, set them free from their solemn promise (the advantage of being a divine vicar is obvious: he could dispense with petty worldly formalities), and they all, except one, voted for Langton; and the Pope wrote a letter informing John of the decision, asking that he would receive Langton in a kindly spirit. John had no such intention, and declared that the new man was an enemy of the kingdom of England, who had lived in Paris and had been the most familiar friend of the King of the French; and this was the man they desired to make the second in the kingdom.

So, in a fury, John sent down to Canterbury two knights, Falk of Cantelupe and Henry of Cornhill, with instructions to drive out the whole body of the monks of Christ Church from their home. These two men most cruelly carried out their orders on July 15, 1207; and the monks fled over the sea to St Omer, where they were given shelter by the abbey of St Bertir, while their lands and goods were seized by the king.

John sent angry letters to the Pope, and Innocent retaliated by instructing some of the bishops to inform the king that unless he behaved more reasonably, he would find his kingdom placed under an interdict. But John would not move from his position, and on March 23, 1208, the interdict was formally proclaimed.

"Then did all the sacraments of the Church cease in England, except the administration of the last rites to the dying and the baptism of children; while the bodies of the dead were carried outside the cities, and there buried in the manner of dogs." The Bishops of London, Ely, Worcester, Bath, and Hereford left the country rather than uselessly remain in an interdicted land. As a matter of fact, a comprehensive curse of this kind could not be properly enforced in a country which was not in the power of the Pope. It was all very well to issue fierce orders at Rome, it was another matter to insist on their observance; and in England the interdict was only partially observed.

Let us see what sort of man was this Cardinal Langton, about whom all this hubbub had arisen. Whether Innocent was fully aware of what he was doing is doubtful; certainly, when he forced Langton on the English people as their archbishop, he was making the happiest of choices. Langton was a scholar and a gentleman already, and his later history was to prove him to be a statesman and a patriot as well. He had been a student in Paris University, where he had gained a great reputation for his general knowledge and wide learning, both in the arts and theology; and as a reward he was given a prebend in Notre Dame, in spite of the fact that he was an Englishman. John was quite right when he stated that Langton was the intimate friend of the French king.

When he found himself elected Archbishop of Canterbury, but unable to approach his cathedral town, or even enter the ports of England, because of the hostility of John, Stephen Langton behaved with commendable restraint. When he heard that the monks had been expelled, he wrote a manifesto to the English nation. In it he was careful to identify himself with the same cause for which Thomas Becket had died. Whatever exactly that might mean, St Thomas was now the most popular saint, and Langton showed that he had the politician's instinct when he put St Thomas on his election programme, as it were. Considering their views, both Langton and the Pope wrote in a very moderate manner of the dispute, and tried to put off extreme measures as long as possible. Perhaps, at the bottom of their hearts, they knew that John was within his constitutional rights in declaring that an Archbishop of Canterbury could not be chosen without his assent: in practice, at least, the Crown in England had never given up this right to approve the bishops. The right of the chapters to elect had always been modified by the necessity of obtaining the king's consent.

It was when John followed up his attack on the Canterbury monks by a general seizure of the property of the whole Church in England (as his retaliation for the interdict), by a general rough handling of the laity, and tyrannical conduct all round on every one within his reach—then it was that the cause of the monastery of Christ Church became only a small part of the great national cause which reached a definite point in the demand for the Great Charter a few years later.

In the meanwhile, in 1209, Langton got the Pope to modify the terms of the interdict to the extent that the churches attached to the monasteries could henceforth celebrate divine service once a week; but the Cistercians, who had offended the Pope by taking this step already without his consent, were specially exempted from this dispensation from the general terms of the interdict. The dispute dragged on somewhat wearily, with attempts at peace on both sides. John tried to entice Langton into his power by offering a safe-conduct if he came to England to negotiate. But the archbishop heard privately that there was a good chance that the promise would be broken and his freedom endangered; so he stayed safely on the Continent.

Then the Pope, after many serious warnings to John of what he must expect, finally excommunicated him in November 1209. This was the most terrible punishment within the power of the Church to inflict. Here are the terms of such a decree—they were the banishment of the criminal from society on earth, and his committal to the worst of fates hereafter: "By virtue of the divine authority conferred on the bishops by Saint Peter, we cast him out from the bosom of our Holy Mother Church. Let him be accursed in his town, accursed in his field, accursed in his home. Let no Christian speak to him, or eat with him: let no priest say mass for him nor give him the communion: let him be buried like an ass. . . . And as these torches cast down by our hands are about to be extinguished, so may the light of his life be extinguished unless he repent and give satisfaction by his devotions." And with all this in front of him John still refused to accept Stephen Langton as the choice of Christ Christ monks, or to allow them to return to their house in Canterbury. As a matter of fact, it is probable that John's guards were so watchful that the papal edict of excommunication was never actually read in England, or, if it ever arrived, there was not a bishop or a priest who dared to declare its terms by a formal publication. "They all became like dumb dogs not daring to bark," says Roger of Wendover. But, informally, of course, every one knew it had been issued. When John's ministers and clerks began to get uneasy at having to risk their own eternal welfare by serving an outcast, then the tyrant proceeded to torture those who dared to complain.

But when Philip, the King of France, at the request of the Pope, began in 1212 to collect an army with which to invade England and depose John, then it was time to do something more practical than scoff. So John, about Easter, 1213, collected an army of sixty thousand men, the main body of which he encamped on Barham Down, just outside Canterbury, to the south-east of the town. It was here that his courage began to fail him ; and he sent off a message that he would be glad to talk things over with the papal legate, who had sent two Knights Templars to the king as he waited in his camp, bearing an offer to show how it was possible to find a way of reconciliation with Rome. So John met Pandulph at Dover on May 13 ; and the papal ambassador drew a lively picture of what was going to happen to John if the French king continued the invasion. All the exiled bishops and priests and laymen were following in his train, and there would be some triumphant scoring at John's expense. So John collapsed rather like a pack of cards, after all his brave words of the last few years. Not only did he swear to accept Stephen Langton as archbishop and to restore all the other bishops to their sees and possessions, but he further surrendered his kingdom to the Pope and received it back as his feudal inferior. The Pope was to be the chief lord of England in a secular sense as well as in the affairs of the Church. What was more to the immediate point, the legate went off to Rome carrying with him, with the treaty of surrender, eight thousand pounds sterling, with which, the chroniclers mentioned, he intended to indemnify the archbishop and the monks of Christ Church and the other exiles for the damage they had received. And so, at the end of June 1213, Langton was able to land in England, six years after he had been appointed Archbishop of Canterbury, and with him came the monks of Christ Church.

Thus, the first phase of the eventful history of King John's reign centres intimately around the monastery of Christ Church, Canterbury ; and although it took a

BELL HARRY TOWER, CANTERBURY CATHEDRAL

far wider sweep than this single house, yet the official root of the quarrel continued there, and we have seen that the last scene of all, the collection of the English army to resist the avenging French attack, and the collapse of John, all took place within a few miles of the city whose archbishop was what they were formally fighting over. Perhaps the deeper root of the quarrel is revealed most clearly in such sentences from the old chroniclers as the following, written under the year 1210: "Then the king made all the bishops of England come before him, and with them all the abbots, priors, abbesses, Templars, Hospitallers, and the agents of the towns belonging to the order of the monks of Cluny, and of all other orders from beyond the sea: and all these were compelled to save their property by paying a sum which is said to have reached the total of one hundred thousand pounds sterling." This is from the "Historia Minor" of Matthew Paris.

There is another illuminating passage from Roger of Wendover's "Flores Historiarum," under the year 1208, where the immediate result of the interdict of that year is vividly described. It is worth repeating somewhat fully, for it will give a feeling of reality to the bare historical facts we have just considered. It will help us to understand the kind of events which followed the action of the monks of Christ Church when they made their election of Stephen Langton; it will give life to the historical names which have entered into the story; and historical names are so apt to be read as the inscriptions on the base of cold marble statues. There was nothing coldly statuesque about such men as King John and some of his contemporaries. "The Bishops of London, Ely and Winchester, according to the instruction they had received from the Pope, approached before King John and did humbly entreat him with tears that he would recall the archbishop and the monks of Canterbury to their church and honour and love them with full affection; for thus would he, they said, escape the ignominy of an interdict; and for his reward, the Giver of all rewards would increase his earthly honours, and at his death would give him eternal glory. When the bishops desired to continue the discussion, the king became almost mad with rage, and breaking forth into words of blasphemy against the Pope and his cardinals, he swore by God's teeth that if any priest dared to lay his land under an interdict, then immediately would he send every prelate of England and all clerics and ordained persons back to the Pope, and confiscate all their property; and he added that if he found any priests from Rome or clerks of the Pope in England or in any of his dominions, he would send them back to their home with their eyes torn out and their noses slit, so that it would be known of a certainty to what nation they belonged. As for the bishops themselves, he told them that it would be well to get out of his presence as soon as possible, if they wished to keep their own bodies safe." So the bishops, seeing no clear signs of repentance in the king, carried out the Pope's instructions and pronounced the interdict. Then, to continue the chronicle: "The King of England, distraught on account of the interdict, sent his sheriffs and other ministers of iniquity, into every part of England, with orders to compel every prelate and all their subjects, with terrible threats, to leave England immediately and go to the Pope to seek justice for the king for all this injury he had received. He ordered all the property of bishoprics, abbeys, and priories to be confiscated, and put it under the charge of laymen; but the greater number of the bishops of the whole kingdom showed discretion in this matter by refusing to leave their monasteries unless they were driven out by violence; and the royal officers, when they heard this, were loath to use violence, since they had not been so commanded by the king; but the property of them all they seized for the king's use, allowing them nevertheless, a scanty portion of food and clothing out of the proceeds. The granaries of the Church estates were locked up, by command of the king, and their contents transferred to the royal exchequer. The concubines of the presbyters and the priests were seized, throughout England, by the officers of the king, until they ransomed themselves under a heavy penalty. Any priests or ordained persons found travelling on the road, were hauled off their horses, robbed, and shamefully ill-treated by the minions of the king; and there was no one to do them justice. There came at this time to the king the officials of one of his sheriffs; and they were leading between them a robber, with his hands bound behind his back: this man had robbed and slain a certain priest on the highway; and the officers asked the king what he desired to be done to the murderer: and the king immediately answered: 'He did kill my enemy, so loose him and let him go free.' Also, the relations of the archbishop and the bishops who had placed England under the interdict, when they could be found, were seized by the command of the king, and when they were spoiled of all their goods, they were thrown into prison. As to these aforesaid prelates themselves, while all these evils were proceeding at home, they were dwelling across the sea, living in luxury instead of making themselves a bulwark for the house of God, according to the word of the Redeemer: 'When they saw the wolf coming, then they left their sheep and fled.'" Such extracts as these, harping so continually as they do on the questions of the seizing or the protection of property, make one inclined to put the strictly ecclesiastical problems on one side as rather an insignificant matter, leaving the problems of finance as the real root of the trouble. The king wanted a revenue; so did the Pope and the monks. The points of doctrine were not so important in their eyes.

With the second part of the quarrel against John, the monks and town of Canterbury had not such intimate relations as in the former part related above. Yet it was really a continuation of the same dispute, of which they had borne the first brunt. For, as a matter of fact, the mere submission of John did not settle the case. He had first to hand over the money which he had promised to pay in damages to the ecclesiastics he had dispossessed by his tyranny. The actual sums were stated in his written deed of submission. "Immediately after the arrival of that person who is deputed to absolve us, we will order a sum of eight thousand pounds sterling as restitution to be delivered over to the agents of the archbishop, bishops, and monks of Canterbury in order that they may return to England now that they are recalled to it with all honour: to wit, two thousand five hundred pounds for Stephen Langton" [to the Bishops of London, Ely, Bath, and Lincoln seven hundred and fifty pounds each], "and to the prior and monks of Canterbury one thousand pounds; and immediately this peace is finally accepted, we will cause, without delay, all the movable property of the archbishop and the bishops, and of all clerks and priests and churches, to be placed in the hands of their agents with full power to administer it freely and to take it in peace. . . . We will restore all that we have taken from ecclesiastics since the interdict, saving the custom of the kingdom and the liberty of the Church. And if any dispute shall arise concerning the amount of the property or the damage owing, then it shall be settled by the legate or agent of the lord Pope when he has heard the evidence. And when all these things have been carried out, the sentence of interdict will be withdrawn."

So, as John could not pay at once, the interdict remained still in force, and it was not relaxed until July 2, 1214, and even then John had not been able to find all the money he owed to the Church. But John now had the Pope as his formal ally, or suzerain rather, and the discontent of the kingdom, clerical or lay, was more difficult to express. It was at last expressed in the vigorous form which drew the Great Charter from John, and Stephen Langton took the leading part in that demand. But that is scarcely the history of Canterbury, except where it more immediately concerned the archbishop and the rights of his church. When his late friend, Innocent the Pope, heard the terms of the Great Charter, he exclaimed, "By St Peter, we cannot allow this insult to pass unpunished," and he issued an edict ordering the rebels against the king, his servant, to moderate their demands, and annulled the Charter. He then sent a writ of excommunication against the barons when they would not come to terms, and when Stephen Langton refused to publish this excommunication, on the ground that the Pope had been misinformed as to the facts by the cunning of the king's agents, the papal messengers at once suspended the archbishop from his duties, forbidding him to enter his church; and off he went to Rome to get the case heard by the Pope. Here he was accused of "showing favour and giving advice to the barons in their attempt to expel John from the throne," and his suspension was confirmed, and it was not until 1218, when Innocent and John were dead, that Langton returned again to Canterbury.

During his absence, Canterbury and the district of Kent had seen itself in the possession of Prince Louis of France, who had been invited by the English barons to lead them against John and to accept the crown if he could get rid of their tyrant king. John came down to Dover to oppose the landing of

THE SCREEN, CANTERBURY CATHEDRAL

the French, but soon retreated; and Louis landed unopposed at Sandwich, and soon only Dover stood out against him in that part of England. Louis took up his quarters at Canterbury, awaiting the arrival of his supporters from London; and when a sufficient force had collected round him, he set out for the capital. It is general history how the unexpected death of John allowed the English barons to return to their allegiance to his young son, Henry III., and Louis then had to make the best way back to France that he could find open. The barons would have allowed him to depart unmolested: but some irregulars in Kent tried to cut up his forces; and we find a body of English knights riding through Canterbury, on their way from London, to his assistance. Louis escaped to France, but soon returned, and his fatal blow was when his fleet in the Channel was beaten by Hubert de Burgh, fighting on the side of Henry III. The French fleet had been under the command of a late monk who had taken to pirating as a profession. This Eustace, "a bloody pirate leader," was captured after this battle off Thanet, as he was hiding in a hold of one of his ships; and Richard, an illegitmate son of the late King John, beheaded him with his own hands and sword; and they carried his head through the streets of Canterbury on a pole. This was in the autumn of 1217.

The first great event after Langton's return to England was in 1220, the fiftieth anniversary of the death of St Thomas; when, on July 7th, the remains of the famous archbishop were translated from their first hasty burial-place in the crypt to the chapel above, which we have already watched in the process of building under the guidance of the records written by Gervase. This ceremony of translation was one of the most gorgeous in the history of the cathedral. The young King Henry was present; he came on to

Canterbury after a triumphant tour round the castles of his newly won realm. Besides the king, there were present the papal legate, Pandulph, and three archbishops, and almost every bishop in England, with the abbots and priors, the earls and barons, and a great gathering of all kinds of people from all over the civilised world so far as it was Christian. Becket was now an international institution, the man who had fought for the privileges of the universal Church, and this cosmopolitan respect for his fame was well represented by the gathering on this occasion. The Pope granted exceptional indulgences to all those who were present at the ceremony itself, or within the next twenty-five days: all these were, by the Pope's grant, to be forgiven forty days of any penance they were undergoing. Further, the legate issued an order forgiving another forty days, likewise did the three archbishops; and each of the bishops remitted twenty days. It was estimated that it was thus possible to be forgiven five hundred and forty days of penance. The generosity of Langton's hospitality on this occasion, to rich and to poor, aroused the enthusiasm of the chroniclers. He built a temporary palace which, of course, the contemporary historians said had not been equalled since the time of Solomon—one of their standards of wonder. Langton, with the approval of all the ecclesiastical magnates present, pronounced that this day of the translation of Becket's remains should remain a feast day for ever.

The great ceremony had been announced throughout Christendom two years before its performance; so there was plenty of time to get the pilgrims together in numbers that had never been seen before, and the whole of the accommodation in the country round Canterbury was packed to overflowing with the travellers. The archbishop had ordered all his manors to provide provisions for man and beast, along the roads by which the pilgrims came; and there is the usual mediæval statement that the wine flowed on tap in the city itself, and poured along the gutters.

On the night before the ceremony the body was taken from its marble coffin in the foundations of the crypt, and placed in a sheet, ready for the transition to the gorgeous shrine which had been prepared in the chapel above. This shrine was of purest gold, and inlaid with the most precious gems. It is not usual to find the names of individual craftsmen recorded in mediæval chronicles; but in this case the names of Walter of Colchester, the sacrist of St Albans, and Elyas of Durham, a canon of Salisbury, are both added by Matthew of Paris to his account of the great people present at the ceremony of transition: he terms them "those incomparable craftsmen by whose advice and skill all those things were prepared which were necessary for the making of the shrine and for its setting up." In one of his accounts, the "Chronica Majora," the former name is alone given, in a marginal note, and the whole management of the translation is there ascribed to him.

This ceremony took place the day a week following the festival of St Peter and St Paul, on the anniversary of the burial of the king, Henry II., who had so much to do with the death of the martyr, St Thomas, a fact which would be undoubtedly in some way significant to the contemporary mind. The procession from the crypt to the new shrine was led by the young king, Henry, only thirteen years old; after him came Pandulph, the legate, the Archbishop Stephen, the Archbishop of Rheims, who was the Primate of France, and Hubert de Burgh, the chief lay minister of the realm. These four carried the coffin to the shrine above, and there mass was said by the Archbishop of Rheims. This placing of St

Thomas's relics in the Chapel of the Holy Trinity is a noteworthy point in the history of Canterbury; for it was this shrine that became the centre of much of its subsequent mediæval history. With that in its place, the history of this city takes a more settled course: it is henceforth established in life, as it were; its period of youthful change has passed away. The shrine itself will be discussed again in a later chapter where the subject of the pilgrimages to Becket's tomb will be discussed more fully.

When the matter of the translation was accomplished, the Archbishop Stephen Langton set off for Rome, where he had important matters to discuss with the Pope. In order probably that this high dignitary might be in the best of tempers, Langton carried with him a fragment of the precious relics of St Thomas; and Walter of Coventry tells us that it was because of this gift that he was received with great honour by the Pope and the cardinals, and by the command of the Pope he at once preached a sermon to the people, before entering the church to deposit the relics.

Langton's business with the Pope was successfully performed: he desired that three important petitions should be granted, and he gained all three. First, he asked the Pope once and for all to tell the Archbishops of York that they had no metropolitan authority in the province of Canterbury; secondly, that the papal claim of the right to present to ecclesiastical offices should never be exercised by "provisions" twice in the case of the same benefice; thirdly, that there should be no other legate recognised in England except himself, for his own lifetime, at least. This last ruling became the fixed custom; and henceforth, until the Reformation, the Archbishop of Canterbury was entitled to be the permanent legate or representative of Rome in England, though the sending of special legates, to perform special temporary duties, continued, and did much to encroach on the monopoly of the archbishops in this office.

The rest of Langton's life was mainly filled with the affairs of the nation in general, which can scarcely be called the history of Canterbury; but there was one other series of all-important events which were intimately associated with the city of Canterbury, and also were of the greatest national interest. This was the arrival of the Friars, and their position in the ecclesiastical world must be clearly grasped as a preliminary to appreciating the significance of their coming to this city.

The Friars were the latest thing in the religious development of their day. We have already, in this brief history, seen how new orders and newly expounded creeds, and new regulations had at various intervals made revolutionary phases in the progress of the Church. The monkish and hermit movements, the Benedictine Orders, the revision of these last by the newer rules of Cluny, the Cistercians, the Augustine Canons, and so on—all had been fresh starts in theological practices. Now there was another great revolution, perhaps the greatest of all. The revolutionaries of the Benedictine Orders had became conservative and reactionary. They had started out with brave resolves on the subject of hard work and self-denying poverty and strict observances of the severest rules of the ecclesiastical law. But they had one by one succumbed to the frailties of human nature. Instead of remaining poor, they had become owners of mighty possessions, which the Orders they had set out to reform (with all their wealth) would have thought riches beyond the dreams of earthly desire. Instead of strict discipline there had come laxity again. The older orders, in short, were degenerates, little better than the still older ones that had already lapsed.

Take the case of Canterbury: there were two

GREYFRIARS, CANTERBURY

great houses in the town professing to follow the rules of St Benedict: St Augustine's Abbey and Christ Church Priory were wealthy bodies of aristocrats or plutocrats who were just as worldly, almost, in their ways of living as the great lay lords and barons who were their rivals in the acquiring of lands and possessions. The people were coming to think of the Church and its officers as a vast system for procuring money out of the common man's pocket. There was an undertone in the world of Christendom asking for some one to reform the Church.

It was at this moment, at the beginning of the 1200-century, that the teaching of two men gathered together in one more attempt to reform this wayward, backsliding institution called the Church of Rome, and its offspring, the Church in England. Francis of Assisi and Dominic of Osma in Spain, the former an Italian nobleman, and the latter a canon of the Church, alike taught that self-denial must be the keynote of serious religion. It was Francis who insisted most on the vow of poverty, but at the beginning Dominic also said that want of worldly possessions could be the only safe foundation on which to build a life-work of fiery preaching, which would show the way of salvation to their fellow-men. It is said that when Francis went to the Pope Honorius, asking his permission to found an order of Begging Brethren who would receive nothing beyond the needs of the passing moment, the Pope looked at the rags of his poverty-stricken guest with sarcastic scorn and replied, "Get thee to the pigs, brother, for they seem thy fit companions." But when Francis took the words in their literal meaning and came back to the Pope with the dirt of the pig-stye added to his rags, then Honorius granted the petition with astonishment, and the Order of Franciscans was founded, the Grey Friars, as they soon were called. They were to wander over the world preaching the faith of Christ, aiding the poor and the sick—asking in payment only a scanty fare for the passing day. There was to be no storing up of riches against the morrow. Such at least was the ideal at the setting out. And the theory (and early practice) of the followers of Dominic, who became known as the Dominican or the Black Friars, was much the same as is the case of the Franciscans. And they arrived almost at the same time. We shall see the sequel.

It was within a very few days of the death of Dominic, in 1221, that Gilbert, a prior of the new Order, arrived in England and went straight to Canterbury, the chief place of the Church, an acknowledgment that they were no heretics, but faithful sons of Rome. Langton, who was then in the city, at his palace, asked Gilbert to deliver a sermon in one of the Canterbury churches; and the result was so pleasing to the archbishop, that the Dominicans became his special care. Thus, when we see, as we shall in the itinerary of the city of Canterbury, a substantial fragment of the ruins of the house which they built for themselves (it is said by the means of money given to them by Henry III.), we can know that we are looking at the first resting-place in England of one of the most important of all the Orders that the Church of Rome has ever produced. It is here we find the origin of the Friars in England.

The case of the Franciscans was very similar. It was St Francis himself who sent off to England a band of four clerks and five laymen to evangelise the land. The fact that five of the band were laymen should remind us that, as in the earlier case of the original monks of St Benedict, it was not necessary to be an ordained priest in order to join the Friars. This was one of the reasons why there was so much jealousy on the part of the ordained clergy. The Franciscan missionaries came straight to Canterbury like their brother Dominicans; and there they became the favourites of Simon Langton, the archdeacon and brother of the archbishop. We shall find the picturesque remains of the Friary which was built for them in Canterbury, spaning over the river, as was the case in the building of the Dominicans lower down the same stream.

Thus we find in Canterbury the ruins of the first houses in England of the orders of the Grey and Black Friars. With the building of these, the main lines of the social and political and ecclesiastical structure of the city of Cauterbury is now complete: the position of the archbishop, the monks of Christ Church, the shrine of Becket, the friars and the general physical outlines of the town and its buildings are all in their places. The municipal history we will leave for a chapter by itself, merely noting that it was in 1233 that Henry III. granted to the citizens the right to hold their city at a fee-farm rent, which meant, in those days, municipal freedom. The rest of the mediæval history of Canterbury will be mainly a filling-in of the details, a modification of minor points, but no great change in general principles; until at last we reach the definite and drastic change of the Reformation of the 15th century, when the heart's core of the city—Becket's shrine—will be pulled out, and Canterbury will cease to have any title henceforth, to be called a "mediæval" city.

So with the end of the reign of Stephen Langton as archbishop we close the early manhood of this city, and enter upon its period of full development. Langton died at his manor of Slindon about July 1228, and was buried in his cathedral, tradition says in St Michael's Chapel, a few days afterwards. The monks of Christ Church, "having procured a licence from the king, chose a monk out of the bosom of their church, Master Walter of Eynsham, by name," to be his successor in the primacy. But when the king heard of the choice he told them rather curtly that their man was useless to him and to the whole kingdom, that his father was a convicted thief, and that he had taken sides against King John in the matter of the interdict. The Pope, on appeal, kindly cancelled the election, after putting Walter through a stiff cross-examination by three cardinals, who put all kinds of theological posers to him. They wanted to know, for example, whether Christ, in his descent into Hell, went in body or only in spirit, and all kinds of subtle points about marriage and the sentence of excommunication; and the verdict was that his answers were bad ("male respondit)." So the archiepiscopal candidate was "ploughed," and Richard Grant took his place.

But with the appointment of Langton's successor it will be convenient to begin a new chapter.

CHAPTER XIV

The Settled Career of Canterbury

WE have thus got all the actors on the stage—the archbishops, the monks, the friars, in settled relations to one another, and the municipality of citizens independent on the basis of a free town (for freedom was then understood to be the right to pay a fixed tax to the king, without the interference of his taxing officers). The subsequent history of Canterbury until the Reformation, as we have said, is more a matter of detail, the examination of the manner in which these general principles worked themselves out. All that can be attempted in a book of this size is now a chapter giving a general view of the chief events affecting Canterbury between Stephen Langton's death and the beginning of the Reformation. There can only be a throwing of straws into the air to show the direction of the wind.

Richard Grant only lived long enough to get into serious conflict with Henry by claiming the lordship of Tunbridge Castle, and when he proceeded to excommunicate everyone who interfered with this right, the monks of Christ Church took the king's side. Richard also had trouble with the abbot of St Augustine's, who refused to acknowledge his right to consecrate him. So Richard set off to Rome, and got a decision from the Pope in favour of his claim on Tunbridge Castle, but he died on the way home to enforce his judgment.

The next archbishop, Edmund Rich (1234-1240), was one of the saintly holders of the see. He was too spiritual for his surroundings of evil-living monks (so he said), worldly popes and a money-extracting king. So he lost his nerve, after trying excommunication on the monks of Christ Church, and gave up the struggle by returning to Pontigny, where he died in 1240; and his reputation for sanctity, and all the rumours of miracles at his tomb, gained him the privilege of canonisation in 1247. The final blow, which had driven him from his office, was a papal demand that three hundred Roman priests should be admitted to English benefices. The persistent attempt of the papal Court to seize the control over the English Church is the dominant note of the ecclesiastical history of this country during the next two centuries. It was as a defence against these demands that we find the English Parliament passing the various statutes of Provisors, and the Pope of 1296 retaliated against the English tight purse by the publication of the bull "Clercis laicos," forbidding any clerics to grant money to the State in taxation, and forbidding the State officials to take it from the Church—it was the principle of the dog in the manger—if the Pope could not get the money, he did his best that no one else should have it. But that again is general history rather than the province of Canterbury. The monks of Christ Church were probably heartily sick that their rebellious conduct had so much to do with the exile of Edmund, by which event they lost for their own church the advantage of being the burial-place of another famous saint, whose tomb in Pontigny soon became a place of pilgrimage, and therefore a valuable source of income to the possessors of the church which contained it. It was by the hands of St Edmund that Henry III. and Eleanor were joined in marriage at Canterbury Cathedral on the 19th of January 1236. The lady had landed at Dover, and proceeded to Canterbury, Henry meeting her on the way, and there was a great gathering at the cathedral to witness the ceremony.

Archbishop Boniface (1245-1270) was one of the gorgeous possessors of the see of Canterbury. He was the queen's uncle, and one of the detested foreigners who were so jarring to English national feelings and so serious a loss to English purses. As a matter of fact, Boniface does not seem to have been altogether a bad sort, for he helped to free the archiepiscopal estates from the heavy debts with which Langton's profuse hospitality had burdened them: he did much to beautify the archbishop's palace in Canterbury. But he lived away from his see as much as possible, finding the Continent more congenial to his tastes; perhaps this judicious absence was not the smallest of his favour to his see, for he was not a man of much importance or learning.

Already the friars had sadly fallen away from the good resolutions formed at their start. Matthew Paris is most cutting when he describes their rapid fall from holy living. Writing under the date 1243 he says: "A controversy arose between the Minorite brethren [the Francescans] and, the Preachers [the Dominicans] to the astonishment of many, for it seemed that they had chosen the path of perfection when they went the way of poverty and patience." But now they had already began to quarrel as to which had the greater claim to holiness—a sure sign that there was not much holiness to squabble over. The Dominicans said that the Franciscans had no claim to be more rigorous than the Dominicans, for they indulged, even in public, in eating flesh and other dainties, whereas the Dominicans were far stricter: it was not enough that the Francescans should go about barefoot, with a rope round their waists. Then Matthew Paris says what he himself thinks of these rival friars: how, within twenty-four years, or so, of their arrival with pious declarations, they had sunk to ruin faster even than the old monastic orders who, after all, had lasted three or four hundred years without any worse results than had happened to these friars in twenty-five, for now, already, in spite of all their avowals of poverty, they had " built in England dwellings which were the equal of kings' palaces in height. Thus they daily make manifest their endless riches by enlarging their luxurious houses and building high walls, which so violate the rules of their early poverty and the basis of their creed. When nobles and rich men are dying—these friars do urge them to make secret wills and confessions in favour of their own Order, to the injury and loss of the proper parish priests. There is now no righteous man who thinks he can be saved except by the counsels of the Preachers and the Minorites. Wishful of obtaining privileges in the courts of kings and nobles, these friars do act the part of councillors, chamberlains, treasurers, bridegrooms, and agents for marriages ; they are also the collectors of the papal extortions ; in their sermons, they are flatterers or reproachers in turn. They despise the authorized orders sanctioned by the holy fathers, St Benedict and St Augustine, and their followers, and set their community before all others. They look down on the Cistercian monks as clownish and ill-bred priests, and the monks of the Black Order they regard as haughty epicures." [1]

Of course, the houses of the friars in Canterbury never reached the size of the Black and Grey Friaries in London ; however, they were sufficiently successful, in a worldly way, to rouse the bitter opposition of the Christ Church regulars and the parish church priests of the town. Nevertheless, the friars were so exceedingly popular with the general laity in their earlier years, that it was a dangerous thing to oppose

[1] For some reason or another, Matthew Paris cancelled most of this passage in a later copy of his history ; but there is no cause for thinking that the general statement was far from the truth.

their will, lest it should bring the opposers into popular disrepute. Thus, we find the monks of Christ Church, in 1294, driven against their will to make a free gift of some land and houses in the neighbourhood of the Grey-friary, which these friars had seized on years ago, and had then refused to pay any rent therefor.

Another instance of rivalry between the houses of Christ Church and the friars for popular favour is shown at this same period; when we find the angry citizens using the churchyard of the Black Friars as a meeting-place to protest against the refusal of the monks of Christ Church to pay a share of the expenses of fitting out men to take part in the war in Wales. Edward had ordered the city of Canterbury to provide twelve horsemen, as its share of the burden, but the monks said they were not liable for any such military tax, and refused to pay. Whereupon the citizens, under the leadership of William Childham, the bailiff, met in the Black friary and passed the following resolutions: "That they would overthrow the pentises, windows, and miln belonging to the monks; that no citizen should dwell in any house belonging to the monks; that all rents belonging to the monks of Canterbury should be gathered to the use of the Commons [citizens]; that no man should send or sell to the monks any victuals; that they should seize all the horses and beasts that came into the city with carriage to the monks; that all such monks as came forth of their house should be spoiled of their garments; that a trench should be cast, to stop all men from going in or coming out; that every pilgrim at his entering should sware that he would make no offering; also that every one of those Commons aforesaid should wear on their finger a ring of gold that belonged to Thomas Becket."

This was militant political action with a vengeance; but we may take it as not an abnormal state in the relations between the townsmen and the monks during this period: the former probably thought that the monks got more than their fair share out of the Becket shrine; and we can imagine all the scandals about the monks being passed round the city with malicious glee. The actual quarrel related above was settled by a compromise brought about by Archbishop Kilwardby, who held the see between 1273-1278. He was himself a Dominican, and had been their provincial prior in England; he was the first of the friars to reach a high ecclesiastical office in the English Church. He attended to his ecclesiastical business better than did most of his predecessors and immediate successors; and had little to do with politics. He was a great deal in Canterbury and a frequent preacher in his Cathedral and busied himself a great deal with the organisation of his province. Indeed, he seems to have been so attached to its affairs that when he was made a cardinal, and therefore compelled to resign the see of Canterbury, he took away with him to Rome all the registers and documents relating to the see. He also seems at the same time to have been attached to five thousand marks in money, valuable church vessels and hangings, and manuscripts, all of which he took off to Rome; and in spite of all endeavours nothing came back to Canterbury. It is possible that these early registers of the archbishopric of Canterbury may still be in existence: but, as it is, all our official documents of this kind begin with Archbishop Peckham, who succeeded Kilwardby in 1279.

Peckham was another friar, this time a Franciscan, of which Order he was the ninth provincial minister in England. One of the popes took a fancy to him in earlier days, and he was made a professor in the papal school at Rome. When he came back to England as archbishop he was filled with high notions of ecclesiastical rights over the lay state; and there is much in his history which will interest the theological and ecclesiastical expert. When an archbishop he still continued to wear the poor clothing of a friar, and if his ecclesiastical theories were haughty, he was humble for himself. He died in 1292, and his tomb is one of the sights of the Cathedral to this day: it stands in the martyrdom transept.

Archbishop Winchelsea (1294-1313) had an exciting career in our national history; and his local affairs in Canterbury were not without exhilaration, for on one occasion, in 1303, a mob of the citizens broke into the palace while the archbishop was in residence, and almost killed a dean who had carried some of Winchelsea's autocratic orders into execution. The official writ of inquiry into this affair states that certain persons "notwithstand the king's ordinance for the preservation of the peace during his absence in Scotland, by night invaded the archbishop's dwelling-place at Canterbury while he was in it, cut to pieces and broke the gates, assaulted his servants and ministers, carried away his goods, and took Richard Christian, the archbishop's dean of Osprenge, whom he had sent to Sellinges, Co. Kent, to make certain citations and do other things that were incumbent upon him by reason of his spiritual office, threw him into filthy mud, and with his face turned to his horse's tail, holding the tail in his hand instead of the bridle, compelled him to ride through the middle of the town of Sellinges, afterwards cut off the tail of his said horse and its ears, and prevented him from exercising the office committed to him by the archbishop." Another account adds that there were "songs and dances" thrown in to enliven the procession as it passed through Sellinges, and they finished up by another rolling in the mud, after the ride. Winchelsea had great struggles with Edward I., but he appeared to have been on generous terms with the humbler folk and gave away two or three thousand loaves of bread each Thursday and Sunday, so one is not surprised to hear that he only just escaped being canonised as a saint. It was during his term of office that the marriage took place, in Canterbury Cathedral, of Edward I., then sixty years old, to the young Margaret of France; and the wedding feast was held in the great hall of the archbishop's palace.

Archbishop Reynolds (1313-1327) seems to have been one of the easy going sort who liked to be on good terms with everyone, and succeeded in changing sides with sufficient rapidity and discretion to live through those troublesome times. When the difficulty of chosing between Queen Isabella and Edward II. became particularly acute, Prior Eastry of Christ Church (who built the screen round the choir of the Cathedral and whose name is often attached to the large window in the St Anselm Chapel, though it was really his successor's work, in 1336), advised him to get over the problem by taking sanctuary in the Cathedral until the trouble was over. The people Reynolds really pleased were the monks of Christ Church, to whom he was most obliging, and they had a good time under his patronage. This is a sample of the things he did which pleased them so much: he gave them the manor of Caldicot and the wood of Thorolt, ancient possessions of the archbishopric; and Reynolds got the Pope's licence for the transfer. The Pope's letter on the subject is of interest; it runs: "The manor of Caldicot, with the adjacent land belonging to it is of the value of ten pounds and is in the possession of the Archbishops of Canterbury for the use of their table, and is situated near Canterbury: this possession the Monks of Christ Church did earnestly desire; that the manor with the adjacent lands might be granted to them for ever for their own use, inasmuch as it was a convenient place for the monks to retire unto and recreate themselves when they had been let blood, or when they were tired and wearied with much labour."

But these Canterbury monks were now, thanks in great part to the virtues of St Thomas, in a well-established position; and they were quite able to look after themselves in a worldly way, without much patronage. The monastery of Christ Church was a little town on its own, as we may see from the list of the inhabitants of the monastery which was drawn up in the year 1322. This list is worth giving at length, for it is a very living picture of the backstairs life of the monasteries, which leaves a fuller impression of the reality, perhaps, than any amount of documents narrating the coming and going of kings and nobles and archiepiscopal dignitaries.

The cellarer seems to have had under him a whole army of subordinates to whom he paid wages in money and in food. Among these officials and servants, inscribed under the cellarer's charge, were: The seneschal of the liberties (who was usually a knight) and his clerk; the steward of the great hall; two janitors of the precinct gates; the pantler and his boy; the doorkeeper of the cloister and his boy; the pantler of the great hall; the vigil curiæ; the scullion of the hall and his boy; the potagiarius (or cook for the delicacies); the scullion of the refectory and his boy; the first and second cooks and their boys; the salter and his boy; the kitchen stoker; the wine measurer; the cook's messenger; the wine-bearer and his boy; the cellarer's esquire, his groom and his carter with two boys; the huntsman and his boy; the porter ot the guest hall and his boy; one odd servant; a gaoler; and two others. That is thirty-eight servants under the cellarer alone.

The other senior officers of the monastery have other servants under their control: thus, in the bake-house there was a master-baker and seven others; in the brewhouse a master-brewer and seven others; in the sacristy there were eighteen officers, including two clerks of Our Lady's altar, one at the tomb of St Thomas, one in the Martyrdom Chapel, four ringers, the embroiderer, a washerwoman, and a plumber. The so-called clerks in this instance were seculars and not priests; in the chamberlain's office there were fourteen officials, including the leather-dresser, the chief shoemaker, the bath attendant, and three men in the laundry; in the treasurer's office there were eight officials including two collectors of rents; in the Infirmary there were four; in the prior's chamber and stable there were over eleven servants; and besides all these there were such various persons as sixteen ringers for the bell tower or campanile, organ-blowers, banner bearer, and general scrubbers or charwomen.

Here we have a list of between one hundred and thirty or forty officials and servants, mainly to administer to the lay wants of the monastery and Cathedral. It will be noted that quite a fair proportion of them were for the personal service upon the monks, who at this time numbered about eighty. This was during the priorship of Henry of Eastry (1285-1331), who has left us a statement of the business affairs of his monastery during the first thirty-seven years of his office. They reveal the vast wealth of the establishment.

When he came into office there were twenty-one law-suits running against the house, a sign of its widely-spread interests and possessions. A sum of over two thousand pounds was spent in these years on the fabric and ornaments of the Cathedral and the monastic buildings. The gifts and "exactions" paid to the king and his family reach the sum of over four thousand pounds. The manors of the monastery had almost another four thousand pounds spent for their benefit. The prior reports that his total expenditure on behalf of the monastery during these thirty-seven years was over twenty-three thousand pounds: this, being changed into its equivalent at present-day prices, would equal about three hundred and sixty thousand pounds sterling. It is by business details of this kind that we can most easily realise what a vast social organism was this monastery of Christ Church; and when we add its ecclesiastical influence to its power as the possessor of material wealth, when we realise that it was a capitalist company as well as a spiritual father, then we can begin to grasp the significance of the name of Christ Church in our history.

It was during Reynolds' time that Canterbury saw a vigorous part of the civil wars between the great Court factions of Edward II.'s reign. Edward's queen, Isabella, had, in the October of 1321, been on her way to Canterbury, when she asked hospitality of Lady Badlesmere, who was then in charge of her husband's castle at Leeds in Kent: there are reasons for suspecting that this pilgrimage to Canterbury was only an excuse for taking Leeds Castle by surprise. She was refused admittance, and when she tried to rush the castle with her few followers they were badly beaten back. Isabella roused her husband to come down and wipe out the insult, and he brought an army which captured the castle and hanged many of its defenders. But Badlesmere was not at home, so he remained uncaptured. It was in the following year that he rode into Canterbury with nineteen knights having armour concealed beneath their fur coats, and thus visited the shrine of St Thomas, with his esquires openly bearing their swords. The citizens made an immediate complaint to the king of this behaviour, which they considered riotous and sacrilegious. When the offender was captured elsewhere, soon afterwards he was conducted to Canterbury and there drawn to the gallows at Blean; and, after hanging, his head was fixed on a pole at the Burgate entrance of the city.

Archbishop Mepeham (1328-1333) got into a serious row with the monks of St Augustine's Abbey, and when he refused to pay the costs of the action which the Pope's deputy decided against him, then he was excommunicated, and since he died at that moment, the abbot of St Augustine's had to absolve the body from the sentence before it could be buried with the full rites of the Church. His fine tomb still stands in the Cathedral at the entrance to St Anselm's Chapel.

Archbishop John of Stratford (born in Shakespere's town), 1333-1348, his successor, has also left us a fine tomb in the Cathedral. He was rather a statesman than an ecclesiastic, and his chief work was in the national history, not in that of Canterbury. The succeeding archbishops: Bradwardine (1349); Simon Islip (1349-1366); Simon Langham (1366-1368), a Benedictine monk; and Wittesley (1368-1374), made no very definite marks in the history of Canterbury or its see: but there are one or two events of their time which must be recorded.

It was in 1357 that the Black Prince came back to England in triumph after his great victory at Poitiers in the September of the previous year. According to Froissart (who is, however, contradicted by other historians) the Prince, after an eleven days' passage from Bordeaux, arrived at the port of Sandwich on the 16th of April, where he disembarked with his party, "and took up their quarters in the town and neighbourhood. They remained there two days to refresh themselves, and, on the third, set out and came to Canterbury. The king and prince remained one day at Canterbury, where they made their offerings to the shrine of St Thomas. On the morrow they rode to Rochester."

The king mentioned in this narrative was that King John of France who was the Black Prince's chief spoil at the battle of Poitiers; he had been able to keep very few prisoners, for the French army was almost five times as numerous as the whole English force. But King John had been brought as his great note of triumph.

In 1363 the Black Prince, in commemoration of his marriage to his cousin Joan, Countess of Kent, founded a chantry in the Cathedral of Canterbury. We shall find the chapel during our itinerary of the church, where it now forms part of the French chapel in the crypt. The endowment of chantry priests about this time became the fashionable form of religious exercise for wealthy people; the priests were to continue to pray for the welfare, alive or dead, of their benefactor. By this process, the advantages of both donor and priests were fitly served; a priest or a religious house was granted an income, and the soul of the donor was made secure for heaven. Thus, in this case we are now considering, the Black Prince, in return for the right to these chantry priests' services, presented to Christ Church his manor of Fawkes Hall (now Vauxhall) near London, which is now a part of the metropolis, but then a village opposite Westminster, beyond the River Thames. The deed of gift says that the two priests are to be fit, sober, and honest men, not given to quarrels in courts of law, neither unchaste nor otherwise notably vicious, and they are to be under the control of the archbishop of the day. The altar of one priest was to be dedicated to the Holy Trinity and the other to the Virgin Mary; and we can still trace the position of these two altars in the chapel.

The other event of the Black Prince's life which is intimately connected with Canterbury was the last of all, his burial in the Cathedral in the year 1376.

BLACK PBINCE'S TOMB, CANTERBURY CATHEDRAL

He had died at Westminster on the 8th of June; the body had lain in state at that place, and then it was taken to Canterbury that it might be buried on the spot, and after the minute directions, expressed in the will which probably he had caused to be written a few hours before his death. "We leave our soul to God our Creator, to the Holy Blessed Trinity, to the glorious Virgin Mary, and to all the saints; and our body we do leave to be buried in the Church of the Trinity [as Christ Church was sometimes called], Canterbury, where the body of that true martyr, the lord St Thomas, does lie, in the middle of the chapel of Our Lady of the Undercroft." It will be noted that this direction was not followed, for the tomb was placed in the Chapel of the Holy Trinity, above, near by, the body of St Thomas. The other instructions for the funeral were apparently obeyed as the will commanded. "We desire, at the hour when our body shall be taken through the city of Canterbury to the priory, that two chargers, covered with our arms and bearing two men clad in our armour, shall go before it; one bearing our arms of war, the other bearing our ostrich feathers of peace; each of these men who bear our banners shall have on his head our helmet. We desire that the herse shall be carried before the high altar where vigils and masses and the divine services may be performed." As we have said, the body was taken after these services, to the Chapel of the Holy Trinity instead of the Undercroft, as the will goes on to direct. "Further, we give and bequeath to the High Altar of the church, our vestment of green velvet embroidered with gold," and many other personal possessions are also commanded in the will to be presented to the Cathedral or certain of its altars. The tomb has the shield of arms, and the inscription written around it, which he also specified in this will.

It was in the spring of this same year (1376) that Simon Sudbury had been enthroned as archbishop in Canterbury. He was not of orthodox opinions for a

WEST GATE, CANTERBURY—SIDE FACING TOWN, INNER SIDE

holder of the see. At least, the story goes that when, five years before his enthronement, he had passed on the road some pilgrims going to worship at St Thomas's shrine, he had spoken scornfully of their waste of time in going on such vain journeys, when they should be showing their repentance by good works. It was on this occasion that the knight, Sir Thomas of Aldon in Kent, in reply made the prophecy, "My lord bishop, why do you seek to stir up the people against St Thomas? By my soul, your life will end in a foul death." If the prophecy was thus made, it certainly was truly fulfilled, as we soon shall see.

But before describing the events which led up to Sudbury's violent death (events which in great part were schemed and begun in Canterbury, though the actual death of the archbishop was in London) we must describe the last great period of architectural building in Canterbury which Sudbury inaugurated. In the city itself he rebuilt the West Gate as it now stands, and he also repaired the walls from this point to the North Gate, just behind the archi-episcopal palace. But it was the plan of the reconstruction of the nave of the Cathedral which was his great work. It was in the December of 1378 that Sudbury published an appeal to the clergy of his diocese, asking for their earnest support in collecting funds for the rebuilding of the nave of his church. The one which was then in existence had stood since Lanfranc began it shortly after the Norman Conquest, and finished it about 1077. It was now in a very ruinous condition ("propter ipsius notorium et evidentem ruinam" run the words of Sudbury's appeal). Apparently during his term of office the work got no further than pulling down the old building. Almost the whole of this part of the church was raised level with the ground, but probably leaving the Norman foundations, and certain parts of the walls of the transepts, and also the main piers of the central tower, while the whole of the north-west tower was left standing until 1834.

The new nave which arose on these foundations

CHRIST CHURCH GATE, CANTERBURY

was mainly put up during the term of office of the prior Thomas Chillenden, and probably under his immediate supervision, for which reason it fitly bears the name of Chillenden's Nave. He was prior between 1391 and 1411, during the archiepiscopates of Courtney (1381-1396) and Arundel (1396-1414), and he may well have had charge of the work before he became prior. As Professor Willis points out, the building operations were carried out by the monks of the priory of Christ Church, while the archbishops assisted in finding the funds; thus Arundel gave the livings of Godersham and Westwell, two Kent parsonages, as an endowment fund to meet the rebuilding expenses; he also gave a thousand marks, as did, likewise, Archbishop Courtney.

This new nave was built, as it remains, in the manner of the last phase of Gothic, the Perpendicular style, when the straight lines of the mouldings and tracery were approaching the rectangular form of the Tudor and Jacobean Renaissance. It remains to us as a monument of the reigns of Richard II. and Henry IV., and the period which we always associate with the stormy days of the Peasant Rising and the Wycliffe controversies which followed the great Black Death of 1349.

Besides the nave, the cloisters and the Chapter House were included in the rebuilding of this period. So that by the year 1411 we could have seen the main outlines of Canterbury Cathedral very much as we see them to-day—with one very important exception, however; the central tower remained for a long time not much higher than the roof-line. It was not until 1495 that the great Angel Tower was completed during the office of Prior Goldstone II., the same prior being responsible for the beautiful main gateway by which the traveller usually enters the precincts from the main High Street of the city. So that this west end of the Cathedral may be, roughly, grouped within the century which saw the beginning and end of the struggle between the White Rose Yorkists and the Red Rose Lancastrians.

We have seen how Archbishop Sudbury's intentions were suddenly interrupted by his death in 1381. The story is a part of our national history which is also an intimate part of the local history of Canterbury, for the Peasant Rising, which was the cause of the tragedy, was specially a product of Kent. The scarcity of labour which followed the depopulation by the Black Death plague of 1349, had enabled the peasants, in some parts of England, to claim a greater share in the products of their labour. At least the peasants were filled with a new pride in their personal rights; there was a spirit of freedom abroad, and circumstances brought it to a head in 1381, when the demand of a poll tax (that is, so much per poll or head, of the population) raised the storm. The peasants of Essex were the first in the field, but by the beginning of June, Kent was stirring. By the seventh day of the month Maidstone was in the hands of the rebels, and Rochester Castle, with its governor, fell into their hands almost immediately after. By the 10th the rebels, headed by Wat Tyler himself, had entered Canterbury in triumph with a joyful welcome from the citizens, who were on their side, having no desire to pay the poll tax. There was no general bloodshed, though the rebels asked the citizens to name any avowed enemies of their cause who were in the town, and two or three of these were immediately beheaded. Or perhaps the citizens suggested the executions to get rid of some objectionable local tyrants or opponents.

The general demand of the rebels may be judged by the terms of some of the charges brought against them in the courts of law after the first panic was over. Thus, to take a case near Canterbury, we find four men in Thanet accused of having "raised a cry that no tenant should do service or custom to the lordships in Thanet, as they have aforetime done, under pain of forfeiture of their goods and cutting off their heads. And also that they should not suffer any distress to be taken under the above-said penalty." It was equally as dangerous to be lawful as rebellious under those conditions. "And also the aforesaid men raised another cry on the day of the feast of Corpus Christi, at St Laurence in Thanet, that every liegeman of our lord the king ought to go to the house of William Medmenham and abolish his house and level it with the ground, and fling out the books and rolls found there, and burn them with fire, and if the said William could be found, that they should kill him and cut off his head from his body under like penalty; and they ordered a taxation to be paid for maintaining the said proceedings against the lordships throughout the whole Isle of Thanet, except the tenants of the priory of Canterbury and the franchise of Canterbury. By virtue of which cry, these same men entered the house of the said William and burnt the aforesaid rolls and books and did no other harm to the said William."

Then we read that "William the Capellan, officiating in the Church of St John, in the Isle of Thanet," incited the people to attack this William.

Of course all these statements are the assertions of these opponents; as is admitted above, the rebels did no personal harm to William, and there was little personal violence which could be definitely ascribed to the peasants' own action.

In Canterbury itself (which remained the headquarters of the Kentish rising after the bulk of the peasants had marched to the general rally in London) there were, says Mr Trevelyan,[1] not more than two or

[1] England in the Age of Wycliffe, by G. M. Trevelyan (Longmans).

three murders: and one gathers that these were settlements of private grudges, and had little or nothing to do with the rebellion and its principles. The events of the rebels' arrival in Canterbury are told in another charge sheet where we read that: "John Sales of Malling, on the Monday aforesaid, came to Canterbury with a great multitude of the enemies of our Lord the King, by him raised and assembled, and feloniously broke open the houses of Thomas Holt, William of Medmenham, John Tebbe, the Castle of Canterbury, the Town Hall of Canterbury, Sir Richard de Hoo, knight, Thomas de Garwenton, and Sir Thomas Fog, knight, and stole and carried away goods, chattels, and muniments, to the value of a thousand pounds, and feloniously set free the prisoners that were in the said Castle and Town Hall; and they say that he was the first and principal originator of the insurrection and levying of all the enemies of our Lord the King."

From another writ we learn that the peasants were also charged with seizing the sheriff of Kent from the Castle, and that dragging him with them, they compelled him to deliver up all the books, papers, and writs of his office; and that these documents they burned. There are many records of such burning of legal documents during this popular rising, for the peasants, with simple-hearted faith, hoped that when these deeds and parliament were destroyed, then there would no longer be any possibility of servitude under their lords and masters. Another charge, says that there were fifty rolls of the pleas of the county and of the Crown destroyed on this day in Canterbury, besides other writs.

Of course, Canterbury was in a very unruly state of mind, and here (from yet another judicial presentment) is the kind of thing that was going on: "they say that on the Monday aforesaid, the said Henry Bongay raised a certain assembly of the enemies of our Lord the King, viz., Nicholas Royle, late servant of Nicholas Glovere, Simon Sletton, tailor, and many others unknown, who came to the house of Robert Sherman, in Canterbury, and feloniously broke open the chambers and chests of the said Robert, and took and carried away divers of his muniments, and also compelled the said Robert, to pay a ransom of ten marks sterling." Again, a body of men broke into the house of William Medmenham, as we have seen, and took away goods and chattels to the value of ten pounds. Then Henry Bongay, who appears to have been particularly wild in his behaviour, also "came with force and arms to the house of William Watshipe in Canterbury, and threatened that he would burn down his house unless he delivered to him the keys of a certain shop and cellar situated near the Church of St Andrew, and feloniously compelled the foresaid William to pay him forty shillings." There is certainly a suspicion of private business about this piratical excursion.

But the main army was soon transferred to London, on which the peasants were converging from the surrounding districts. All this time they were maintaining that they were fighting on the side of the king, the boy Richard, and his parliament, and it was his traitorous councillors on whom they preferred to ask that justice should be done, and one of their most hated enemies was Simon Sudbury, the Archbishop of Canterbury. During their brief stay in Canterbury (it was only one day) they had surrounded the monastery of Christ Church with their angry cry that the monks must soon choose a new primate, for the present one was about to be executed by them in London. It was during Mass that they broke into the Cathedral to make this announcement, and it is said they went there even before they had visited the Town Hall to demand the allegiance of the city officers, the mayor and bailiffs, so marked a man was Sudbury.

As the Kentish peasants passed through Maidstone, on their way to London, they added John Ball to their ranks. He had been lying in prison, whither he had been sent by Sudbury for preaching rebellion against the established orders: "beguiling the ears of the laity by invectives, and putting about scandals concerning our own person, as also those of other prelates, and (what is far worse) using concerning our Holy Father, the Pope himself, dreadful language, such as shock the ears of Christians." Ball, if he had lived to-day, would have have been labelled as a "dangerous agitator" and accused of various evil opinions by the orthodox press. He seems to have been set on the putting down of the tyranny of lay lords and church dignitaries. But the point that concerns us here is that when he joined Wat Tyler at Maidstone, it did not tend to lessen the anger against Sudbury.

Two days after leaving Canterbury the peasants had encamped on Blackheath: this was the 12th of June. Here it was that John Ball preached them a sermon with the famous couplet for his text:—

"When Adam dalf and Eve span,
Who was then a gentleman?"

The listeners cried out that when Sudbury's head was off they would make Ball their chancellor and archbishop in one. Soon they were in possession of London, and Sudbury, who was in the Tower, was surrounded and tried in vain to escape through their ranks. There was scarcely any private plundering, it was justice they clamoured for—according to their lights: they even hanged a man who was discovered stealing a silver cup. Within a few minutes of their breaking through the gates of the Tower, Sudbury's head was off on Tower Hill, and with the head of Hales, the Lord Treasurer, was paraded through the City on pikes, and then mounted over London Bridge. But all the other momentous events connected with these belong to the national history, and we have only to pick out what particularly belongs to Canterbury. After Sudbury's death London became a scene of murderous riot, probably in great part the work of discontented persons who seized their opportunity, although they had no sympathy with the original rebellion. The final crushing of all rebellion, just or unjust, was not long in its accomplishment; but there is one interesting record of the position in Canterbury on the 1st of July when we read: "John Gyboun of Maidstone came to the Town Hall, before the bailiffs of the City of Canterbury, and required the said bailiffs to make levy of the whole community of the said city, to resist the lords and justices assigned to keep the peace of our Lord the King in the county of Kent." But it was a last despairing effort to get the more established orders to give help to the peasant's cause; and we soon find that the aiders and abettors of Sudbury's death were being brought before the justices.

After Sudbury's death, the aristocratic William Courtney succeeded (1381-1396). His stage was mainly the national history; but he was, as we have seen, interested in the rebuilding of the nave of his Cathedral, which was in progress during his time. And he also procured from the Crown a charter licensing four fairs every year within the precincts of Christ Church priory, each to last for the nine days following "the four principle feasts of peregrination," these being: Innocent's-day, Whitsun-eve, the eve of Becket's transition, and Michaelmas-eve. Although these have long since disappeared from the Cathedral precincts, it is probable that, at least, the annual

October festivities outside the walls are a survival of the Michaelmas fair ; and if the traveller goes the giddy circle of the roundabouts, he may remember that his pastimes are mingled with the deeds of this Archbishop Courtney of Richard II.'s reign. When the French threatened to invade England, Courtney took vigorous measures to compel the clergy of the city of Canterbury to furnish their share of men and armour. Courtney also had a dispute with the citizens as to the right of their serjeants to come into the Cathedral bearing their maces, and it was agreed that henceforth the maces should be left at the gates whenever the serjeants had business within. This was a distinct rebuff to the citizens; and there was another decision against them when Courtney ordered the bailiffs to cesae from meddling in ecclesiastical cases, such as the punishment of adultery ; and if they disobeyed his ruling he threatened to put the city under an interdict. His tomb is near that of the Black Prince in the Trinity Chapel.

Thomas Arundel, who succeeded him (1396-1414), also saw the continued rebuilding of the Nave, and his memory has lasted in the Arundel Tower, though the present one is not the same Norman tower in which this archbishop placed his five bells, and thus gave it his name. He was banished for high treason by Richard II. ; and is said to have lectured the king at great length, before his departure, on the extravagance and greed of the Court. On the victory of Henry IV. and the murder of Richard II., Arundel returned to his post. During the last year of his office Henry IV. was buried in the Cathedral on the Trinity Sunday of 1413, when Henry V. was present. Henry IV. had given considerable funds for the rebuilding of the Nave.

But the archbishops of the succeeding period were great statesmen and wealthy magnates of the whole nation, rather than peculiarly bound up with the history of Canterbury itself. Both Courtney and Arundel had been Chancellors of England. Archbishop

EAST SITE OF CANTERBURY CATHEDRAL

Chicheley (1414-1443), of humbler birth, paid considerable attention to ecclesiastical affairs, but not particular attention to Canterbury. During his long term of office nothing of great importance seems to have happened in the way of local history. Sigismund, King of the Romans, was in Canterbury in 1416, and while in this city he met Henry V. and signed a treaty of alliance with him. Chicheley has left to posterity his handsome tomb in the choir.

Archbishops Strafford (1443-1452), Kemp (1452-1454), Bourchier (1454-1486), Morton (1486-1500), Dean (1501-1503) must be passed by mere naming. During this time, about 1495, the great central tower was finished by Prior Goldstone II., and called the Bell Harry Tower, after a bell presented by Henry VIII. From this date the outlines of the Cathedral have remained to this day almost unchanged, except for the North-West Tower, which remained as Lanfranc had left it until it was entirely rebuilt in 1834, as we now have it.

During these years Canterbury saw a good deal of reigning monarchs. Between 1439 and 1456 Henry visited Canterbury eleven times, as a pilgrim or otherwise ; and his Queen Margaret also accompanied him. Edward IV., his successor, was also at least six times in Canterbury between 1460 and 1471. In 1469 he came for the purpose of hanging Nicholas Faunte, the mayor of the city, because he had given assistance to Falconbridge, termed Robert the Bastard, who had been an ally of Warwick the King-maker, the uncle of Falconbridge, and a Lancastrian. With Nicholas, the mayor, died many others for their rebellious designs. For this misconduct of the mayor, Edward took the governorship of the city of Canterbury into his own hands and put a custos, or warden, in charge until the following January, when he restored the liberties of the citizens and their own officers.

Archbishop Warham (1503-1532) deserves a a longer date, both on his own account, and because he is the last archbishop of Catholic Canterbury : he may be regarded as the symbol of the end of the mediæval history of the city. He was apparently a man of complex and charming character. Gorgeous, for example, in his entertainment of others, he was frugal himself. He was most generous to Erasmus, and he saw the Reformation proceeding before his eyes and against his will. Happily for his peace he died just before the crisis came. But we can only record the facts of his local history.

Dugdale gives a lengthy account of the ceremonials, and mainly the feasting, at his enthronement in 1504. It takes a big folio page of the book to record all the officers; beginning with Edward, Duke of Buckingham, who was "hygh stewarde of the feast, and Sir Edward Poynings as chamberlain. The order of service of the meals was most precise: "The lorde archbishop sittynge in the middle of the hygh boorde alone, whiche was serued in this order: first, the duke on horseback; ii. The heralds of arms; iii. The Seruer. iv. The service every dishe in his order." The first course consisted of the following; "Frumentie ryall and mamononie to potage; Lyng in foyle; Cunger p. in foyle; Lampreys with galantine. Pyke in latmer sauce. Cunger. Halibut. Salmon in foyle. Carp in sharpe sauce. Eels rost. Samon baked. Custarde planted. Lecke florentine. Frytter-dolphin." Then came a set-piece: "A subtyltie as the last dish serued at the same course, of three stages, with vanes and towres embateled, and in the first our lady, and the king presentyng the sayde lorde in the habite of the maister of the rolles, vnto Saint Paule, sitting in a towre betwixt Saint Peter and Saint Erkenwalde." And the figures made elaborate speeches in Latin verse, expressed by rolls proceeding from their mouths. Then came another course, longer than the last, and then more "subtilties." "In the first, the sayde lorde kneelyng, ravished as he goeth to masse, before the Pope sytting on a throne with cardinals about him, with other bishops puttyng the pall upon his neck, the pope extending his hande to the ende of the pall with these verses." Then we are told in full what the Duke had for a repast in his own room when he had started the archbishop at his first course. Then follows what the brethren of the monastery had. The frugal Warham must have had difficulty in maintaining his reputation in such a maze of feasting.

In 1518 Warham received the papal legate, Cardinal Campeggio, at Canterbury. It was the latter's first visit to England; he had come to collect money for a Crusade against the Turks. In 1520, during the month of May, the archbishop was receiving the Emperor Charles V. and Henry VIII., who were discussing foreign policy, and the great hall of the archbishop's palace was the place of their banquet. The whole visit was evidently very well mounted, to use a theatrical phrase, which perhaps is the most appropriate term for the occasion, for at this moment the sovereigns of Europe were trying to make the most vivid appearance in the eyes of their fellows. An account of the present meeting says that Charles, the newly-elected emperor, came to Dover, "where the King met him, and did accompany him to Canterbury, and were received together, ryding under one Canapie, at St George's Gate at Canterbury, and Cardinal Wolsey, riding next before them, with the chiefest of the nobility of England and Spain. And on both sides of the streets stoude all the clerks and priests, that were within twenty myles of Canterbury, with long Censures, Crosses, Surplesses, and Copes of the richest, and so they rode, still under the Canapie, until they came unto the west door of the Church, where they alighted and were entertained there and wayghted on by the bishop of Canterbury, and so sayd their devotions and went into the archbishop's Palace upon Whitsunday. And one night of the sayd Whitsun-week there made in the great Hal of the sayd Palace wherein danced the Emperour with the Queen of England, the King of England with the Queen of Arragon, the Emperour's Mother. This triumph being donne, the Tables were covered in the sayd Hall, and the banqueting dishes were served in, before which rode the Duke of Buckingham, as server, upon a white Hobby, and in the midst of the Hall was a partition of boords, at which partition the Duke alighted off from his Hobby and kneeled on his Knee, and that done took again his horse back, until he was almost half way unto the table, and then alygthed and did the same as before; and then rode to the Table where he delivered his Hobby and served kneeling at the table where the Emperour was. And the King with his retinue kept the other end of the Hall."

Charles had come on this visit that he might get Henry's ear before the latter met Francis I. of France. And to make matters surer Charles promised Wolsey (when they met at Canterbury) that he would give him a pension of 7000 ducats and all the influence that could be used in the direction of procuring for him the papal throne itself. So that Wolsey, at least, must have considered this visit to Canterbury one of the most memorable times of his life.

Warham then accompanied Henry on his immediately following visit to Francis at the Field of the Cloth of Gold. In 1522 the Emperor was again in Canterbury, but Warham was too ill to meet him, though Henry was again there as his host and fellow-schemer against Francis, to whom Henry's heralds were at the very moment reading a declaration of war. There had been some exterior reason for the former visit of 1520, for that was the third-hundredth's anniversary of the transition of the relics of St Thomas to the tomb in Trinity Chapel. But this second visit was purely political, without any special excuse to cover their scheming.

It was in 1525 that Canterbury was profoundly stirred by the news that a serving-maid in the parish of Aldington (it was this living that Warham had given to Erasmus), about twelve miles from the city, had begun to speak prophesies. There had been some kind of trances, and in one of these she had referred to the death of her master's child. When this event took place within a short time, her reputation as a prophetess was established, and pilgrims rushed to the shrine of Our Lady at Court-at-Street, where she gave audiences. The news of a rival miracle-worker brought the ecclesiastical authorities of Canterbury quickly to the spot. Commissioners were appointed to examine her case, one of whom was the cellarer of Christ Church, a Dr Bocking, one of the monks. They decided that such a distinguished person as Elizabeth Barton, for that was the name of the maid, should come to Canterbury; and she entered the convent of St Sepulchre of that town as a nun. So long as the "Holy Maid of Kent" kept to purely ethical, religious and medical visions, and preached on such themes alone, all went well: and for several years she was a triumphant success as a prophetess, with almost a European reputation. But then, it would appear that she became the convenient tool of statesmen and ecclesiastics who had big schemes in their hands which they saw Elizabeth might further.

Henry had made up his mind to divorce his wife, and in the January of 1533 had married Anne Boleyn without getting the Pope's consent. This was a defiance of the Church of Rome. The Maid of Kent had already prophesied that if he entered this unholy new marriage "he would not reign in his Realm one month after, nor rest in God's favour the space of an hour." That, in its turn, was defiance of the King of

England. So Elizabeth Barton was taken to London with Dr Bocking and other monks and priests who were accused of being behind her utterances; and she, with five of the others, including Bocking, the Christ Church monk, were executed at Tyburn during April 1534.

If is a little difficult to get at the real truth: men were so apt to lie to please the King; and they were very cautious in what they said of the Maid. There is an interesting letter to Cromwell from the prior of Christ Church, saying what he thinks of her: Father Resby one of the Grey Friars had recommended her to him. The prior says he had seen her six or seven times; and she was often with Warham, and she had spoken to both of them as to the evil effects of the King's marriage with Anne. She is "usually sick about the conception of Our Lady and lives three or four days without meat or drink. Last year when she so lay I was called to see her, but she only spoke like any other sick person."

The truth probably is that the Romish party egged on this simple Maid to prophesy events which might tell in favour of their own case. The mighty Church of Rome was indeed in a parlous state when she had to go to a Holy Maid of Kent to find aid.

By this time Warham had died (August 1532), protesting against the attacks on his Church of Rome which were now gathering on all sides. He was buried in the tomb which still stands in the Martyrdom transept of Canterbury Cathedral, and as we look at it we can feel that it is one of the mementoes that mark the end of mediæval Canterbury.

He was succeeded by Thomas Cranmer, and with that event it is necessary to begin a new chapter in the history of the town, for the whole mental constitution of the place was changed during his term of office.

CHAPTER XV

The Reformation: the end of the Pilgrimages

DURING the last three hundred and fifty years of the history with which this book is concerned, the main undertone of it all has been that continual stream of pilgrim life passing before the shrine of St Thomas the Martyr. At regular intervals there have been those times of greater torrent, at the jubilee years. It will soon cease, for the shrine of St Thomas is about to be destroyed. A few years before its destruction there had arrived in the town a pilgrim who had a very fluent pen and very quick, observant eyes, and he put his experiences on paper. The pilgrim was Desiderius Erasmus, who arrived in Canterbury in 1513.

This account by Erasmus of his visit to Becket's tomb has become a classic of its kind, and it must be given in some detail here,[1] for it is one of the most illuminating documents in the history of Canterbury, and a typical pilgrimage as it was conducted at St Thomas's shrine. It is written in dialogue form as a conversation supposed to be taking place between one, Menedemus, and another Ogygius. The latter, when asked if he had passed unheeded the shrine of St Thomas of Canterbury,

[1] It will be found translated in full, with much other useful information about Canterbury, in "Pilgrimages: Walsingham and Canterbury" by J. G. Nichols (Murray 1875).

replies that most certainly the had commited no such blunder, for that pilgrimage was not to be surpassed in reputation by any in Christendom. He goes on to tell his friend that he found that Canterbury was the chief city of Kent, and in it were two monasteries both following the rule of St Benedict: these were, of course, St Augustine's Abbey and Christ Church Priory, though Erasmus says (through Ogygius) that the latter is called St Thomas's; evidence of the supremacy of the Saint. His description of the Cathedral is enthusiastic and impressive; it "raises itself to the sky with so much majesty that even from afar it brings holy awe to the minds of those who see it. . . . Two great towers are there which seem to hail the traveller when yet afar off; and the country round does ring with the wonderful sounding of their bells."

The narrator then continues to tell of the progress through the church, and what he saw therein. It was by the south porch he went in—where the modern traveller of to-day still enters, and over its doorway he saw the statues of the three knights who had committed the deed of martyrdom. When the narrator is asked why so much prominence to these murderers, he replies, "So that no courtier shall ever again lay his hand upon a bishop or upon the riches of the Church," a moral that was very soon to be forgotten when, a few years afterwards, Henry VIII.'s nobles and favourites gorged themselves with the lands of the monasteries and religious foundations. But Erasmus, if he had lived to see the seizure, would have scarcely counted these monastic houses as a legitimate part of the Church—they were, rather, an excresence according to his philosophy.

The pilgrims then entered the nave, where all, without exception, were free to come and go. It was empty, except for a few books chained to the pillars, and one monument, of which Erasmus did not know the name. For the rest there was nothing but "the vastness of the building" to arrest the eye. Then they came to the steps leading up to the choir, as they do now. But for the moment they turned aside into the martyrdom transept, where they were shown an altar before which "the holy man is said to have breathed his last farewell to the Virgin." As a matter of history it is known that the altar was built after the murder—but the story had changed to the form in which it was thus told to Erasmus. On this altar the pilgrims were shown the point of the sword which had dealt the fatal blow to Becket, the same sword with which the traitor priest had scattered the archbishop's brains. "The sacred rust of this piece of iron we did piously kiss for the love of St Thomas."

Then they went down into the crypt. "It has its own priests. There we were first shown the cleft skull of the martyr; the forehead is left bare, so that it may be kissed, but the rest is covered with silver." Then followed the inspection and worship of many other relics, also in the crypt. There was a strip of lead bearing the name "Thomas Acrensis," that is, Thomas of Acre, for there are some who say that Becket was born at Acre, and his mother a Saracen; his sister founded a chapel to him in London and, certainly, it was called St Thomas of Acre. There were also "the hair shirts, the girdles, and the bandages, with which that prelate subdued his flesh, striking horror with their very appearance and reproaching us for our indulgence and our luxuries." "And perhaps even reproaching the monks?" says Menedemus, slily.

Then they were conducted to the choir entrance, and going inside they were shown, on the north side, chests full of the many other relics of other saints and sacred places possessed by Canterbury [as well as its masterpiece, St Thomas; "skulls, jaw-bones, teeth, hands, fingers, entire arms, on all which we devoutly bestowed our kisses, and it seemed that this showing might last for ever, had not my unruly companion broken into the zeal of the showman." This is a reference to John Colet, the famous Dean of St Paul's in London, who was with Erasmus during this journey. The writer goes on to describe Colet in a few vivid words: "A learned and pious man, but not so well affected towards this part of religion as I could wish." "Some Wycliffite, I suppose," Menedemus asks. "I do not fancy so, though he has read Wycliffe's books." When the relic arm was displayed by the priest, with the flesh still clinging to it, Gratian Black (for that is the name under which Erasmus disguises Colet) "drew back from kissing it, and, indeed, showed signs of disgust." Whereupon the priest shut up his treasures.

Then came the visit to the altar, with its picture above, and rich vessels and ornaments upon and beneath it. There was no kissing of these, says Erasmus, and he began to wish that he had such beautiful things at home. Then into the sacristy, by which he probably means St Andrew's Chapel. "Good God! what a sight there was of vestments of silk and golden candlesticks! There also did we see the pastoral stuff of St Thomas," but this last was disappointing in length and workmanship. Then, the pall of silk, but coarsely made, and entirely lacking in gold or jewels, and a napkin with signs of real blood on its dirty surface. "These tokens of the simplicity of olden days we kissed very willingly." The writer goes on to mention that this last group of relics was not known to every pilgrim; he adds that he had gained his privilege from the friendship of Archbishop

Warham, a man who is "courtesy itself": learned, simple in manners, full of piety, is the estimate of Erasmus.

Then they approached, by another flight of steps, to the tomb of Becket in Trinity Chapel, and there they were first shown a full figure of St Thomas "gilded and adorned with many jewels." It was the sight of so much wealth that roused the anger of Colet, and he debated this question with the attendant priest: if Thomas was so kind to the poor while he lived, would he now resent it if some needy woman, with starvation before her and her children, took some fragment of all this mass of riches to relieve her poverty? That was the awkward poser that Colet put to the priest, and got no answer but sour looks, while Erasmus says that he felt very uncomfortable and put down a few pence as an offering, telling the priest that it was Colet's usual chaff. Then there is a passing meditation as to the ethics of all this ecclesiastical display, and Erasmus comforts himself with the thought that, after all, it is mainly accumulated by gifts from kings and princes, "and would have a worse destination in gambling or in war" if it came not to the churches; and a richly furnished church is better than a mean one which looks like a stable.

But the prior, fortunately, came forward at this awkward moment and opened the shrine for the pilgrims' eyes. This was the final end of the pilgrimage; the place where the body of St Thomas was said to rest. However, says Erasmus, it was not possible to see the bones except by climbing a ladder, and that was not permitted. The shrine was covered by an outer wooden case which the prior raised by pulling ropes. "Inestimable treasures were opened to view," writes Erasmus. "The least valuable parts was of gold, but every part glistened and shone with sparkling, rare and very large jewels, some of them larger than a goose's egg." The prior pointed out each jewel with a white rod, telling its name in French, its value, and the name of its donor; and a party of monks led the worship of the pilgrims meanwhile.

Erasmus says he was then conducted back to the crypt and shown the shrine of the Virgin Mother closed round by iron screens. He confesses he had never seen such riches before: "When lamps were brought we beheld a more than regal sight," richer even than the Lady of Walsingham, even on the outer surface—"her hidden riches are known only to herself." This shrine was shown only to the privileged few, men of rank or with intimate introductions, as in the case of Erasmus.

Then, for the last visit in the Cathedral, the pilgrims were taken back to the sacristy where a box covered with black leather was produced, and all present knelt in worship immediately it was opened. It contained a few fragments of dirty linen; "with these, so they told us, the holy man was accustomed to wipe the perspiration from his face and his neck, and the runnings from his nose." Once more Colet began to show signs of disgust; and, to make matters more obviously embarrassing, the prior offered Colet a piece of the linen as a gift, thinking he was doing a gracious service to a man of such high reputation. When Colet "disdainfully replaced" it in the box, with one of his little pouts or half whistles, as was his habit when annoyed, Erasmus once more felt exceedingly uncomfortable. But the prior, "like a sensible man, pretended not to notice it, and, after offering us a cup of wine, he courteously dismissed us."

Having thus gone the round of the pilgrimage to all the treasures of the Cathedral, Erasmas and Colet set out for London by way of Harbledown, where they were waylaid by the aged inhabitants of the hospital of St Nicholas (which had been founded by Lanfranc and is there to this present day) who rushed out to hold before them "the upper part of a shoe, bound with a brazen rim, and set with a piece of glass resembling a jewel. People kiss this relic and give some small coin in return." Whereupon Colet asked what all this meant, and he was driven to the last stage of indignation when the reply came that it was the shoe of St Thomas. Were they never to escape from this senseless and fraudulent relic worship? "Do these brutes think that we should kiss every good man's shoe?" But the more tolerant Erasmus adds the characteristic note: "For my part I pitied the old man, and gave him a small piece of money by way of consolation." He further adds the reflection: "I must own that these things had better be left undone, but when a thing cannot be at once corrected, I am wont to gather from it whatever good I can. . . . Thus, this saint, when he was alive, by his example, his learning, his preaching, encouraged piety and the relief of the needy, and now, when he is dead, he is of almost greater use. For he has raised that most magnificent Cathedral, he has gained the greatest respect for the priestly order throughout England. Finally this fragment of his shoe supports this little fellowship of poor men."

This essay by Erasmus is one of the most illuminating historical documents that ever was written. It is particularly useful to the student of Canterbury, because it at once gives a picture of the saintly relics worship which had gone on for so many hundred years (for Becket was not the only saint, be it remembered); it is an account of a fairly typical example of those incessant pilgrimages which had been going on before Becket's shrine all during its existence; and, on the other side, it shows that spirit of ridicule and impatient contempt for relics and formalities, which was the new spirit of the Reformation, now on the brink of history. This unending collection of relics must have been a strain on the credulity of pilgrims even in less critical times and of less critical nature than Colet's. Here are some of the relics which they had to accept and worship at Canterbury: there were whole arms of eleven saints, such as St Gregory, St Mildred the Virgin, and Hugh of Lincoln; there were the heads of St Blasius, St Fursaeus, and St Austroberta; there was part of the arm of St Jerome and another piece of the arm of St Paulinus; there was the bed of the Virgin Mary, and the wool of her own weaving; there was a fragment of the rock on which the Cross stood, another piece from the Holy Sepulchre, others from the manger, the scourging column, and the stone when Christ was translated to heaven; there was Aaron's rod, and a piece of the clay of which Adam was made. The list seems very wonderful and startling even for mediæval imaginations, but we must remember that Canterbury was one of the very first pilgrim centres in Christendom. In England there was only the shrine of Our Lady at Walsingham to come near it in attraction. And in all Europe there was scarcely one which surpassed it; there was Rome, of course; and Compostella with the body of St James, and Loretto with its Santa Casa, the home of the Holy Family, they said; there was the shrine of St Martin at Tours. But the monks of Christ Church would have thought twice before they exchanged their treasures for any of the sacred collections of their rivals; and there was no more prized mark of pilgrimage than the lead broach bearing the words "Caput Thomac"—the head of Thomas—or the ampulla, the little bottle, also usually of lead, which contained some of the holy water which had been mixed with the blood of the martyr, which had got considerately diluted before the time of the Reformation, one may imagine. These were the most common of the tokens carried back by the Canterbury pilgrims; just as they took a scallop shell from Compostella, or a palm branch to show they were from the Holy Sepulchre.

Such was the system of saint worship which was to come to the ground in England with a crash during the archbishopric of Cranmer (1533-1556). The history of the Reformation of course belongs to the story of England; here it will be only possible to describe the effect it had on the city of Canterbury, and indeed the bare recital of these facts will do more to illustrate the larger subject than any amount of generalisation and discussion of principles.

If one had asked a citizen of Canterbury what was the chief event of the Reformation, he would have replied, without hesitation, that it was the destruction of Becket's shrine, and that the other two great things were the dissolution of the abbey of St Augustine and the priory of Christ Church.

When Cranmer suggested an easy way by which Henry could get divorced from Catherine of Aragon, and thus be free to marry Anne Boleyn, his almost immediate reward was the archbishopric of Canterbury in 1533. That same year, within a month after the marriage to Anne, the previous marriage to Catherine was pronounced illegal—rather a cart-before-the horse manner of proceeding, but Henry made his reputation by violent methods. The next year, as we have seen, the Holy Maid of Kent and her fellow-believers, or fellow-impostors, were executed; the glove to Rome was thrown down in the arena of history; the fight began in dead earnest. The desire to get free from his marriage led Henry by steps to a general attack on the Pope and all who owned his authority, and the king who had won the title of "Defender of the Faith" finished his royal career by seizing every tangible piece of ecclesiastical wealth and privilege that he could persuade the English Parliament to vote into his hands. Soon Bishop Fisher and Sir Thomas More, the late Chancellor, had been beheaded because they refused to acknowledge that Henry was supreme head of the English Church under Christ. The head of More was brought to Canterbury by his daughter Margaret Roper, and buried in St Dunstan's Church,

ROPER HOUSE

near by the Roper's house, of which the doorway still stands in St Dunstan's Street. The first right which logically followed, when Henry was declared the pope of England, was the control of the monastic houses; for the Pope of Rome, as we have seen, had always had a very direct hand in their government. So the visitation of the monasteries began, which took the form of a set of commissioners sent round the country with instructions to bring back the worst report against monastic institutions that they cared to put on paper. The monks were no saints, and their role in life was played out. Still one feels that the commissioners would have reported against them had they been companies of angels. In 1536 the lesser religious houses were dissolved. In Canterbury this meant that the Black Friary, and the Austin Canons at least, were confiscated and passed into the hands of the Crown who sold them to laymen. It would appear that the Grey Friary had already gone the same way two years before, having got itself badly involved with the Maid of Kent; certainly we find a letter of the year 1534 by which a certain priest is licensed to collect money "for the grey friars of Canterbury who have no lands nor rents."

It was in 1536 that the first move was made which shook the reputation of such observances as the worship of St Thomas, for in that year a royal proclamation abolished "superfluous holidays"—which were held to be all those holy days which interfered with harvesting. This abolition cut into the feast of the Translation of St Thomas on July 7. So the number of the pilgrims on that occasion fell rapidly off. Thomas Cromwell, the king's chief minister at this time, soon instructed the clergy that "they should not set forthe or extoll any images, reliques, or myracles for any superstitution or lucre, nor allure the people by any inticements to the pilgrimage of any saynt . . seeinge all goodness, helth, and grace ought to be both asked and looked for only of God . . . that they do rather applye themselves to the kepying of Goddes commandments and fulfilling of his works of cheritye, persuading them that they shall please God more by the true exercising of their bodilie labour, travaile or occupation and providing for their familyes, than yf they went about to the said pilgrimages; and that it shall profitt more their soules helth yf they do bestow that on the poore and nedy which they would have bestowed uppon the said images or reliques."

That was the new spirit which, right or wrong, was undermining the wealth and glory of Becket's tomb. In 1538 the festival days in honour of St Thomas were abolished by decree, and only the ordinary services for those days were to be read instead; and the faithful were horrified when they saw the archbishop Cranmer leading the way in obeying this order, "by not fasting (as was the custom) on the eve [of the feast], but supping upon flesh in his parlour with his domesticks. This appeared a strange unusual sight to all that were present."

In September of this year, 1538, the shrine itself was destroyed. We are told that the vast wealth of its gold and jewels filled two chests, each of which needed six or eight strong men to carry it from the church, and all this was seized by Henry VIII. In a proclamation which was published within a month or two, Henry tried to make out a case against Becket which would excuse the confiscation and sacrilege: "Forasmuch as it appeareth clearly that Thomas Becket, sometime Archbishop of Canterbury, stubbornely to withstand the holsome lawes established against the enormities of the clergy by the king's highness most noble progenitor King Henry the Second, for the common wealth, rest and tranquillity of this realme, of his forward mind fled the realme into France, and to the Bishop of Rome, maintenour of these enormities, to procure the abrogation of the said lawes, whereby arose much trouble in this said realm. . . . For these, and for other great and urgent causes long to recite, the king's majesty, by the advice of his counsell, hath thought expedient to declare to his loving subjects, that, notwithstanding the said canonisation, there appeareth nothing in his life and exteriour

TOWERS AND S. PORCH OF CANTERBURY CATHEDRAL

conversation whereby he should be called a saint, but rather esteemed to have been a rebel and traitor to his prince." The proclamation then goes on to order that Becket shall no longer be entitled a saint, but only Bishop Becket; that all his images throughout the realm shall be turned out of their churches; that his feast days shall be no longer observed, and all reference to him in the service book erased. St Thomas was to be blotted out in brief. Another proclamation of 1539 points out that the pieces of the skull in the shrine itself and the skull in the crypt, of which Erasmus has told us, made more than one skull—in other words, there was an imposture somewhere—as the same proclamation shows was the case of many other supposed sacred relics in other churches; for example: "the Blood of Christ, so called in some places, was but a piece of red sylke, enclosed in a piece of thyck glass!"

There is an elaborate tale, which may or may not be true, that this deposition of the saint was preceded by a formal trial, to which the dead man was summoned by the proclamation of the king's heralds, standing by the side of the shrine; and when, after thirty days' grace, the dead man neither answered nor came forth, then the case was heard at Westminster with an advocate to represent Becket. As might be expected, under these circumstances, the verdict went against the saint and he was declared a traitor, and his bones ordered to be burnt, and the offerings at the shrine forfeited to the Crown. There are several gaps and contradictions in the evidence for this story of a formal trial, but the result was the same, as we have seen.

With the shrine gone, the dissolution of the monastery of Christ Church was but a secondary thing. This happened in the year 1540, where a commissioner went down to Canterbury and received from the prior and about twenty-four of the monks a formal surrender of their property and privileges, and in return they received the promise of a yearly pension to last during their lives or until they got other ecclesiastical offices of equal value. In all, fifty-three members of the monastery appear to have received pensions; the prior got eighty pounds a year and a prebendal stall, and six others got prebends, while ten of the monks were made minor canons. All the chattels, the plate and jewels of the priory were counted by the commissioners, and all that was especially valuable was sent to the Tower of London. Out of the possessions of the dissolved priory, the Crown endowed a Chapter of Secular Canons to serve the Cathedral under the presidence of a dean, and this constitution remains to this day. In some ways there was rather a change in theory than in practice, and the same squabbling between the Church and the city continued much as before. But there was the radical change that the old communal monastic life was broken up, and the buildings which had been shared collectively by the monks were divided into separate establishments, and allotted amongst the canons. To-day, of course, when the old priory buildings are in ruins, and newer residences have been called for, even the husk of the communal life has gone and Cathedral clergy now live in those entirely separate houses which we see around the Close.

The dissolution of the Abbey of St Augustine happened in the year before the surrender of Christ Church, but we will discuss the details in the separate chapter on that abbey, merely mentioning here the important distinction that in this case no religious body took the place of the monks, and the buildings were given over to lay uses: so one of the most important centres of ecclesiastical life—

not only in Canterbury, but in all England or even Europe—disappeared.

With these events—the destruction of Becket's shrine, and the dissolution of the two great monasteries, and some of the smaller religious houses—Canterbury ended its career as a mediæval city. Its subsequent history rather lacks that unity which it had under the supremacy of the Church. The archbishops ceased to have that intimate connection with their Cathedral which had been much more marked in early days, but which had existed to some extent as late as the time of Warham. Of course, one does not mean that there was any absolute break in the continuity of things: it is only a matter of estimating broad tendencies. Whereas, the earlier history of Canterbury has been most conveniently grouped round the archbishops and the Cathedral Church, henceforward the story will be more easily linked with the municipal history of the city, with the affairs of its corporation and citizens; or with the later history of St Augustine's Abbey, after it became a royal palace. This manner of treatment will be followed here, and the later history of Canterbury will come at the end of the two chapters which will now be devoted, in the main, to the distinctive histories of St Augustine's and the City, respectively.

CHAPTER XVI

The City of Canterbury and its lay affairs

ALONGSIDE of the history of the ecclesiastical Canterbury which we have followed in this book, there has been all the time a more or less separate life progressing beyond the walls of the monastic houses and their great churches. The two courses of events were continually mixed together, but, on the other hand, there was a strong rivalry between the city and the Church which makes their respective histories detached things in many ways. The outlines of the history of the city—as a lay community—will be given in this chapter.

The early foundations of the municipal story have been already noted: the Roman city; the royal borough of Ethelbert; the state of affairs at the time of the Domesday survey, when it was still in the special domain of the Crown. But by this time there had been drawn some of the important boundary lines of those private jurisdictions or estates which were marked off from the general domain of the kings. These special jurisdictions were for various reasons considered to stand without the government of Canterbury. This manner of private exemptions is a marked feature of mediæval society, and it will be useful to give a list of those semi-private areas which existed in Canterbury in these early days, for it will give a certain anatomical structure to the town.

Within the walls there were the following more or less distinct districts: (1) *The Borough of Staplegate:* a small patch of the city which lay to the south-west of Northgate.[1] The tradition ran that this was the spot where Ethelbert first entertained Augustine and his monks, hence the name of Stablegate—the earlier form meaning in Anglo-Saxon (it has been suggested) "stable" or a "resting-place." Here they lived until the king was converted and gave up his own palace, and in commemoration of this conversion, the piece of land was forever exempted from the control of the city officials and their jurisdiction. It is interesting to find Hasted writing, as late as 1800, that Staplegate was then "inhabited only by poor and undisciplined people, who fly hither, as to a sanctuary, and shelter from the liberty of the city." Here we have a case like the notorious district of Alsatia, which was a similar place in London. (2) *The Ville of the precincts of the archbishop's palace*, which was, from its first giving by Ethelbert to Augustine, reserved from the authority of the civic rule, even after it became separated (by Lanfranc, chiefly) from the connection with (3) *the Christ Church monastery*, which made another special district. (4) *The White or Augustine friary district* off St George's Street; (5) *Kingsbridge* (*or St Thomas's Hospital*); and (6) *Cokyn's Hospital* we shall visit and discuss in the Itinerary.

Outside the walls were: (7) *The Priory of St Gregory*; (8) *St John's Hospital*; (9) *the Abbey of St Augustine*; which also we shall consider in the Itinerary. (10) *The Borough of Longport* was the

[1] Hasted, writing in 1800, defines it: "This district at present is bounded on the east by the street leading from Northgate to Palace Street, on the south by the end of Palace Street, and a part of King's Street, on the west by Knott's Lane, and on the north by that part of the parish of Northgate within the walls."

original plot of ground which Ethelbert gave for the building of the abbey, and will be more easily understood in the next chapter. (11) *Smith's Almshouses;* (12) *Doge's Chantry;* and (13) *St Laurence's Hospital* will be also mentioned in the Itinerary.

Such were, comparatively early in its history, the main divisions of the city of Canterbury, besides the division into six wards, which took their names from the six principle gates in the city walls. We will now consider the structure of its central city government.[1]

By the 1000-century Canterbury was under the control of a Portreeve, who was probably elected by the king in the earlier period, and afterwards, perhaps, elected by the burgesses from a list of names approved by the monarch. In later documents the portreeve becomes named as Præfectus, but this is only a change of title, the functions remaining as before. At a period which Mrs Green defines as "at least as early as the thirteenth century" but which other authorities have not ventured to put earlier than the end of the 1300-century, we find the Government in the hands of two Ballivi or Bailiffs, who preside over a Burghmote or city court of justice, and administer it with the assistance of twelve burgesses, and beyond there was a greater council of thirty-six "probi homines or Jurati." By this time all these officers and councils seem to have been elected by some more or less democratic process, though "democracy" then meant only a limited number of recognised burgesses of the town, of course. Six members of the Council of twelve were aldermen. The aldermen were, originally, the private owners of the jurisdiction of

[1] On the municipal condition of Canterbury see "Historical Manuscript Commission," vol. 9, page 131, and also Mrs J. R. Green's, "Town Life in the fifteenth century." These volumes contain much about the lay history of Canterbury.

their respective wards, that is they paid a definite rent for the right to administer the affairs of the ward—in much the same way that they would have paid the rent of a manor. We find in Canterbury wards much the same state of affairs as in the history of London, for example. These wards may have even begun as the private estates or manors of which the aldermen were the lords. A ward may have been, in short, a manor in a large town. But in later days, the alderman, even when he purchased or inherited his aldermanry, as was the usual practice, only acquired the right to certain dues in the ward. We find in Canterbury the abbey of St Augustine's possessing a ward, just as we find the Aldgate Ward in London held by the priory of Holy Trinity. There were six wards in Canterbury, and the aldermen at first held them "in capiti" or direct from the Crown; afterwards, when Henry III. practically leased the city to its citizens, the aldermen held their wards from the city. "The wards, however," says Mrs Green, "still remained the property of certain families in the county of Kent, estates which could be bequeathed by will and which descended for generations from father to son. Their hereditary governors need not be either freemen or inhabitants of the city, and might moreover make their profit if they choose by leasing out the post." As an example of this last right, we find, in 1285, that William de Godstede, the alderman of Westgate ward, had leased it to the rector of Sturry (about two miles from Canterbury), at one hundred shillings per annum rent, while alderman William was only paying the city three shillings and fourpence a year. Then aldermen had charge of the police arrangements of their individual wards, and in their collective capacity it was their duty to act as the adversory council of the Portreeve or Mayor, to make bye-laws, and to pass all the accounts of the city.

It was in the time of Henry III. that a great step towards municipal freedom was taken, by procuring from the king the right to hold the city "in fee farm" at a rent of sixty pounds a year, to be paid in two instalments. In other words, instead of being under the power of the sheriff of the county who had collected the city's contribution to the royal exchequer, the citizen now collected the money by their own officers; and, further, it was fixed at a definite sum. In this grant of Henry III. there seems to have been included the right to choose the bailiffs by the vote of the citizens; it is possible that this was their first popular election, whereas before they may have been selected by the king.

In the time of Henry VI. there was (1445) a violent dispute as to the proper manner of electing the bailiffs, and Cardinal Beaufort, who was in the city at the time, was bribed to use his great influence to get the matter decided. It ended in the king granting a new charter by which the bailiffs were both supplanted by a single mayor who took their place as the chief officer of the city. It was in the charter of Edward IV. that Canterbury was made a county by itself, and henceforth possessed a sheriff of its own. Further changes in the city constitution were slight until we come to the municipal reforms of the 1800-century; and even now the mayor, aldermen and councillors of to-day are, in their main structure, as they existed during the mediæval period.

A great deal of the mediæval history of the municipality of Canterbury concerns the fiercely fought quarrels between the city and the monks of Christ Church as to their respective rights and duties in the town. We have already seen an instance of this when the citizens met in the Blackfriary, in the time of Edward I.

One frequent cause of trouble was about their respective duties in repairing the city walls. During the time of Hubert de Burgh's justiciarship, in Henry III.'s reign, we find a record that he gave the monks a certificate to the effect that the timber, which they had recently supplied for the defence of the city, had not been due from them as a right, but only given by their free will and good pleasure. Even the wall which lay outside the extensive grounds of the monastic buildings of Christ Church, belonged to the city, and there was for a long time a public way running between the walls and the priory enclosure. It was in 1413 that the prior of Christ Church leased (for six shillings and eighpence a year) one of the towers of the wall, a postern, and the public land, intervening at that spot between the walls and the priory. In 1492 the drastic change was made by which the city sold to the priory the whole of the wall between Burgate and Northgate, that is, all the wall which lay immediately outside the grounds of the priory. Presumably with the wall also passed the possession of the intervening public ground (pomœrium) which had separated the priory from the wall. This open space or pomœrium had been mainly left clear for military purposes, but by this time the country was getting more settled, and the defence of the walls was no longer an urgent problem. Thus the city wall became also, at this spot, the wall of the priory and the Cathedral domain. We will now notice other instances of disputes between the two societies which were not so quietly settled.

In 1428 some officials of the Christ Church kitchen department had gone to the seaside and purchased some fish before it was brought to the Canterbury stalls. This, said the citizens, amounted to the serious offence of forestalling the market, so they seized the fish which the monks had bought. In this case the disputing parties agreed to abide by the decisions of two arbitrators, and the bailiffs gave a bond as surety for that course. But the matter was not always settled in this peaceful manner. Thus in 1473 there began a gigantic struggle in which physical force took a prominent part as well as the gentler voice of the law, and the affair went on for thirty years before it was settled. It turned on the rights over the "Rosier" or Rose Garden which was a meadow beyond the ctiy walls. Both the citizens and the monks claimed it as being their property, or at least that they had special rights of jurisdiction over this district. In 1500, on the 16th of July, the citizens decided to bring the matter to a point by testing their rights. So the mayor, accompanied by about two hundred armed men, sallied forth from the city and began to cut down trees and close water courses in the aforesaid meadows, and they also made a general onslaught on any monks who could be found in the neighbourhood. They set on a monk named Thomas Ikham "being late afore sore sike and wulking in the fields for his recreation, and then and there put him in grete juberdie of his lyf." The citizens frank greeting to the wandering Thomas was "Yeld the, horeson monke; comest thou her to be a captayn this daye." They then proceeded to "assault, bete and yll intrete some servants of the prior, and carried them in custody into the city, where they confiscated their belongings and imprisoned them for three days. Then they seized Sir Thomas Jure, a priest of the almonry, whom they chanced to meet during their triumphant career, and assaulted him, also, and took his hawk, which he was carrying on his wrist. And all these proceedings were carried through with language which was fully worthy of the physical violence used.

The next day the campaign took a new turn. So far the fish market had been in the little square outside Christ Church gate, where it was most convenient for the customers from the priory. Presumably to spite the monks, the mayor now ordered his market to be removed to another part of the town. When the monks sent all the way to the new market to buy a "hallybutte" the bearer was robbed by the citizens of his purchase as he went back to the priory gate. When the monks sent all the way to the seaside to get fish the result was

CHRIST CHURCH GATE, CANTERBURY

the same: it was seized on the return. And the mayor and his men continued the process of using the meadows as their own. They left no stone unturned if they could annoy the monks. They thought of the happy idea of staying away from the Cathedral services. "While it hathe ben used of a laudable custom of the mair and other citizens that at the feste of Christmas have assembled theym selfe in the church at the tombe of Archibysshopp Sudbury, ther saying divers orysons and prayours for the sowle of the same Byshopp, for the greate actes he has don to the seide city, the same maior and citizens, for the greate malice and grugge as they owed to the seid priour and convent, at the fest of Christmas last passt absented themy selfe from the seid church, and withdrew there prayours from thense and kept there prayours and orysons under the prisonhous called Westgate of the seid cite," which was especially appropriate to Sudbury's worship, for he had built this gate during his term of office as archbishop. They also failed to come to the cathedral with the king's usual Christmas messenger bearing the annual gift to the shrine of St Thomas.

When charged with all these misdeeds, the mayor did not deny them, but said the prior had been just as bad himself, for he had seized the municipal mace out of the hands of the City official, and had turned sewage into the City ditch, to the hurt of the town.

The fish-market suit cost much time and money before it was settled; and the corporation records contain many details of the journeyings to attend the courts of justice at Westminster, and the treating and bribery that went on to secure a verdict. For example, we find the mayor sending back a messenger to Canterbury for something useful in "makyng frends," and his fellow-citizens send him up two "troughts" and ten capons to distribute as he sees fit.

Another dispute of about the same time was progressing between the City and the Abbey of St Augustine, also concerning the matter of boundaries and landed property. The first notice of this trouble seems to be in the year 1480 (but there had been another similar case settled between them about 1417) when the city revenue is charged with the expenses of its representatives going to Westminster to appear as witnesses before the courts. In this year (1480) the arbitrators sat for a month in London; and we find them meeting at the sign of the Panyer in Paternoster Row to give final judgment. They were plentifully supplied with dainties all this time, three meals a day served in the French manner. There was not the same bitter feeling against the St Augustine monks that there was in the case of those from Christ Church: if we can judge by a case in 1479 when we find the City purse charged with drinks for the use of these rivals in another suit. When the city representatives returned home to Canterbury, after the arbitration settlement recorded above, a complimentary supper was given in their honour.

The whole civil records positively ouse with generous drinking, during this period specially. Every opportunity was seized with eagerness. Thus in this same year, 1480, when the news arrived at the mayor's house that the archbishop's deputy had seized the tithe of the aftermath from the King's Mead, his worship immediately gathered together an armed band and marched to the scene of this ecclesiastical violence to save the town property. It was only a mile to the place; but his first gallant action was to order drinks all round, sixteen-pence worth of wine, at the City's expense. Then he made a speech defying the Archbishop and all his men—and, for all we know, came quietly home again. When they were not feasting themselves, they were judiciously supplying the wants of their witnesses and advocates. Thus, in 1496, when there was further disputing with St Augustine's, we find the city treating Sir John Fyneux, its representative, to a breakfast before the conference: the repast consisted of a swan, two geese, five capons, two lambs, four rabbits, gurnards, roach, salmon, brawn, a rump of beef, red and white wines, claret, beer, and ale. In 1498 this same man and Sir Edward Poynings, were entertained lavishly for three days, while they collected evidence concerning the procedure which had been followed in the matter of the election of some City officers: one item of this feasting is a trout which cost seventeen pence, which, in modern values, is equal to ten shillings.

A common subject in the City account books is the entertainment of monarchs and great lords and statesmen. Thus, we find Margaret, Duchess of Burgundy,

HOUSES OF CANTERBURY WEAVERS

Edward IV.'s sister, being sumptuously treated by Canterbury, in 1480, on Barham Down, as she was passing on her way to London, and she is again feasted in the same year on her return journey, this time having Edward, the king, with her. We have seen how Canterbury hesitated whether to accept the Yorkist Edward in place of the Lancastrian Henry VI., and how a mayor of the City got himself hanged by Edward for making up his mind on the wrong side. In 1485 Richard III. paid his first visit to Canterbury after his coronation, and he was received by Lord Cobham and the principal citizens who rode out to meet him. The citizens had collected a purse of money to present to the king; but having a doubtful title, he was on his good behaviour and graciously refused the coin, and they made him a present of meats and other things instead. While the purse was, by the unanimous vote of the mayor and his brethren, presented to Dr Langton, the Bishop of St Taffy's, whom they evidently considered likely to have influence with Richard: it is quite possible that Richard got the money discreetly passed on to him after all.

The citizens were always generous with their hospitality where it seemed a paying investment. They feasted Henry VII. in 1485, 1487, and 1500; and at other times also, as, for example, in 1503, when his eldest son, Prince Arthur, came with his father, and the City revenues had to find money to tip the Prince's "hensshman" to the amount of three shillings and fourpence, as well as a like amount for the King's. The Prince himself got a present of a silver-gilt cup, which cost £4, 16s., and was filled with nobles amounting to £13.

The city records give some behind-the-scenes details concerning the visits of Henry VIII., and Charles V., and Wolsey, which we have already noted elsewhere. Thus, in the accounts for 1521-2 we find: "The xpens of curyage of sand for the stretes ayents the Emperour and Kyng comyng to the citie xxx^{s} vii^{d}." Wolsey was always received with great consideration; in 1517 we find him in the city at the end of June, when he was presented with capons, pears, walnuts and cockles. In 1521, when the cardinal was on his way back from a great diplomatic visit to the Continent, the citizens of Canterbury sent out a canopy to cover him during his stately entrance into their town, and the civic book tells us that they had to pay for the "mendyng one of the rodds of the canopye broken at my Lord Cardynallys comyng home from beyond the see." They had borrowed this canopy from the citizens of Sandwich; it was the precious one which the Barons of the Cinque Ports used at the royal coronations.

During the ecclesiastical turmoil of the Tudor period we have the barbarous notes of religious bigotry entering into the City's records. Thus in 1539 there is this ghastly assertion of Christian grace and meekness: "Paid for half a tonne of tymber to make a payre of Gallaces to hang fryerstone [Friar Stone, who had refused to acknowledge the supremacy of Henry VIII., over the Church] . . . for a load of wood and for a horse to drag hym to the Dongeon. For ii men that sett the ketyl and parboyled hym. To ii men that caryed hys quarters to the gate and sett them up. For a halter to hang hym. To the woman that scowred the ketyll. To hym that dyd execucion iiii^s^ viii^d^." When the Catholic Mary came to the throne they burned people in Canterbury for asserting much the same thing that they had burned them for denying under Henry VIII., and forty-one Protestants were burned during the Marian persecution; the fires were in a field near the present south railway station, where a monument stands to their memory to-day. During this reign the citizens had to treat and feast Cardinal Pole, as their ancestors had feasted and humoured Cardinal Wolsey. For example, the accounts of 1555 show: "To my Lord Cardynall and my Lord Chancellor at their going to Calys to treat a peace between the Emperor and the French King, in bere, brede, wine, capons, chekyns, mottons, veales and frute. For a grete porpos gevyn to them at their return from Calys."

The reign of Elizabeth brought Canterbury a rather exciting time. As for the visits of the queen herself we shall cross her path when we consider the history of St Augustine's Abbey. The citizens received an entirely fresh addition to their ranks by the settlement of the Walloons who had been driven to England as exiles owing to the persecutions of The Duke of Alva. Elizabeth, who was always ready to do anything that would annoy Spain, gave these refugees a licence to settle in Canterbury if the archbishop did not object. It is recorded that there came "eighteen housekeepers, besides children and servants." In 1568, Elizabeth granted to them the crypt of the Cathedral as a place of worship (a tradition has it that the crypt was also given as a place for their weaving, but this seems uncertain), and this use has been continued from that time until to-day, when the successors of these exiles still hold their services there. To continne their history beyond the time of Elizabeth, we find that by the year 1634 there were 900 communicants belonging to this sect. In 1665 there were said to be 126 master-weavers, out of a total community of about 1300, while they employed 750 English in their trade. In 1676 they were granted a special charter, at which time they numbered about 2500. The revocation of the edict of Nantes 1685, drove many more Protestants out of France and increased the number of the refugees at Canterbury. But, by the end of the 17th century the silk trade had moved up to London and occupied the district of Spitalfields, and in 1799 we find only ten master-weavers left in Canterbury, and only 80 communicants in the church of the undercroft. At this last date the total population of the City was about 9000.

To go back to the date where we introduced this digression on the foreign silk weavers. During the early Stuart time Canterbury had both Royalist and Roundhead leaders for its close inspection. Charles I. we shall meet in our chapter on St Augustine's, but Cromwell has more directly to do with the City itself. Its sympathies were, from the beginning of the national struggle, on the side of the popular party, for as early as 1628 we find the citizens refusing to billet the soldiers of the royal army. In 1642 the Parliamentary army was in the town, and doing damage to the Cathedral. On the Christmas day of 1648 there were serious riots in Canterbury, for the Puritan Mayor, Michael Page, had incited the unruly element of the City to insult those who were going to the service at the Cathedral. This riotous conduct was quieted down very quickly, but apparently, the Parliamentary "Committee of the County" seized the excuse for marching soldiers into the town "who, though they heard by the way that all was quiet, chose to march in as conquerors, and, finding the gates open, took them down and burned them, threw down several parts of the wall, and committed many to prison on suspicion." Cromwell himself was in the City in 1651 and treated the Corporation to a banquet. In the following year a national Committee was appointed to devise means of raising money for the use of the Commonwealth; some religious fanatics in the army—so it is thought—suggested that one good way would be to select a few cathedrals which could be put up for sale, demolished, and sold as building material. The Committee actually decided on Canterbury as one of the doomed places; but it was such a monstrous scheme that nobody started on the work of destruction, or attempted the sale.

When the Restoration of Charles II., 1660, took the fickle popular fancy, it was in Canterbury that he passed the first three nights after his landing at Dover on his way to London. But with his reign the history of Canterbury gets more sober and uneventful than ever. Almost everyone of the archbishops between Juxon, 1660, and Sumner, 1848, was enthroned by proxy, if at all: and many of them never entered Canterbury at any time during their term of office, and Lambeth Palace was now the real centre of their activities, such as they were. For the Church was not now the supremely important organ of society that it had been during the days to which we have devoted our space in this book; and the only few events which Hasted, the Kent historian who wrote about 1800, can call "remarkable" in the history of Canterbury after the Restoration of Charles, are such things as an earthquake in 1692, and a flood in 1776, and the prosecution of the master and mistress of the City workhouse in 1737. So it seems well to close our history, lest the brilliant colouring of the Middle Ages, with their picturesque ceremonies, their gorgeous robes and all the trappings of feudalism and craftsmanship and religious faiths, may be blurred by the drab shades of commercialism and outworn superstitions. Let us leave Canterbury in our minds as a place whither pilgrims go, where abbots and priors and monks do dwell.

CHAPTER XVII

The Abbey of Saint Augustine

THE abbey of St Peter and Paul, as it was at first called, or St Augustine's Abbey as it was named afterwards, is such an important place in the life of Canterbury that it demands a short chapter wherein its career can be sketched as a whole, with more attention than could be devoted to it in the general narrative. St Augustine's was the greatest rival to the priory of Christ Church and its Cathedral Church. In its earlier career St Augustine's looked like coming out the victor. But this part of its history we have already seen (Chapter III.). The real reason which led to the foundation of this Abbey was probably that there might be a place for royal and archiepiscopal burials outside the walls of the City, for the early Saxons followed the Roman custom of refusing to allow burial within the limits of a town. It was the consequent gathering together of the bones of such sacred persons as St Augustine and his immediate followers and their royal patrons, that at first gave the Abbey such a pull over the archiepiscopal church. This was changed when Archbishop Cuthbert (740-758) procured from the Pope the licence which allowed the archbishops to be buried in the precincts of their own Cathedral; and Jaenberht (d. 791) was the last archbishop to be buried at St Augustine's.

Bede has recorded for us the words which were placed on St Augustine's own tomb: "Here resteth the Lord Augustine, first archbishop of Canterbury who erewhile was sent hither by Blessed Gregory, bishop of the City of Rome, and being helped by God to work miracles, drew over King Ethelbert and his race from the worship of idols to the faith of Christ. Having ended in peace the days of his ministry, he departed hence seven days before the kalends of June in the reign of the same king, A.D. 605."

The building of the monastery began in A.D. 598. Ethelbert held the Christmas of 605, the year of Augustine's death, at Canterbury, and, on the 5th of January following, he handed over to the monks the monastery as it then stood, and all the endowments he had given it. These two charters of this year are still in existence, but one, at least, is not above suspicion; though even if of later date, they may be copies of the originals. But the Abbey was not sufficiently advanced for dedication until the year 613. It was re-dedicated by Dunstan in 971, with the name of St Augustine added to its former patrons, and this last name is the one by which it has been generally known during its history.

In spite of the privilege of burial which was granted to the Cathedral the Abbey still possessed the more venerated relics; and Canute (about 1030) added the remains of St Mildred at the same time that he presented to St Augustine's the lands of Minster Monastery in Thanet, which had been ravaged by the Danes. The tale goes that when the Abbot of St Augustine's prayed to the saint that she would move to St Augustine's, she refused at first, but at last allowed him to take up her body by night; whereupon the abbot was pursued by the men of Thanet, who were unwilling to lose so precious a patroness.

A more material privilege had been granted to the monks a few years before this, when King Ethelred the Redeless, in 1003, had given a charter establishing a five days' fair to be held in the precincts of the Abbey annually at the season of the anniversary of the translation of St Augustine. This fair apparently continued to flourish until the time of Edward I., when it was stopped, on account of the disturbances which took place, and because the bailiffs of the city claimed such heavy dues on the bread and ale brought to it.

The abbey collected a vast number of privileges and estates during the course of its history until it came to rank as one of the most famous Benedictine monasteries in Europe. Its position may be judged from the fact that the Abbot of St Augustine's, from the time of Edward the Confessor, had the right to wear the mitre, a privilege which made him to all intents free from the jurisdiction of the archbishop, and gave him the rights of a bishop so far as the abbey extended. This privilege had been won from the Pope during a visit to Rome made by Abbot Egelsin in 1063; when, says the chronicler Thorne (who wrote the history of the abbey about the year 1400), "he was the first of all the abbots of this monastery who was ordered to use the mitre and sandals according to the pontificial law." A few years before this his predecessor, Abbot Wilfric, had been granted the privilege of sitting next to the Abbot of Monti Casino (the head of the Benedictines), whenever he was present at the General Councils of the Order. In other words, this Abbey of St Augustine was the second in rank in the most famous of all the monastical Orders.

It was such privileges and ranks as these which caused the long-standing jealousy of the archbishop and the monks of the neighbouring Christ Church: and even when the privileges were formally granted, it by no means followed that their jealous rivals would allow them to be exercised. For example, when Egelsin came back with his grant of the mitre, it was not long before he had to fly from the country immediately the strong Lanfranc was made archbishop; but mainly, perhaps, because he had taken sides with the English Stigand against the Norman invaders. St Augustine's suffered the fate of the other English monasteries at this time. "In the year of our Lord 1070," says Thorne, "William the Conqueror violated his promises in many ways, for he ordered the monasteries of all England to be searched, and the money and also the charters, which he had promised to respect, he ordered to be taken from the churches where they were lying securely, and to be transferred to his Treasury." When Egelsin fled, Abbot Scoland, a Norman (though by some his name is spelt Scotland) succeeded by the favour of William and Lanfranc. With such powerful supporters he was able to do great things: and began a similar rebuilding of the abbey and its dwellings as was going on at the same time at the Cathedral under Lanfranc. The ruins of the church which we shall see in our walk through the present abbey grounds, are of this period. He was also active in getting back again any lands of the abbey's domain which had been lost: thus he persuaded William to compel his half brother Odo, Earl of Kent, to restore the manor of Plumstead; and to give them a charter by which they won back the borough of Fordwych, which Egelsin had granted away to Hamo the sheriff. And William continued the process of adding new lands to their temporal possessions.

We have already seen in a previous chapter how the next abbot, Wido, was placed in his chair by force, and the monks who refused to admit him were driven out of their house by Lanfranc's orders. Wido almost completed the rebuilding of the great abbey church which Scoland had begun. His successor was Hugo de Floriac, who was a kinsman of William Rufus and had formerly (before he became a monk of St Augustine) been a bold knight who had fought for the Conqueror and his son in both Normandy and England. This Hugo had chanced to attending at St Augustine's for prayer while he was visiting Canterbury with William Rufus: he was seized with a great desire to become a monk of the house; and the abbot admitted him. Out of the wealth he brought with him, he entirely rebuilt the chapter-house and the dormitories and a part of the church.

In the time of the next abbot, Hugh de Trotesclive, the abbey contained sixty monks. During the term of Sylvester, his successor, there were fierce struggles with the archbishop Theobald, who refused to consecrate the new abbot, as we have seen in chapter ix. This Sylvester made a regulation that on the first day of every Lent there should be received into the abbey as many poor people as there were monks in residence, and that these poor should be maintained during the whole of Lent at the expense of the abbey. This is one instance of the economic function of the monastic houses; it is a feature of the social organisation of the mediæval times.

We are now in the times of almost continual friction between the monks and the archbishops concerning their respective rights. As early as 610, the abbey had declared there was a papal bull decreeing that no bishop should intrude in the abbey, unless when the monks cared to admit him of their free will, to perform services in their church. But the ecclesiastical rivals have not been above forging documents to prove their case after their own desires. Then there was a claim of another bull of A.D. 955 by which Pope John XIII. forbade the monks of Christ Church to interfere with the abbey; and afterwards he took St Augustine's under his immediate protection—which meant that the archbishops were to be deprived of all jurisdiction over their rivals who lived but a few yards from their palace door. The position was rather ignominious. Matters got worse, of course, when, as we have seen, the abbots got a mitre; and although the first Egelsin had to fly abroad, the privilege was confirmed again in

1173, and henceforth maintained. Henceforth the abbot of this proud St Augustine's could, in many cases, pronounce excommunication or reconsecrate desecrated churches. A mitred-abbot was also usually summoned to sit in the House of Lords as a peer of the realm, beside the barons and the bishops. It is unnecessary here to give the details of the squabbles between these rivals, but an instance during the year 1253 is given by Matthew of Paris in his chronicles. Here we find the archbishop of that time, Boniface, staying at St Albans, when a monk of St Augustine's arrived bearing a letter which the abbey had received from the Pope, so that they might serve it on the archbishop if he became troublesome. The letter was to the effect that Boniface "was not to disturb the abbot of that house or the conventual brethren by visiting, suspending or excommunicating them, which he proposed and previously attempted to do." According to the chronicler, Boniface "after carefully reading the letters ordered them to be burned." What the Pope's letter said was this: "We are bound to look with a favourable eye on the monastery of St Augustine's, Canterbury, of the order of St Benedict, because it belongs without any intervening party to the Church of Rome. . . . Enjoining you by these apostolic papers not to molest any more the persons of the said monastery . . . but in reverence to us, and to the apostolic chair, to yield to them and their monastery their rights."

In 1277 the abbot Nichol Thorn was detected in the sharp practice of forging bills to support the case of the abbey; the crime was so gross that he went to the Pope and asked that his resignation should be accepted. The friction was so great when Edward I. and his family visited St Augustine's, in 1289, that the monks refused to allow the archbishop to dine with them there. It was in the time of the next abbot, Thomas de Fyndon, that the quarrels between the archbishops and the abbey reached a climax. Fyndon grouped all the numerous parish churches in the possessions of the abbey into three deaneries, obviously as an assertion of his episcopal rights over these possessions, which he thus was beginning to subdivide as a bishop would his see. For two months and more nothing was said; then the archbishop, the chapter of Christ Church, and the archdeacon of Canterbury, all appealed to Rome against Fydon's action. In the end the latter had to give way, and restore all the parishes to the archbishop's jurisdiction and ask pardon. It was he who built the Great Gateway which still stands; and got a licence from Edward II. empowering him to embattle it in 1309. The temporal majesty of the abbey may be appreciated from the account of the great feast which this same abbot gave to a company of 4500 persons including the prelates of the county and 65 knights.

The vast possessions of the abbey included ten whole parishes, and parts of a hundred more: it had fourteen rectories in its gift, and appointed to fourteen vicarages. The kings were not slow to ask as much as they could get of this wealth. We find Edward III. borrowing from the abbey 50 marcs in his twelfth year, 100 marcs four years later, and 200 four years after that. Richard II. also twice borrowed 100 marcs from the monks. Another sign of their great riches can be deducted from the account of the sums which William Welde had to pay before he could get a confirmation of his appointment as abbot in 1389. There was a long delay during which the king had to be paid £1418 as his share of the vacant estates; the Pope's chamber got 600 florins; the cardinals' chamber got another 600 florins; the Pope's attendants got 405 florins; and the servants of the cardinals got 46 florins; and over and above these were the expenses of the proctor who had gone to Rome to procure the election. All this period of its history, the Holy Court of Rome was making a very handsome income out of its spiritual duties, and this little bill of St Augustine's is a good example of what was going on.

The abbey went on, without any very drastic change in its affairs, until it was surrerended to the Crown in the reign of Henry VIII.; as had happened to its rival Christ Church. The deed of surrender was signed by the Abbot Essex and thirty monks, all of whom received pensions during their lives. The total revenue of the abbey at this time was £1413 gross and £1274 net.: which sums, of course, would be immensely higher if translated into the values of to-day. In the case of Christ Church Priory, Henry had to provide for the endowment of a chapter of dean and canons to serve the Cathedral; but in the case of St Augustine's there were no ecclesiastical uses left to provide for: so the buildings were retained by the Crown and treated partly as a royal palace; all through its previous ecclesiastical career it had been the usual residence of the monarchs when they had occasion to stay in Canterbury. Queen Mary I. granted it to Cardinal Pole for his life. In Queen Elizabeth's time it was again leased, but we find her here in 1573, keeping her court and entertained with much magnificence by Archbishop Parker on her birthday which happened during her fortnight's stay in the Abbey. The birthday festivities took place in the great hall of the archbishop's palace which Parker had almost entirely rebuilt during his holding of the see (1559-1575). Parker met her at the west door of the Cathedral, attended by the bishops of Rochester and Lincoln; and after kneeling to say the Psalms and the collects, the whole party processed up the Cathedral, with the queen under a canopy supported by four knights, and the dean and canons on either side: and then evensong followed.

It was at St Augustine's that Charles I. received his wife, Henrietta Maria, for the first time on her arrival in England, June 12, 1625. They had been already married by proxy; but their meeting at St Augustine's was their bridal feast. During the civil war of this reign, St Augustine's was in the possession of another tenant, Lady Wotton, whose name has remained as the title of the little green outside the abbey gate. The Parliamentarians sacked her residence, but she remained here until she died in 1658. When Charles II. returned to England at the Restoration of 1660, he landed at Dover, and it was at St Augustine's that he spent his first few nights in England, before he passed on to London.

The abbey, after this, gradually fell into ruin and was used for various uneventful purposes, such as a brewery. In 1844 it was partly restored and partly rebuilt into the form of a college for the training of missionaries, which it still remains.

St Augustine's Abbey held an important place in the everyday life of mediæval Canterbury: through its wide patronage over the parish churches of the city; through its fairs; through its courts of justice which it had a right to hold concerning the affairs of its tenants; in all these and other ways it must have loomed continually before the eyes of the townsmen. The borough of Longpoot (the name exists to this day as the title of the street leading to St Martin's) was the original manor which King Ethelbert had given to Augustine and his fellow monks; and it remained in possession of the abbey until its end, and was under its rule as distinct from the jurisdiction of the city councils. In Domesday Book it is described as being in the immediate possession of the abbot; and it adds that there were "seventy burgesses in Canterbury City who belong to this manor."

CHAPTER XVIII

Itinerary of Canterbury

PART I.—ITINERARY OF THE CITY

IN the preceding chapters a general sketch has been attempted of the many lines of the historical development of Canterbury. We will now approach the subject from the topographical side; and visit the chief places in the city and its immediate neighbourhood, as far as possible in historical order. In the course of these visits it will be convenient to mention a few further historical details which it has not been possible to weave into the general story. The Cathedral will be left to the last, which is out of its historical order of course, but it will be better understood when the main features of the city have been seen. Besides, it is the proper climax; everything seems rather small, if seen after the mighty church.

The Church of St Martin. This is undoubtedly the best spot to begin a journey through Canterbury. This tiny church was here when archbishops and their Cathedral had not begun their existences in this town. With its squat tower, narrow body, and weather-beaten surface it really looks its great age. For its early history see chapter iii. In the west wall of the nave there are the vestiges of two Roman windows which apparently were lengthened at a later period by Saxon or early Norman masons. The composition of the pink plaster has been an important element in ascribing these parts to the Roman period. There is also, probably, other Roman masonry in the lower part of the wall of the nave; it is shown in the south-east corner near the Norman piscina. In the north wall of the nave is a Norman doorway. In the chancel there is certainly a great deal of Roman brick in

FONT IN ST MARTIN'S CHURCH

the walls, some of which is perhaps as it was laid by Roman builders, or it may have been used by the Saxon builders who rebuilt the church in the time of Augustine. The remains of the square-headed door in the south wall seem distinctly Roman; and the round-headed one by its side seems as distinctively Saxon. Only the first twenty feet of the chancel is of this ancient period (whether Roman or Saxon); for after that comes the east end of the chancel as it was added during the 1200-century, in the Early English style of architecture. The tomb, which is called Bertha's, on the north side, is not earlier than the very end of the 1100-century. The most famous thing in this church is the beautiful font which stands at the south-west corner of the nave: it is of three parts; the lowest of linked rings, the next of a continuous scroll-work; the third and highest of intersecting arches. The two lower are certainly older than the top one, but can scarcely be of the King Ethelbert period to which tradition ascribes this font, saying it is the one used when he was baptized by Augustine. At least, these lower parts may be of Saxon date; and the uppermost tier seems of the Norman period at the latest. The whole font may thus be the pieced-together fragments of an earlier one which was broken and completed in later styles. The monument in the tower is of Sir John Finch, a Speaker of the House of Commons in the reign of Charles I.

On leaving St Martin's Church and going into the Longport Road, we may see facing us the homes of *Smith's Hospital*, founded in 1657, for five men and four women. In *Ivy Lane* (leading out of Chantry Lane which goes to the south) a group of cottages, No. 30-48, on the south side of the Lane: these may be as early as the period of the Dissolution or of the later Tudor reigns. They are worth glancing at as a glimpse of old secular Canterbury. In Chantry Lane, on the west side a little beyond Ivy Lane, once stood that *Chantry, founded by Hamon Doge*, in 1264, which gave the street its name until this day. Doge, who was the rector of St Paul's church (which we shall soon reach during our walk) here established an institution of two chantry priests who were to pray for ever for his soul and his parents, and also for the eternal welfare of the abbots of St Augustine's Abbey and all connected therewith. One priest was to carry on his devout exercises on the premises in Chantry Lane, and the other was to pray at an altar in St Paul's Church. It is a good example of a common mediæval custom. Hasted says that some parts of the building were still standing in 1799 when they were used as a cottage: it is said that there are still remains of it standing, incorporated with a cottage in this lane. Farther along Chantry Lane, almost at the corner where it reaches Watling Street, once were the precincts of the *Nunnery of St Sepulchre*: a house of Benedictine nuns which was founded by Archbishop Anselm, about 1100, on a corner of the domain of the Abbey of St Augustine. The chapel of the nunnery became, apparently, the parish church, or at least the nave of the chapel was used for that purpose. Hasted says there were still ruins of this nunnery to be seen in his time: but even the parish church has disappeared. The nunnery became famous in its later history (as we have seen in chapter xiv), on account of its sister, the Holy Maid of Kent whose prophecies brought her to a sudden end in Henry VIII.'s reign. Farther along the Watling Street (here called the Old Dover Road), to the east, is the site of the *Hospital of St Lawrence* on the right, just before we reach the County Cricket Ground which bears its name. There are perhaps a few fragments of this ancient building still contained in the walls of existing cottages. But it has practically disappeared. It was founded in 1137 by Abbot Hugh of St Augustine's Abbey: mainly as a hospital for the leprous monks of his house and those afflicted with contagious diseases, but it was for the use of outside persons also, as appears from the fact that there was to be room for "sisters" as well as brothers amongst the sixteen inmates for whom it was intended. It apparently survived the Dissolution, being a charitable rather than a religious house; and was for a time used exclusively for women; but it was gradually filched into private hands. Returning to Longport, by turning down Monastery Street we reach

St Augustine's Abbey. At the corner of Longport we pass the *Cemetery Gate*, built by Ickham in 1399—since much restored. The cemetery of this abbey was for the early part of its career the chief burial-place of the city. Continuing along the street northwards, we enter the abbey at the Great Gate. The history of the abbey we have discussed in chapters iii. and xvii. We are still in a part of Canterbury which takes us back to the very beginning of the Saxon period. As in the case of St Martin's Church, St Augustine's was in existence during the life of the first archbishop; and, to begin with, it was the most important building in the neighbourhood. The most important present remains are: (1) The *Great Gateway*, by which we entered, as we see it to-day is the one built during the office of Abbot Fyndon, about 1300. The chamber above it was the *State Guest Room* of the abbey; and when it became a royal palace after the Dissolution, it had many famous visitors (referred to in chapter xvii.). The *College Hall*, to the south of the gateway, is of 1309 building; it was the great festival hall of the abbey when it was entertaining famous guests (for it was not used as the ordinary dining-room of the monks); the warden's chair at its north end is of 1500-century Flemish work. The *Guest Chapel* beyond the hall has been very badly restored and enlarged. The *crypt, or under-croft, of the modern*

LADY MARY WOOTON'S GREEN

library, has some fragments of old masonry in its exterior walls; but the columns are new, and the whole has been restored beyond recognition. In early days, it was the undercroft of the *Great Hall* of the Abbey, which has now been replaced by the modern library. Continuing across the grounds to the south-west, we reach a few remains of the *cloisters*, which show some pieces of wall which appear to be of Saxon building. Continuing a little farther south, we come to the remains of the *Abbey Church*, as it was rebuilt under abbots Scotland and Wido about 1090. The total length of this great church was 320 feet, the nave being 175 feet (the total length of cathedral nave is 188 feet). Only the foundations now remain, and these have been cleared so as to reveal the crypt chapels under the choir, and the bases of the crypt piers and columns; they were all built in the Norman period, as stated above. Several hundred feet of *the exterior walls of the Abbey* still stand between the two remaining gateways which we have seen. Beyond the ruins of St Augustine's great church, across a small field, we see standing in solitary decay the only remaining fragment of the

Church of St Pancras. This church we have already mentioned as existing in the days of King Ethelbert, and probably before his time. The existing ruins show that it was probably built in the time of Augustine himself, very largely out of Roman material, of which four Roman columns and many bricks still remain in the ruins: these materials may have been part of an earlier pagan temple which is traditionally said to have existed on this spot. The piece of ruined window and wall which stands up so prominently is, of course, a part of a much later mediæval building, which was raised on the older Saxon foundations. But the Saxon foundations still exist.[1]

[1] See a fine paper by Mr St John Hope in "Arch. Cant." vol. 25, p. 222.

Outside the Great Gateway of St Augustine's we are in the picturesque *Lady Wooton's Green*, and by walking along Broad Street, to our left and right we get some of the most impressive glimpses of the *City Walls*, which at this place are also the walls of the Cathedral precincts. The City Walls were erected more or less in this form, with the twenty-one towers, in the time of Richard I.: though, of course, they had been there, less substantially, long before. It was perhaps at this rebuilding that the area up to the present Westgate was enclosed; though it was probably earlier, perhaps during Lanfranc's energetic term of office, or even during the reign of Harold who fell at the battle of Hastings. In that part of the Wall which directly faces us as we stand in Lady Wotton's Green, was the famous postern or small gate called *Queningate*, which there is every reason to believe was made for Queen Bertha to leave the palace when she went to worship at St Martin's Church, as we have discussed in chapter iii. Near this gate once stood the *parish church of St Mary of Queningate* a Saxon foundation which had been presented to the Priory of Christ Church by Hugh Magminot, together with eleven houses in Canterbury: it is an example of how the religious communities acquired their wealth. This parish church had disappeared before the Reformation. Bearing to the left we reach the end of *Burgate* where stood the city gate of that name, which was one of the main entrances to the early city in Saxon times. In the yard of the Saraçen's Head Inn, at the left-hand corner of Burgate, can be seen another fine piece of the City Wall. There was once the *parish church of St Michael Burgate* near by: but it had disappeared long before the Reformation probably. The priory of Christ Church owned it. In Church Street, to the east of us we find the delightful

Parish church of St Paul; probably of Saxon

foundation but now showing nothing earlier than the work of the 1200-century (and everything has been much restored) in the two columns between the nave and north aisle and one between the choir and north aisle. The font of Purbeck marble, of the 1200-century also, is now disused, but will be found at the end of the south aisle. This church was originally in the patronage of St Augustine's Abbey, and so it at first had no cemetery, since, like all the parish churches of the city which were in patronage of the abbey, it buried its dead in the great cemetery of the monks. Still skirting the Wall we reach *St George's Street* at the end of which stood another *gate* of that name, called also Newingate. Again continuing round the Wall, we see it here rising above the cattle-market yards. In a short distance we pass the spot where the ancient *Watling Street* pierced it, and there stood *Ridingate* or Radingate as it was once called. There is said to be Roman masonry still beneath the surface on the south side of this gate; which is one of the reasons for the argument that the wall was in this position in Roman times. Watling Street was second to none in importance throughout the Roman and early mediæval periods: but its passage through the City of Canterbury was somewhat forgotten by the substitution of the High Street, with its continuing streets of St Peter's and St George's, as the main thoroughfare of the town. Near this gate once stood the parish church of *St Edmund Ridingate*; but the parish was united with St Mary Bredin as early as 1349. St Edmund's had probably begun its career in Saxon days: it was in the possession of (perhaps built by) Hamo, whose father came to England with William the Conqueror: he gave it to St Augustine's Abbey by which it was given in 1184 to the Nunnery of St Sepulchre.

Beyond Ridingate we mount the Wall and have

below us on one side the *Moat*, and on the other, the public gardens of the *Dane John*, which itself we soon reach, and can ascend for a view of the city. This mound was probably a defensive structure of some kind; but there is conflicting authority as to whether it was raised by the Britons, the Saxons, the Danes or the Normans. It has been suggested that the real name should be the Donjon or Castle Keep. Perhaps this is correct; and the safest theory may be that this mound (which has been much raised in recent times) was a part of the earlier castle which William the Conqueror either raised or enlarged on this spot: there is some evidence that in earlier days the Abbey of St Augustine had some kind of fort here to which the monks could retreat, during the dangerous times of the Danish invasions. At least, in the Domesday Book we are told that William the Conqueror acquired this spot from its previous owners, the archbishop and the abbot of St Augustine, to whom he gave in exchange the holdings of seven and fourteen burgesses, respectively. But the wording is a little vague, and it is not certain that any fort was already there. This Dane John mound must be considered as one of the three which once stood here in a group—a smaller one was just beyond the walls; and the third was where the railway station has supplanted it. We now continue our walk to

The Castle. This later Castle is the one which was begun by Henry II. The keep, of which we now see the ruins, was finished about 1174. In size it was the third largest in England, only Norwich and Colchester being bigger. The Castle was enlarged by various kings; by Henry III., who had a passion for building operations, and by Edward I. in 1300. Louis the Dauphin of France took the Castle without resistance when he invaded England in John's reign. It fell into disuse in the time of Queen Elizabeth, but remained in the possession of the Crown (latterly for use as a prison) until the end of the reign of James I., who granted it to a private owner, and it has remained in private hands ever since.[1] Near the Castle once stood the *parish church of St Mary de Castro* (in the patronage of St Augustine's Abbey), probably first built in Saxon days. There was another *parish church of St John Baptist*, which once stood in the middle of St John's Lane, but it was united to the parish of St Mary de Castro as early as 1349. It also belonged to St Augustine's.

Just outside the Castle walls, across the end of Castle Street, stood the

Worthgate, one of the oldest of the city gates, of which the Roman foundations have been discovered, and existing pictures seem to show the arch still Roman in almost modern times though this was probably a reconstruction using Roman materials. But this criticism does not apply to the foundations, so we are fairly justified in taking this gate as the south entrance to the Roman city of Duroverum, as Canterbury was then called. It was the gate which opened out on Stone Street, the Roman road which led to their landing place and castle at Lymne, on the coast near the present Hythe. On the other side, north of the Castle, is the little parish church of

St Mildred. This is one of the oldest parish churches of the city, and stood in Saxon days, though the existing building is in the main of the Perpendicular style. But there is a good deal of Roman material to be found in the structure, such as the tiles in the south wall. Some people consider that there are remains of a Saxon arch at the west end of the nave. This church was in the patronage of the

[1] See article on "Kentish Castles," by Mr Harold Sands, in "Memorials of Old Kent" (Bemrose & Sons), edit. Mr P. H. Ditchfield.

Abbey of St Augustine ; and we have seen that it was here that some of its monks went after they were turned out of their Abbey during the quarrel with Lanfranc. Izaak Walton in 1626 was married in this church to Rachel Floud who was a descendant of Cranmer the archbishop ; her grandfather being the Thomas Cranmer whose monument is in this church. Leaving the circuit of the later wall of the city, and proceeding up *Stour Street*, we pass on the right, mainly off a side lane,

Maynard Hospital, an ancient foundation for brothers and sisters of fifty years and upwards "of good and honest conversation and unmarried." This endowment seems to have been on this spot since its first foundation by John Mayner (afterwards corrupted into Maynard) in the reign of Henry II.: although the inscription given its origin as 1317. The present building is probably, in the main, of the time of Queen Anne, 1708 ; though the inscription over the door says it was built in 1788. It is a most interesting survival of a mediæval charity. Like all such, it was dedicated to a saintly patron, in this case to the Virgin Mary. By a short passage from the west side of Stour Street we reach the precincts of

The Greyfriars. We have discussed (in chapter xiii.) the first arrival of this religious order of friars in the reign of Henry III., as they were passing through Canterbury, on their way to London. At first they were entertained by the Priory of Christ Church for two days ; when they removed to the Poor Priests' Hospital (which we shall visit near-by), the members of which gave them part of their land on which to build a friary. In 1270, or thereabouts, an alderman of the city, named John Digg, presented to them another plot of ground lying between the two branches of the Stour river ; and it was probably at this time and on this spot that were erected the buildings of which we see the ruins to-day. These are, mainly, the picturesque house, bridging over the Stour, which is of about that period in architecture in the Early English style; it may even date from their first settlement. There are also extensive remains of the precinct walls, with a small 1200-century doorway. The view towards the back of the Eastbridge Hospital is exceedingly quaint and beautiful; one of the finest in the city. In the Greyfriars' Church was buried the rebel Lord Badlesmere, whose hanging we have noted in a previous chapter. The friars, as in other towns, were much petted by the citizens and nobles, who desired the honour of burial in their church. The Friary was dissolved in 1534, and sold by the Crown to laymen. Richard Lovelace, the poet of Stuart days, once owned it and lived here.

There is also a *Bridge* which shows possible Saxon masonry; which may well be the remains of the bridge over the Watling Street whose line must have crossed the Stour at this spot, though the old road has now been blotted out at this part of its journey. Near-by the entrance from Stour Street, through which we came, we find the

Poor Priests' Hospital. There had been an earlier charitable house here, as we have seen, when the Greyfriars were entertained in it about 1224. In 1240 it was refounded or enlarged by Simon Langton, the archbishop's brother, and other benefactors; and the Abbey of St Augustine soon after gave further help. It was for the maintenance of priests who could not find livings for themselves, when in their old age or sick. It was not dissolved with the other houses in Henry VIII.'s time; and continued until it was surrendered to Queen Elizabeth, and by her regranted to the citizens of Canterbury to be used as a Poor's House. The buildings, such as remain, are now used for business purposes. Much of the 1373 rebuilding still remains. The chapel has become a dwelling-house, with floors added: and in the upper rooms are the king posts of the roof. The hall of the hospital also stands, with floors inserted; while the bell in the turret is probably still the one which was placed there in 1373. It is recorded that this building (under Thomas Wyke the master) was the first time the hospital had been constructed of stone. We now continue along the same street until we reach the *High Street*, where, on our left we reach

Eastbridge Hospital, also called St Thomas' Hospital or Kingsbridge Hospital. Here we have another important house built over the river Stour. It took its name from its nearness to the bridge which carries the High Street over the river. There was probably an earlier foundation; which may have been refounded or added to by Thomas Becket. Soon after he died it was certainly dedicated to him, perhaps by Archbishop Hubert Walter who presented some tithes and property to it; but he then addressed it as an established institution. It was for the entertainment at a cheap rate of poor pilgrims who came to visit the shrines of the city; it specially looked after those who were sick. It had many subsequent patrons, such as Archbishop Hubert Walter. In Edward III.'s time Archbishop Stratford drew up fresh rules (for the administration seems to have got somewhat slack) and the hospitality to pilgrims was to be more carefully arranged. By the time of Elizabeth, since there were no longer pilgrims, it had naturally fallen away from its earlier work; although it had escaped the great dissolution period of Henry VIII.'s reign. Archbishop Parker inspected it, and found that the hospital had been divided up into separate tenements for private persons: he made stricter rules. But a few years later it had all lapsed again and Elizabeth confiscated it, and gave it to a private owner. But it was recovered and refounded by Archbishop Whitgift as nearly as possible to fulfil the purposes of the early charity, with educational benefits added thereto. The present building possesses a Great Hall of the first half of the 1200-century, with some wall-paintings, rather faded, of Christ in glory and later and ruder ones of the Martyrdom of St Thomas. The crypt below is of the same date and contains interesting pillars with circular capitals. The chapel overlooking the High Street is mainly of the 1300-century, with the Decorated windows of that period and a fine wooden roof: there is also in it a beautiful deed of 1245, bearing the seal of the hospital.

Opposite Eastbridge Hospital, on the other side of the main street and overlooking the river, are the *houses of the Canterbury weavers* which at least date from the time when the Walloon and French refugees came here (as we have seen in chapter xvi.), and are probably in great part still of 1400-century main structure; although now considerably restored, and altered. The houses have again been restored to their original use as a weaving factory. Continuing along St Peter's Street westwards we pass a great number of interesting *domestic dwellings* which yet have their main structure of the 1500-1700 centuries. No 37 is usually regarded as a typical dwelling of a French silk weaver. No 49, the King's Arms, should also be noticed. No 53 is the original home of *Cogan's Hospital*, which was established in 1657 by Peter Cogan, who gave his house for the dwelling-place of six widows of clergy, with endowments for their maintenance. This institution has been removed to another part of the city. On the N.E. side of the street is.

St Peter's Church. This parish church was founded in the Saxon period ; when, it must be remembered, it was outside the walls, which did not then extend beyond the bank of the Stour which we have just crossed by the East Bridge. All the city where we now are was not enclosed until the Norman period (or the closing days of the Saxon Harold, at the earliest). The church still has a tower, in the main, of early Norman building (though altered), with Roman tiles built into it: there is an interior Norman arch facing as one enters the door ; and the square font is probably Norman also. This church was in the patronage of the priory of Christ Church. At the east side of the entrance gate is a charming Tudor or earlier domestic dwelling, with gables, and figure-brackets supporting the overhanging top storey. We now continue westwards to

Westgate. This is the only one still standing of the seven gates of the mediæval city. It has always been the most important of these from the days when it was first built, as part of the extended walls, probably in Lanfranc's time, as we have seen. In its present form it stands as it was rebuilt, 1380, by Archbishop Sudbury, who lost his head during the Peasant Rebellion of the following year. The traveller should certainly climb to the top, for it gives the finest view of the whole city. The clustering red roofs, which surround it on all sides, and the quaint main street leaving it both ways, will make one realise the pilgrims' days: it was through this gate that the majority of them first entered the town. The gate contains a small museum. Through this gateway have passed many memorable processions. The Black Prince's triumph after Poitiers and his burial herse were in the days of the earlier gate. But when Henry V. marched through Canterbury with the prisoners he had captured at Agincourt, 1415, it was through this gate, as we have it to-day, that he left to continue his journey to London. And since then, almost all the famous visitors we have already noticed have passed under the same archway. By the side of the gate, on the south-west, is the parish church of

Holy Cross. This church was originally part of the gateway itself, being built over the road, which also was the case at Northgate. The dedication of this church, to the Holy Cross, led Mr Godfrey-Faussett to suspect that this part of the Wall of the city was originally extended by Harold; for Holy Cross was the dedication of his special abbey at Waltham and his battle cry at the battle of Hastings. When Sudbury rebuilt the gate in 1380, the church was built on its present site. It has been recently practically rebuilt, and is only of slight interest: the font is of the same date as when the church was first removed here. The church was under the patronage of the Priory of St Gregory, on the other side of the city.

Passing through the gate (or by its side, for the wall has gone at this side of the town) we pass into *Westgate Without* and its continuation, St Dunstan's Street. Here again, are many fine old houses. There is the *Falstaff Inn*, with its elaborate iron-work sign holder, hanging from its 1400-1500-century front. In the adjacent *North Lane* Nos 59, 60 and 63 are interesting overhanging houses of the smaller kind. In *St Dunstan's Street*, on the west side, is one of the most beautiful houses in the city: it is now usually called "*The House of Agnes*," because it has been said to be the basis of a word picture which Charles Dickens drew of the home of one of his characters: there is probably some good ground for this connection. But the house itself, of course, is much earlier, and bears the date 1563 on its front. It is said to have been once, in a still earlier form, a house for the use of pilgrims. Continuing westward, we see on the other side of the street, a *gateway of* 1500 (now part of a brewery); which is all that remains of the house where lived the *Roper* who had married the daughter of Sir Thomas More; she brought from London the head of her father, which had been stuck on a pike on

London Bridge, after his execution in 1535; and it was buried in the family vault of the Ropers on the other side of the road in

St Dunstan's Church. This is another parish church which perhaps dates from the Saxon period, though it may have been one of Lanfranc's foundations. In this instance there is perhaps a little Saxon masonry still remaining, at the north-west angle of the nave where the chapel joins it, and also beneath the lancet window on the north side of the chancel. There are windows of the Decorated period on the S. side. But the whole interior has been badly restored, 1879, though the open wood roof of nave is good. The round tower at south-west corner is still an ancient thing, and so is the north porch. The chapel by the side of this last was built, in 1330; it contains a 1200-century chest. The story goes that it was in this chapel that Henry II. took off his robes before doing penance at Becket's tomb; but, of course, the date of its erection spoils the tradition, though it may accurately apply to some other part of this church. The chief, if somewhat morbid interest in the church is that the head of *Sir Thomas More* is buried in the vault under the Roper Chapel, at the south-east corner of the church. There are also some tombs of the Roper family. It is well worth travelling the mile beyond this extremity of the city, in order to visit

The Hospital of St Nicholas Harbledown. This is undoubtedly one of the most vivid pictures of the mediæval period remaining in this neighbourhood. It stands on the slope of the steep hill on the Watling Street, or London Road, as it passes through the little village of Harbeldown. The hospital was founded here by Archbishop Lanfranc, within a few years of the Norman Conquest, as a hospital for leprous men and women, and although now devoted to other uses, it still remains to this day, after over eight hundred years, as a means of maintenance for a group of brethren and sisters, with a master and prior. The residential part of the house is now quite modern, but the chapel still remains in large part as it was built by Lanfranc; it has been respectfully treated, and looks well repaired and yet old. There are two arches and

BLACK PRINCE'S WELL

three pillars, on the north side of the nave, of the Norman period, and on the south side there are pillars of the later Early English style. There is a splendid open wooden roof, a font of about the 1400-century, two pew seats of the 1200-century, and remains of wall paintings, especially in the splay of the E. window, but signs of them are all over the church walls. It was at this hospital that Erasmus and Colet called as narrated in chapter xv., and the box is shown in which Erasmus is said to have placed his contribution. This chapel must not be confused with the parish church higher up the hill. Near the Hospital is the well which tradition says (untruly) supplied water to the Black Prince as a cure on his death-bed.

We now return the way we have come to the point where we crossed *King's Bridge or East Bridge* in the centre of the city. This bridge takes its name from the King's Mill which stood by its side, probably one of the three mentioned in Domesday book. There is in existence the grant by which King Stephen gave this mill to the abbot and monks of St Augustine's in return for the hundred marcs which he "took from them on account of my necessity." On the left hand, almost opposite St Thomas's Hospital is the modern (1882) rebuilding of *All Souls'* ; now a Sunday School, but in its old form it was one of the parish churches of the city, in the patronage of St Augustine's Abbey. By taking the lane on the same side of the main street we can soon reach the remains of the

Blackfriary. The Black Friars settled on a spot very like the Grey Friars' home farther up the stream. We have seen in chapter xiii. how they arrived in Canterbury, and were so welcomed by Stephen Langton the archbishop, in 1217. This friary was built for them, perhaps with the help of Henry III., and was their first house in England (unless Oxford can claim that distinction). Their history was very similar to that of the Grey Friars. They were both popular favourites and had many patrons who were buried in their church. The friary was dissolved with the rest in the deluge of 1536, and passed into private hands. The great hall, now used for modern business purposes, still stands, covered with ivy, in rather solitary but dignified massiveness on the bank of the Stour. There is also standing the refectory, now divided up into various dwelling-houses, and in part fitted up as a chapel; it is of about the year 1300 building, with alterations of a hundred years later; there is a window in the Decorated style overlooking the river. As recently as 1800 a great part of the friary was still standing, with its three gates. We have seen (chapter xiii.) how the citizens of Canterbury held an indignation meeting in the friary against the injustice of the Christ Church monks.

Farther down the Stour stream is the descendant of the *Abbots Mill*, which is recorded as being in the possession of St Augustine's Abbey in King Stephen's time, when the abbot of that day bought it and presented it to his abbey, or rather, for the special benefit of the sacristy, after it had ground all the corn required by the monks, and a tithe had been paid to the almonry. Near-by is said to have been a house of the *Knights Templars*.[1]

Continuing along the street that once skirted the City Wall, we soon reach North Gate Street at the end of which, just outside the precincts of the Cathedral, once stood the *North Gate*, which had a church over it (as in the case of West Gate); this was the *parish church of St Mary Northgate*, it has been rebuilt near-by (1830) when the gate was destroyed; this modern church contains a few relics (windows and glass and a brass) of the older church. It was originally in the patronage of the priory of St Gregory, near-by. This was the gate which opened on to the road to Reculver, and here the monarchs were received when they landed at Margate, as they sometimes did on arriving from the Continent. There is no trace of the gate now. Continuing along the street we come to

St John's Hospital. This is another ancient institution which was founded by Archbishop Lanfranc,

[1] "Biblio. Topo. Brit." vol. i. p. 446.

1084. In this case it was for infirm, poor, or blind men and women. According to Eadmer, Lanfranc "built, beyond the north gate of the city, a handsome and spacious house of stone, and added to it several dwelling-houses, with a large courtyard. All this he divided into two, placing men in one part and women in the other: he gave them daily food and clothing at his own expense, and appointed attendants and watchers who might see if they lacked anything, or if the men and women mixed. And on the other side of the road he built a church in honour of St Gregory the Pope, in which he placed canons who were to live according to the rules, and minister to the souls of the above-mentioned inmates." (The house of the canons we will consider later.) This Hospital of St John, we enter through the (restored) gate of the late 1400-century, with its handsome timber-work, and the chamber above the passage. We find ourselves in a large courtyard with grass in the centre, surrounded by the dwellings of the inmates who still receive their pensions and maintenance from the property of Lanfranc's endowment of more than eight centuries ago. But the dwelling-houses are modern, of about 1850. However, the kitchen of a 1500-centuries building remains, with the old Communal Dining Hall of the hospital above it, of the same date. The hall contains chests of the 1200- and 1300-century and a few interesting pieces of pewter table-vessels and other utensils belonging to the hospital; also some charters, one of 1348. On the opposite side of the courtyard we may see substantial remains of what were probably the Norman walls of the hospital; or they may have been a part of the chapel. This Norman gateway, with a window of the same period, near above it, and the massive surrounding Norman masonry, all take us back at least as early as 1145 when there was a fire in the hospital, or probably to Lanfranc's first foundation. The chapel which is at present used (dedicated to St Gregory) is a building of various later dates, but the doorway is of Norman date, though it was rebuilt in its present position, probably a removal from the earlier chapel. The font is probably early 1200-century though some authorities say that it is of the Saxon period: it has an Elizabethan cover. Such are the present remains of the hospital which Lanfranc founded as a companion to his lepers hospital at Harbledown, which we have seen still exists to this day also. Both the institutions are important glimpses into mediæval life. Such little communities had special exemption from the laws which governed the world outside. For example, St John's Hospital had the rights of sanctuary; and as late as 1500 we find the city council paying men to watch the premises, in order to prevent the escape of a felon who had fled there for refuge; "the guards are instructed to watch "ne evaderet per noctem." It is an instance of the ecclesiastical privileges which clashed with the civic interests so often throughout the history of the Middle Ages. We now turn to glance at the adjacent

Priory of St Gregory. There are still some mere fragments of it to be seen in the neighbourhood of No. 137 Northgate, over the road—a piece of a wall and the side of a gateway. Until nearly 1800 there was a ruin of a chapel to St Thomas the Martyr still standing in one of the adjacent gardens behind the street front. But it is the history rather than the substance of their religious foundation which remains. As we have seen, it was founded by Lanfranc at the same time as, or perhaps a few years before, the Hospital of St John was founded by him. One of the most important duties of these regular canons was to attend to the spiritual wants of the inmates of the Hospital. These canons were probably the first "regular" canons to be established in England: a kind of halfway-house between the full monk and the secular priest. The members of this order were usually called Austin or Black Canons, because they wore the black gowns of the order of St Augustine. Soon after their institution they had a dispute with the full Black Monks, or Benedictines, of St Augustine's Abbey, concerning the right to possess the body of St Mildred, which both claimed. They were a wealthy body for in Domesday Book (1086) they are entered as possessing in Canterbury alone thirty-two dwelling-houses and one mill, and twelve tenants paying rent to them. Here is one example of the kind of endowments which such a religious house received: in the manor of Northfleet Kent, the canons of St Gregory had the right to take four acres of the best wheat, and four acres of the best barley grown in the manor. The priory was dissolved with the other religious houses in the time of Henry VIII.; at first it was given to the archbishops of Canterbury, but they eventually sold it and it passed into lay hands. At the time of the dissolution, there were thirteen canons being maintained in the priory, and they possessed a clear annual income of £122 between them, quite a large sum in those days. Returning now to the city end of Northgate, we skirt outside the west walls of the Cathedral precincts on our left, and then reach the houses which enclose the archbishops palace, in Palace Street. On our right as we crossed the line of the walls, where Northgate formerly stood, is the *Borough of Staplegate*: this square of ground (enclosed by the road we are in, and on the opposite side by Knot's Lane, and on the north side by the street which runs where the walls formerly stood) is probably the first patch of land which Ethelbert gave to Augustine and his fellow monks before he gave up his Palace to them. To this day it has certain exemptions from the regulations which bind the surrounding properties, and we are probably historically justified in holding that these few remaining exemptions are the remnant of the privileges which the first Saxon king of Canterbury granted to the first archbishop. Continuing along Palace Street, we pass on our left the old *Gateway of the Archbishops' Palace*: that which we now see is the gate which Archbishop Parker built during his extensive reconstruction of the Palace in the reign of Queen Elizabeth; its old brick front is now sadly concealed by stucco. Leaving the Palace for consideration with the Cathedral precincts, we find on our right

The *Parish Church of St Alphege*, which dates from before the Norman Conquest. There are still traces of Norman masonry in the west pier on the north side of the church. The tower is of the 1200-century at which time the whole church appears to have been remodelled. There is an Early English window in the south wall, and one in the north wall; and three of the Decorated period in the south wall, of which same period is the west window. There are several handsome Late Perpendicular windows of the rebuilding which took place in 1468. The font is of this same century. There is a stair in the north wall, apparently leading to the rood loft, with a well-carved canopy over the entrance. From immemorial times, this church has been in the patronage of the archbishops who lived on the other side of the road.

In Palace Street is also an *old house of the late 1400-century* [restored], with richly carved woodwork in the Early Tudor style. Continuing along Palace Street, we reach Guildhall Street at the south-west end of which we find the *Guildhall*, now with a very modern-looking exterior of stucco: but the interior is older than the outside would lead us to think. The Guildhall was certainly there in the reign of Henry VI.; it was almost entirely rebuilt in 1495, and again it was rebuilt in the time of Queen Anne, as we now know it, in the main. The council room with its beamed roof is probably of the 1495 rebuilding. It was in Henry VI.'s time that we first read of it by its present name of "Guildhall"; before that, it was called the "Speech House." It now contains the City's Sword of State, which was presented by James I. in 1607; and the Mace which was presented, probably by James II.

We are now in the *High Street*, almost exactly in the centre of the area enclosed by the mediæval walls as they were since the Norman period at latest. This was also in the Roman city, of course, and it was a few yards up the High Street, towards the west, that heavy *Roman foundations* were discovered lying across, or rather, under the surface of the present street. This building must have stood just under the Roman walls which kept to the east bank of the Stour, which flows under the High Street a little farther west. Opposite the spot where these Roman foundations were discovered is the ancient house which was once the "*Fleur-de-Lis*" *Inn*. It has low windows overhanging grotesque brackets: and there is a 1200-century window, and a part of a Tudor staircase. On the same side of the High Street, farther east, is a fine building (45 High Street) with a Tudor period front of deeply embossed figures on a squarely projecting upper part overhanging two square bay windows. This was once an Inn (which the Fleur-de-Lis still remains) called "*The Crown*." The ceiling of the upper room, is a very fine example of the Elizabethan period. Still farther east, at the corner of Mercery Lane, and extending along its west side, was the most famous of all Canterbury pilgrims' inns. This was "*The Checquers of the Hope*,"[1] mentioned

[1] The name describes the sign—the chessboard on the barrel-hoop, *i.e.* there were both games and drinks provided.

in the epilogue to the "Canterbury Tales" [but this part was not written by Chaucer himself]. The building was largely destroyed in 1865 by fire; but a piece of the old wall still forms the corner of Mercery Lane although remodelled, and some of the vaulting remains inside the shop premises. The entrance to the old inn was from the High Street, whence one entered a large courtyard surrounded by a wooden gallery, by which the bedrooms could be reached. This inn was for the use of pilgrims who, being neither very noble nor very poor, were not invited to shelter in the religious houses of Christ Church and other like places. The Checquers was built at least as early as Chaucer's time, probably far earlier. Many of the houses in Mercery Lane are far older than they seem from the front: in main structure some of them are of the 1300-century. It is recorded that Prior Chillenden rebuilt the Merceria about 1400: it is not very certain what was the extent of the work done at this time. Leland says this same prior "builded of new . . . the faire ynne in the High Streate of Canterbyri" — it is not clear to which this refers: or it may be a mistake for the Merceria rebuilding. The house fronts of most old towns are very deceptive: it is such a common thing to find that a modern front covers a more ancient framework and interior.

Returning down Mercery Lane, we cross the High Street to St Margaret's Street. We have left on our right a little way down the High Street, rather beyond the front of the "Checquers," the *site of the old parish church of St Mary Bredman*, now destroyed. It was in the patronage of the priory of Christ Church and was probably founded before the Norman Conquest, for Hasted says (writing 1799) that the building was then "seemingly of the early part of the Norman times." The name denotes that the Bread-market was near it.

In earlier days it was called St Mary Andresgate, because the four roads here crossed near St Andrew's Church. It was the parish church of the Guildhall, so here the Mayor and Council attended a service on his election day. As a companion to it, on the opposite side of St Margaret's Street end, a little way towards St George'e Street, is all that remains of the *parish church of St Andrew* (now used as a Sunday-school). In its present form it dates from 1774. In mediæval times it stood in the middle of the High Street, where it had been founded probably in the Saxon period. It was in the patronage of St Augustine's Abbey. Going along St Margaret's Street we reach, abutting into the street on the west side, the

Parish Church of St Margaret. This is usually considered to have been founded in the Saxon period. It was in the patronage of the Abbey of St Augustine, by which it was presented to the Poor Priests' Hospital in 1271, and went to the Archdeacons of Canterbury when that hospital was dissolved. The present church is the one that was so much restored in 1861, by which its interest has been sadly damaged; but the apsidal end, standing out to the street, still has a quaint mediæval appearance. There are Perpendicular columns in the nave, and the windows are of the Decorated and Perpendicular periods.

Continuing along the street we find a most interesting cluster of *old houses* at the corner where St Margaret Street crosses *Watling Street.* Some authorities hold that this spot was the south-west extremity of the early Roman walls. Certainly massive masonry of the Roman period has been unburied at this corner. In any case, we are now in a very old quarter of the City; and the *Queen's Head Inn and Nos.* 5, 6, *and* 7 *St Margaret's Street* are very good examples of mediæval houses, which date at least from the Tudor times, and perhaps from the 1400-century. To the eastwards of this corner, half way between Watling Street and St George's Street, lies the

Parish Church of St Mary Bredin. This is now in a modern form, being entirely rebuilt in 1867; but its history goes back probably to a Saxon foundation. It was certainly built or rebuilt by William Fitzhamon, the grandson of a man, Vitalis, who came over to England with William the Conqueror. It was probably this Fitzhamon who presented the church to the nunnery of St Sepulchre, beyond the walls on this side of the city, which held it in its patronage until the time of the Dissolution by Henry VIII., when it passed to the lay patronage of the lords of the adjacent manor of the Dungeon. Hasted, writing in 1799, says: "It is a very small building, seemingly ancient. You go down into it by several steps, which makes it very damp."

We now make our way south-east to the walls at St George's Terrace, and, walking northwards along their top (above the Cattle Market), we arrive at *St George Street.* Turning along it, towards the centre of the city once more, we soon find on our right the delightful

Parish Church of St George. This is a capital example of the parish churches of the town. The tower is still mainly Norman, but the history of this church probably goes back to the Saxon period. The east end of the south aisle is of the late 1300-century; and the font is of the 1200-century, with a cover of the Stuart period. The arcade between the nave and the north aisle is part of the church of St Mary Magdalene, which was removed here when the latter was pulled down. St George's was in the patronage of the priory of Christ Church all through its mediæval days, and passed to the Dean and Chapter at the Dissolution.

Continuing westward along St George's Street, we pass many *old houses.* Turning in at a passage on our left, we find the only remaining ruins of the

White Friary. Here was the house of the White Friars, or Austin or Augustine Friars as they were also called, who settled here about 1325. At least in that year we find the archbishop writing a complaint that these friars had built themselves a chapel in which they openly tolled a bell, and said public Mass, and received oblations, all which was to the damage of the rights of the parish church of St George, which we have just visited, and its patron, the priory of Christ Church. The friars had deposited themselves on a piece of ground which paid tithes to the parish church and a rent to the priory, and when they started to build themselves a church thereon, it looked extremely likely that they would defy both these superiors, or at least damage their interests. However, an arrangement was come to, and they bought out the parish priest's rights for nine shillings a year. They extended their premises by renting, in 1356, a further piece of ground from Christ Church Priory. On the Dissolution under Henry VIII., that king granted their property away into lay hands. Only a fragment of this friary remains, a piece of wall and a doorway of the early original buildings of 1325 or thereabouts. The site is now mainly occupied by a school called the *Simon Langton School*, so called because it is endowed with the estates which were originally given by that donor to maintain the Poor Priests' Hospital, whose history and buildings we have already considered.

Continuing along St George's Street, we see more old houses, such as the one which is now *Baker's Hotel*, bearing the date 1632 on its (restored) front, but which is still earlier in other parts of its structure. Near by, at the eastern corner of the lane running south-east, is a house (of the 1400- or 1500-century) in which *Christopher Marlow* was born, 1563: his father was a member of the shoemakers' guild of the town, and had been married at St George's

Church over the way, where also Christopher was baptised. Crossing St George's Street, we find the very picturesque *Butchery Lane*, which once bore the sweeter name of Angel Lane, because of the view of the angel steeple of the Cathedral which can be seen as one goes down the lane northwards. At the end we reach *Burgate*. Going to the right, on the south side of the street we find the solitary tower which is all that remains of *the parish church of St Mary Magdalene*. This tower is of the 1503 rebuilding, but a church existed here in Saxon days. It was in the patronage of St Augustine's Abbey until the Dissolution. Close to this church is the modern *church of St Thomas*, of the Roman Catholic order, where an attempt has been made to reproduce the famous shrine of St Thomas Becket over the altar of this church. Almost opposite this church are some *old houses*, one of which has been traditionally called *the house of Mr Wickfield*, who lived in Charles Dickens' "David Copperfield": it is now occupied by offices of the Town Clerk. And all around us are ancient houses from the 1400-century onwards; and the same will be found in *Sun Street*, if we continue to the west, past the Cathedral gates and Marlow's statue.

We have now made a more or less complete circuit of the city, and have noted the most important historical buildings and sites which it contains. The traveller who is really serious will extend his excursions over a larger area, and at least visit the *Bigbury Camp* (about 2½ miles), which was probably the fortress where the Britons waited to receive Julius Cæsar when he marched on Canterbury, or whatever there was then to be found of it; also *Patrixbourne* (about 4 miles), where there is a Norman church; *Hackington* (near the north railway station), with its church of St Stephen, where, as we have seen in our history, Archbishop Baldwin talked of establishing his secular canons, which so roused the monks of Christ Church; to *Fordwich* (3 miles), once a borough with a mayor of its own, whither the tide came up the Stour and made it the port of Canterbury; and many other places which will give a living setting to this city of Canterbury. But there is not space to deal with them here; and we must now proceed to visit the heart of Canterbury, the Priory of Christ Church, and its Cathedral Church, with the memories of its treasured saint, Thomas Becket.

PART II.—*Itinerary of Canterbury Cathedral and the Priory of Christ Church.* We now enter the Cathedral precincts. A cathedral is the church which contains the chair (*cathedra*) of a bishop. This church which we are now to visit is the successor of the building which Augustine adopted as the place of his episcopal chair. The priory of Christ Church which grew up around it, and whose remains we shall also visit, was the community of monks who performed the services of the Cathedral. The Cathedral Church was the essential element of the whole group, and the priory was subsidiary. So we shall visit the Cathedral before the Priory, whereas, in the case of such a church as Westminster Abbey, or the smaller church attached to St Augustine's Abbey in this city of Canterbury, it would be more logical to visit the monastical buildings first, for these two churches were only the private chapels of the monks. In the case of Christ Church, the monks of the priory served a church which was, technically speaking, the parish church of the whole diocese.

(A) The Cathedral

There will be an attempt here to point out the chief features of this building, as much as possible in a logical historical order. For this reason, although visitors will probably enter by the great west doorway, they must remember that the nave and west end of the Cathedral are now the newest parts of the building. So it is better to go straight down into the

Crypt. The part nearest us as we enter is the oldest substantial part of the Cathedral: it is the crypt of the new choir which was rebuilt by the combined management and work of Archbishop Anselm and Priors Ernulf and Conrad, somewhere between the years 1096 and 1130. This part of the crypt is the most complete portion of their work which remains. Observe the square-headed capitals of the supporting pillars, with strong massive carving beneath (which carving is usually later than the pillars themselves). This part is usually called *Prior Ernulf's Crypt*, for it was probably all built under his supervision, as the foundation of the new choir. The early Norman crypt of Lanfranc's choir was entirely swept away, unless some of its columns were used by Ernulf. But Ernulf's work only covers a part of the crypt, for the east end has a sudden change in its style which marks *the later crypt*, which was built between 1179 and 1184 as the foundation of the Trinity Chapel which William the Englishman built at that date. Note the higher vaulting and the huge piers inserted to bear the additional weight of the higher choir above. We are now approaching the Early English style of building, whereas Ernulf's crypt is pure Norman. This whole crypt was dedicated to the Virgin, and the *chapel of Our Lady Undercroft* stands in the middle, with its later Perpendicular screen round it. Just east of this shrine lay the body of Becket from its first burial until it was translated to the chapel above in 1220. *The Black Prince's Chantry* was built in the south aisle of the crypt and endowed by that prince on the occasion of his marriage, 1363. This chantry endowment was for two priests, and one can still see the remains of the two altars at which they prayed. The chantry chapel is now used as the *French Chapel*: it is built in the late Decorated style of 1363. The crypt was given over to the French and Flemish refugees who began to arrive in Elizabeth's reign. Whether they used it for secular as well as religious purposes is a debated point, but certainly the south aisle of the crypt became a chapel for their services, which still continue to be held there. In the adjacent *St Gabriel's Chapel*, under St Anselm's tower, are some exceedingly fine wall-paintings, probably of the early 1200-century. They are not often shown to visitors, but reproductions of them can be seen in the library of the Cathedral. At the entrance to this chapel is what is left of the *tomb of the Countess of Athol* (d. 1292). Having thus seen the main features of the crypt, we will now enter the

Choir. This part of the Cathedral, as we now see it, is in the main the building which was put up by William of Sens between 1175 and 1178. We have seen that he left Ernulf's crypt untouched below, and with it also was left standing a fair amount of the lower outer walls. This combination is most typically shown to this day by a piece of arcading in the lower part of the south aisle near the south-east transept. Here we have side by side an arcade arch of about 1120 (Ernulf's and Conrad's building), and one of 1176 (William of Sens' work). In the north aisle, corresponding to this at the other side of the choir, there is another fine piece of arcade of the Norman building of Ernulf's work with later main shafts of Conrad's time. There is also a great deal of the earlier work left in the exterior aisle walls of the choir and in the walls of the two choir transepts; and the towers of St Anselm and St Andrew are practically entirely of Ernulf's and Conrad's period. In the face of these various walls can be seen features (in the shafts, etc.) of the two periods—see, for example, the north-east corner of the south-east transept. In such cases William of Sens made use of masonry of the earlier choir which had survived the great fire of 1174. But the central core of the choir is entirely William's own work, as it was built between 1175 and 1178. Before considering any of its contents, let us ascend the steps in the aisle outside the entrance to *St Anselm's Chapel*, with *Archbishop Mepeham's* (d. 1333) tomb at the entrance, and *Prior Oxenden's famous window* (1336) inserted in the Norman (1110) walls of this Anselm's tower, so called because it contains the tomb of St Anselm somewhere in its foundations. There are also wall paintings (early 1100-century) in this chapel), and at the top of these steps we find ourselves in

Trinity Chapel. This is completely the work of English William, who succeeded William of Sens after the latter's accident. Trinity Chapel was erected under his supervision between 1179 and 1184, including also the east chapel or Corona, and also, as we have already seen, the crypt underneath. Here we have one of the finest examples in England of the combination of the round and pointed arches, which we call the Transition style of architecture.

Having thus seen the structure or anatomy of the choir and east end of the Cathedral, we will now turn to their chief contents. This Trinity Chapel, where we now are, was infinitely the most important place of the building during the Middle Ages, for it was here that rested the *chief remains of St Thomas Becket* after the body was removed from the crypt in 1220. In the centre of Trinity Chapel was the famous shrine which all Christendom came to worship. The steps up from the choir are still worn with the feet and knees of the pilgrims who crept up them, and we can also see the like signs in the stones before which the shrine stood. Now it has all gone—swept away by the violence of Henry VIII. and his wealth-grabbing favourites. To the west of the shrine lay, and still remains, a piece of early Italian mosaic pavement. But the most important survivals of Becket in the Cathedral are the 1200-century stained-glass windows which surround Trinity Chapel, more especially the middle window of the Corona, and the second, third, and fourth windows in the north aisle, counting from the Corona. These were probably placed there soon after the translation of Becket's body to this chapel: they depict incidents and miracles concerning Becket, as well as other scenes. These windows range from medallions, which are untouched mediæval work, to the entirely new insertions of the modern windows of the clerestory. Some of the Trinity Chapel glass has been scattered in other windows of the Cathedral.

To the south side of Trinity Chapel is the *tomb of the Black Prince* (d. 1377), with trophies hung over the canopy, namely, his helmet, gauntlets, and shield and velvet coat ; these are, perhaps, the same ones which were used at the funeral, though it is not likely that they were those used by the prince when in active warfare. On the other side of the chapel, exactly opposite, is the *tomb of Henry IV.* (d. 1413), *and Queen Joan of Navarre* (d. 1437), and on the other side of the adjacent aisle is the chantry *chapel of Henry IV.*, which was built, following the instructions of his will, "that ther be a chauntre perpetuall with tweny prestis for to sing and prey for my soul." The architectural features of this chapel show the fan-vaulting of the 1400-century. The other chief objects in Trinity Chapel are: *tomb of Archbishop Courtney*

(d. 1396), next east of the Black Prince's tomb; opposite Courtney's tomb, on the other side of the adjacent aisle, is (probably) the *tomb of Archbishop Hubert Walter* (d. 1205)—not of Archbishop Theobald, as was formerly supposed; on the other side of the chapel, facing Courtney's, is the tomb of Wotton (d. 1567), the first of the deans after the Reformation abolished the priors. The brick structure next on the east of Courtney's tomb, is the resting-place of *Coligny, Cardinal Catillon* (d. 1571), the brother of the Admiral Coligny, who was massacred on St Batholomew's Day. In the centre of the Corona is *the Patriarchal Chair*, wherein the archbishops are enthroned. Its age is uncertain; tradition takes it back to St Augustine, but it is probably one which was made for the great translation service of 1220, when Becket's body was brought from the crypt. On the left side of the Corona is the *tomb of Cardinal Pole* (d. 1558) the great Catholic churchman of Queen Mary's anti-reformation period.

We now enter the *main body of the choir*. The chief tombs of interest are: *Archbishop Chicheley* (d. 1440) nearest the stalls on the north side; *Archbishop Bouchier* (d. 1485) next but one eastwards; *Archbishop Sudbury* (d. 1381) opposite this last on the south side of the choir, who lost his head during the Peasant Rebellions, as we have seen in the history; *Archbishop Stratford* (d. 1348) next westwards; *Archbishop Kemp* (d. 1454) next west. The *screen round the choir*, separating it from the aisles and nave was built by Prior Eastry (1304-5). The wooden *Stalls* are uninteresting except those of the Dean and Canons, at the west end, which apparently date from about the second half of the 1600-century. There is much *Stained Glass* in the windows surrounding the Choir, but much of it is modern imitation. The finest old windows are the clerestory windows between the south-west and south-east transepts; and the first clerestory window of both the north-east and south-east transepts where they join the Choir on their east sides.

Passing into the *N.-E. Transept* we see remains of fine glass in the Rose Window. In this transept we can see the names of Lanfranc and Queen Ediva as they were inscribed on the wall when their bodies were removed here after the fire of 1174.

Returning into the north aisle of Choir eastwards, we find on our left *St Andrew's Chapel* (now used as the choir vestry) under the tower of the same name, which still remains substantially the same tower as Ernulf and his successors left it about 1120.

Returning down the *north aisle of the choir*, we find in two of the windows early *mediæval glass* which may be as early in date as the end of the 1100-centtry, but perhaps the first half of the 1200-century.

Continuing westwards, we reach the *N.-W. Transept*, or *the Martrydom Transept*, the scene of Thomas Becket's murder, already described in detail in Chapter X. The lower part of the walls and the stone floor near the spot of his death are probably remains of Lanfranc's church which he began in 1070. This is therefore the oldest masonry which we have yet reached, but it is only a fragment, preserved out of respect for the martyr, when the Lanfranc nave and transepts were rebuilt by Prior Chillenden. In this transept are: the *door from the Cloisters* through which Becket's murderers came; the *tomb of Archbishop Peckham* (d. 1292); and that of *Archbishop Warham* (d. 1532), the last of the Catholic archbishops before the break with Rome. The great *Stained Glass Window* of this transept (presented by Edward IV. when he visited Canterbury in 1465) was finished about 1470-80. It was terribly damaged by Puritan fanatics, and only remains in parts, but portraits of the donor and his family, including the two princes murdered in the Tower of London, are still there, and much interesting heraldry. Leading from this transept is the *Dean's Chapel*, of about 1460 building (Prior Goldstone I.), so called because five of the deans are there buried.

When we came out by the doorway from the north aisle of the choir, we entered that part of the Cathedral which is almost completely the work of the Perpendicular period of architecture. *The nave and its two transepts and the south-west tower and maindoor* are the product of the latter part of the 1300-century and the first half of the 1400-century. We have told in the history how Prior Chillenden had the chief hand in the building of the *nave* between 1378-1410, after he had pulled down the old nave and transepts of Lanfranc's building. He left only a little of this latter work in the Martyrdom Transept, in the centre of the piers of the great Central Tower, in the plinth of the side aisle walls, and a good deal of the walls of the transepts; but of all these remains there is practically no outward trace, for they have been covered by the later masonry. The best sight of Lanfranc's work can be seen (from the cloisters) at the north-west outside corner of the tower, and on the outside west wall of the Martyrdom Transept. The great *West Window* of the nave contains much mediæval glass, the top part of the same period as the building of the nave; the rest is mainly older glass taken from the chapter house and the clerestory of the choir, and there is a row of royal shields at the bottom. There is little of interest in the interior of the nave, except the structure itself.

The *S.-W. Transept* contains a large south window filled with stained glass, which in the main has been collected from mediæval medallions and borders which were in the choir transepts formerly before they were broken by the Puritans. The *Chapel of St*

Michael (replacing an older altar to that saint), which is built from the east side of this transept, is of about 1410 construction. Its chief interest is the *tomb of Archbishop Stephen Langton*, the main author of the Great Charter of John's reign. The wall of the later chapel now cuts across the older tomb, which apparently must have been first placed entirely outside the Norman building. There is also an alabaster *tomb of Lady Margaret Holland* (d. 1437) and her two husbands, a good work of the early 1400-century, erected by the wife who died last.

The *S.-W. Tower* of the nave is of Prior Goldstone I.'s time (1449-68), with a *Great West Door* porch probably of the same time as the bulk of the nave ; the statues over the door are of the middle of the 1800-century. The north-west tower (a 1834 copy of the companion tower) was built when the Lanfranc Tower, which had stood until that date, was pulled down. *The Great Central Tower* (*The Bell Harry Tower or Angel Steeple*, the latter its older name) was finished by Prior Goldstone II. about 1495, or a little later. Chillenden had probably carried it no further than the level of the roof of his new nave.

With this we end our statement of the main features of this great cathedral church. We now proceed to visit the remains and sites of the chief parts of the monastic buildings of the Priory which surrounded the Cathedral.

(B) The Priory of Christ Church

The official entrance to the Priory of Christ Church was through the *Court Gate* at the north-west corner of the precincts, near the joining of Palace Street and Northgate Street. The architectural features of this gate give us the keynote to the main periods of the foundation of the monastic buildings as they stood through the chief part of their history. For this gateway is still essentially of the period of Lanfranc's erection, soon after the Norman Conquest; with the chamber above it added in the time of Prior Chillenden. Lanfranc and Chillenden were the two main builders of the Priory; the former in the 1000-century, the latter in the second half of the 1300-century. So this entrance gate gives us a convenient summary of the architecture of the whole Priory—the work of other periods being comparatively a matter of detail. On the left of this Gate lie the present buildings of the *King's School*, on the site of the older *Mint Yard or Almonry*, which was really outside the priory walls; it was the place where the charities of the monks were destributed to the poor.

Passing through the Court Gate, we find in front of us the fine *Green Court* or Curia which was also one of the main features of the older Priory. It divided the whole precincts into two main parts; the monks' dwellings and personal public rooms lay round the Cathedral to our right on the south; while on the north side of the Curia lay the domestic offices of the priory and the dwelling houses of the secular servants—such, for example, as the *Brew-house*, the *Bake-house* (which are now the choristers' school and a residence of a minor canon), the *Granary*, and the *Barn*. Immediately to our left as we enter the Gate, is the modern hall, which has taken the place of the Norman *Aula Nova* (1100-century), of which only the famous *Norman staircase* now stands, the chamber above being built in 1848. This Aula was the building in which, it has been stated, the monks entertained the poorest of those pilgrims who were lodged in the priory itself.

Continuing along the west side of the Green Court we come to *Chillenden's Chambers*, in which the middle-class pilgrims were entertained by the Priory. This part of the hospitality was under the charge of the cellarer. This was an additional building which did not exist in the earlier times of the Priory; it was built by the prior whose name it bears. We now find on the south side of that Green Court a rather confused mass of more or less ruined buildings which are not open to the general public, and some of which will be better seen from the Cathedral side. Suffice it here to say that between Chillenden's Chambers (and the South side of the Green Court) and the Cathedral, lay most of the important buildings of the Priory—the Great Dormitory, the second and third Dormitories, the Infirmary Cloister, the Great Cloister, the Refectory and the Chapter House. We shall visit most of these later.

Continuing to the south-east corner of the green Court, before turning down the passage, called the *Dark Entry*, to the Cathedral, we observe on the east side of the green Court a row of buildings, now the *Deanery*. This was formerly part of the *Prior's Mansion*. It had been the site of the *Bath House* in the early Norman days, when the private apartments of the prior were not very extensive. But, as the wealth of the Priory increased, and, more particularly as the famous pilgrim guests were more and more frequent and of highest rank, still larger premises were built for the prior and for the accommodation of the famous guests whom he kept under his own charge. So we find this south-east corner of the Green Court surrounded by buildings (or their ruins or sites) of the kind necessary to meet this change in circumstances. The present buildings of the Deanery, of Prior Goldstone II.'s time, were still used in his day for the entertainment of the last of the pilgrim guests.

The passage of the *Dark Entry*, which we now pass through, was probably the main door of the *Prior's special precincts:* his actual personal dwelling is probably marked by the remaining ruins on our left (to the east of this passage) in the Deanery gardens. On our right, at the west side of the passage, we see beautiful double and triple groups of columns which formed the east side of the Norman *Infirmary cloister*. Overlooking this cloister on its south side, we see the *Baptistry* or *Lavatory Tower* (which latter was its real name), which was built as part of the water system laid down in the Priory about 1160: it was much remodelled, especially in the upper part, which was rebuilt by Chillenden about 1390. On the west side of the cloister stood the *Great Dormitory*, which we shall see from the great cloister on its other side. On the south side of the Infirmary cloister going to the east side of the Lavatory Tower, was once the *private Chapel of the Prior* (built about 1250) of which the vaulted passage, on which it was built, still remains, with a modern brick building over it. A passage led from this prior's Chapel to the wall of the north-east transept, where a hole in the wall allowed the prior to watch the performance of the services in the Cathedral. Between this Chapel and the St Andrew's Tower stood and still stands the *Treasury*, much as it was when first built in 1135. On the north side of the cloister formerly stood the *Second Dormitory*, with the *Third Dormitory* (which was the name given to the lavatory accommodation of the priory) parallel with it on its north side, and overlooking the Green Court. On the east side of the cloister was the end of the great building of the *Infirmary*, of which five Norman piers and arches can still be seen if we turn through the archway on our left. This department of the Priory was commodious, for it was the dwelling-place of all monks who were for any reason relaxed from the full discipline of the house, and not merely the sick. It extended a considerable way beyond the level of the present Cathedral end; the east portion was a chapel. The whole Infirmary was in the form of a church, with nave, aisles and chapel or chancel. The arches which still remain were those on the south side of the nave. Besides the piers and arches, which stand in ruins as we have seen, there are also remains of the Infirmary in the adjacent house of one of the clergy, where the walls of the *Table Hall* (or dining chamber of the Infirmary) form part of the more modern dwelling: this had been built, 1338-1370, on to the north side of the Norman Infirmary. At the east end of the Infirmary quite detached from it, was one of the guest houses for distinguished pilgrims: it still stands as part of the house of one of the clergy of the Cathedral. Its name, *Meist'omers*, is of uncertain derivation.

Beyond the end of the Infirmary arches we find ourselves in that open part of the Cathedral Close which formed *the Private cemetery of the priory*. This extended round the south side of the Cathedral until it ended in a wall which ran across from the west corner of St Anselm's Tower, and shut off this monks' cemetery from the public churchyard which lay beyond for the use of the citizens, who entered it by the *Cemetery Gate*, which, in its present form, was built by Prior Goldstone II. in 1517. *The Norman Gate* which connected the two cemeteries was removed to the wall of the gardens, further west, where it can still be seen.

We have still to visit the most important parts of the Priory buildings, to which there is now no public entry from the Green Court, whence we should have visited them in more logical order. The centre of the monastic life of every monastery was *the Great Cloister*. In this Priory it stood on the north side of the nave (it is reached by a doorway in the Martyrdom Transept, the same through which Becket went when followed by his murderers). In its present form this

Cloister is as it was rebuilt by Prior Chillenden about 1400, to take the place of Lanfranc's earlier cloister. The lower part of the west end of the *Great Dormitory*, which overlooked the north-east corner of the cloister, is still standing of the 1070 building (we have seen that the other side of this Great Dormitory overlooked the Infirmary cloister). This fragment of the Dormitory has been incorporated with the new Library building. On the east side, also, opening through an Early English period doorway from the middle of the Cloister, stands the *Chapter House*, the centre of the official life of the Priory, as the Cloister was the centre of its social life. The present chapter house is the one as it was rebuilt during the 1300-century, the upper part being of Chillenden's time, finished in the year 1411. On the north side of the cloister stood the *Frater* or *Dining Hall* of the Priory. On the west side stood the *Cellarer's department*, with the *Buttery* at the north-west corner.

We have now sketched the main features of the Priory: all the details can be grasped at leisure when its general structure is understood. The visitor will be well advised in following this general sketch before attempting the multitudinous details of a fuller examination.

(C) Thr Archbishop's Palace

When Lanfranc divided up the property of the Priory between the priory and its monks on one side, and the archiepiscopal see on the other, he also built for himself and his successors a *Palace* outside the premises of the monks, to take the place of the residence which the former archbishops had been entitled to as formal abbots of the Christ Church monastery. This palace and its precincts extended all along the west side of the Priory precincts, from the west end of the

Cathedral to the Court Gateway by which we entered the Priory grounds; and out to Palace Street on the west side. Of the Palace there is nothing which goes back to mediæval times except its site: the oldest standing relic being the *Great Gateway* of Archbishop Parker's erection, which we saw in Palace Street. The Great Hall of the Palace, which we have several times had to visit in our history of the previous chapters, stood very near the north-west corner of the Great Cloister: and it was by a door in this corner of the Cloister that the chief intercommunication existed between archbishops and their Cathedral. It was the door through which Becket passed when he left his palace to enter the Cathedral a few moments before his murder.

THE END.

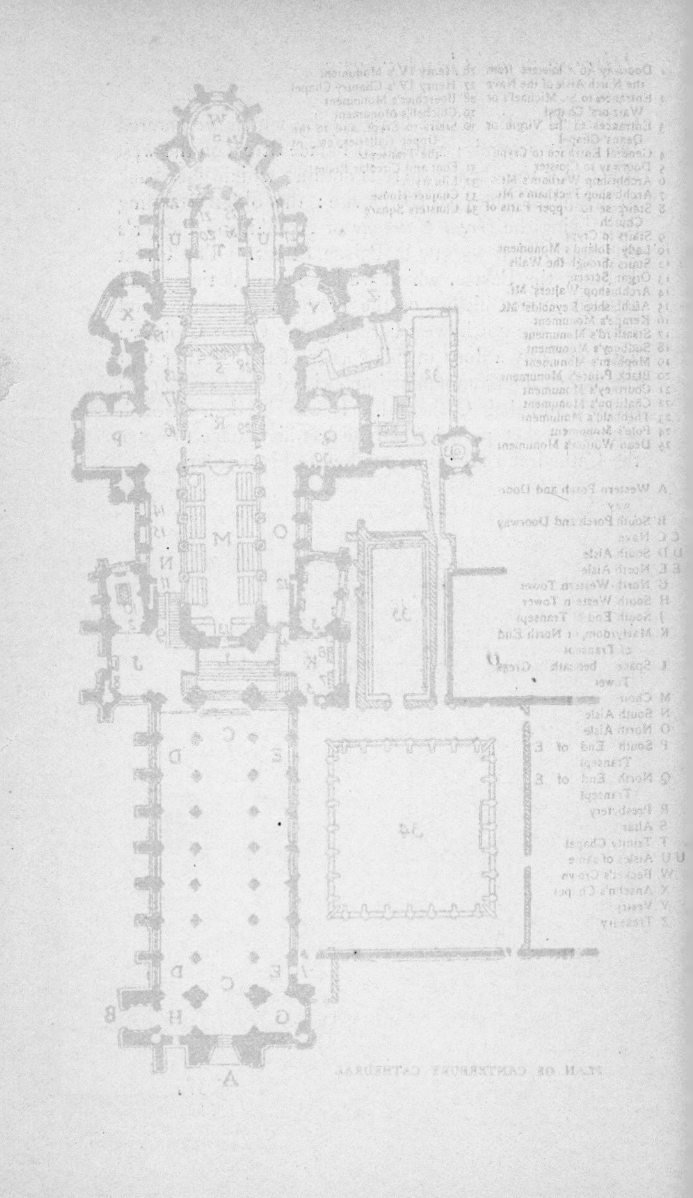

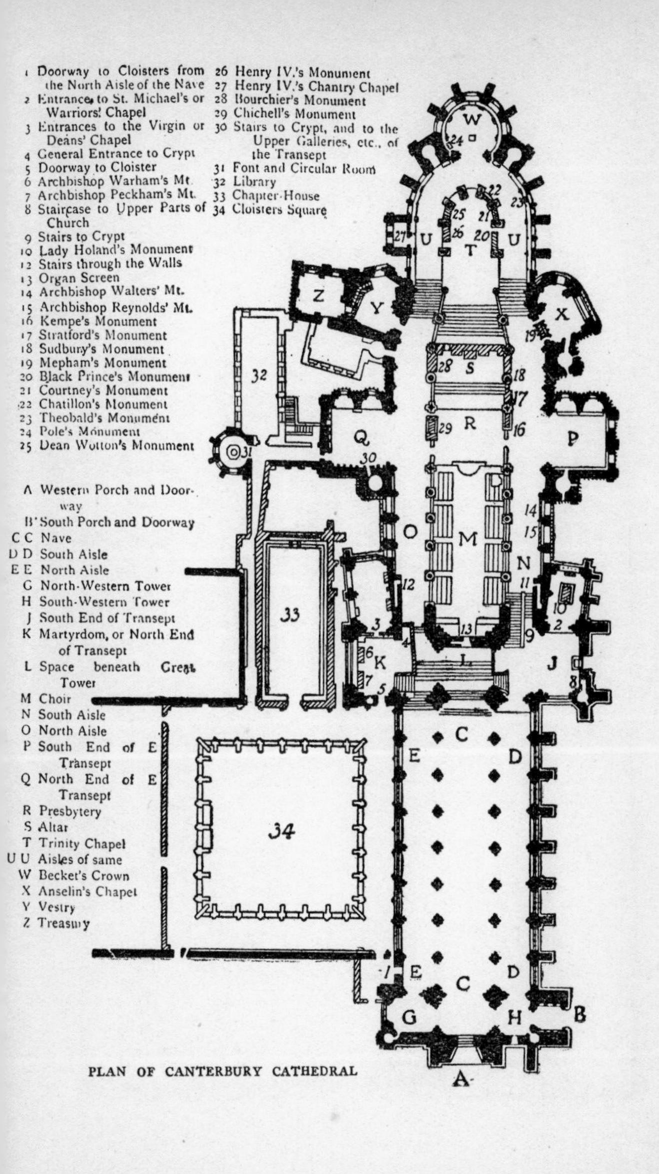

PLAN OF CANTERBURY CATHEDRAL

INDEX

Index

N

O

P

R

PRINTED BY
TURNBULL AND SPEARS,
EDINBURGH

MUSKINGUM COLLEGE LIBRARY
DA690.C3 T3
Taylor, George Robe/The story of Canterb
mustk
3 8152 00087 1074